EXPLORE
KAUA'I

An Independent Traveler's Guide

Blair Pruitt

Mutual Publishing

*Mahalo to Amanda Jones, Ph.D.,
for her support and assistance
with proofreading.*

Copyright © 2002
by Mutual Publishing

Library of Congress Catalog Card
Number: 2002104571

ISBN-10: 1-56647-560-0
ISBN-13: 978-1-56647-560-0

First Printing, June 2002
Second Printing, October 2004
Third Printing, May 2006
Fourth Printing, November 2007

Design by Mardee Domingo Melton and Julie Matsuo

Except where otherwise credited, all
photographs in this book are by Blair Pruitt

Main front cover photo by Douglas Peebles

Mutual Publishing, LLC
1215 Center Street, Suite 210
Honolulu, Hawai'i 96816
Ph: (808) 732-1709
Fax: (808) 734-4094
Email: info@mutualpublishing.com
www.mutualpublishing.com

Printed in Korea

FOREWORD

Visitors to Kaua'i find that their time on this marvelous island is always too short. With its many attractions, activities and natural beauty, Kaua'i offers more adventures than most people can experience in one stay. This book is written as a guide that will enrich the readers' Hawaiian experience and aid them in making the most of their precious time here.

The concise text serves vivid descriptions, accurate directions and insights for the curious and adventurous traveler. Hikers can use their GPS receivers by inputting the coordinates of latitude and longitude provided for many destinations and waypoints. Clear, large maps make it easy for drivers and hikers to find their way by omitting extraneous detail. Highway mile markers, as well as important landmarks, are shown on the maps.

The Hawaiian language is covered early in the book with the hope that a basic background in Hawaiian pronunciation and meanings will lend further understanding when reading the following chapters. I have given history particular importance because an understanding of how things were and came to be leads to an appreciation of the culture and sights the traveler samples. Recounts of history begin with the birth of the Hawaiian Island chain 70 million years ago. Kaua'i's history is given prominence as it intertwines with the history of the other Hawaiian Islands.

This book is for travelers who want to know more about the land and sea they are visiting, the people who live here and how events shaped the island to what it is today. It is meant to be your guide while you explore Kaua'i, and later, a reminder of your visit that will bring back treasured memories until you can return to the "Garden Island".

Certainly, travel is more than the seeing of sights; it is a change that goes on, deep and permanent, in the ideas of living.

—Miriam Beard

TABLE OF CONTENTS

MAPS

INTRODUCTION

Kaua'i matches almost everybody's concept of what a Pacific island paradise should be. First of the Hawaiian Islands to be formed, first to be discovered by the Western world, Kaua'i is the last of the major islands to face development.

Shrouded in mist in the unpeopled heartland is Wai'ale'ale, the extinct volcano that gave the island a birth by fire 5 million years ago. Now cool, dark and a mile high, Wai'ale'ale wrings moisture from the trade winds and stores it in the Alaka'i Swamp. Birds that exist nowhere else on earth find refuge in Kaua'i's swamp and upland forests. Their songs ringing and running water gurgling are all that breaks the silence of the lush wilderness. From this high-altitude cache waterfalls plunge into lacy streams. Joining others, the streams gain force as rivers, radiating from their fountainhead to carve valleys and canyons from crumbling lava.

Northwest of the Alaka'i Swamp, the battle of Kaua'i's fiery origins against the elements' never ceasing onslaught manifests itself in the Nā Pali coast. Cliffs form jagged ramparts rising 4,000 feet above the sea. The sea crashes against the razor-edged cliffs, reclaiming what it spawned. Misty days endow the wild and beautiful region with a dawn-of-creation look.

Contrasting the tropical landscapes of much of Kaua'i is the Waimea Canyon. Often called "The Grand Canyon of the Pacific," Waimea Canyon offers awe-struck gazers vistas as impressive as that of its namesake.

On the dry leeward side of the island, the landscape lifts from bluff, ledge and beach through tilted sugar cane country to peak in sharp ridges. The sunshine that attracted plantation owners lures visitors to golden beaches and low-rise resorts.

The north shore is a luxuriant ribbon of tropical vegetation, lava cliffs, sandy beaches and primordial peaks.

Most of Kaua'i's residents live on the eastern shore, in an area rich in history and legend. Early Polynesians settled the area; their royalty made it their domain. The independent nature of Kaua'i's people is the hallmark of their history. Kamehameha the Great failed to conquer the separate kingdom of Kaua'i with force.

Kaua'i is an adventurer's paradise waiting to be explored. This book is a guide for the traveler who wants to see and experience the best that Kaua'i has to offer. Its detailed descriptions and accurate directions are written to help readers make their own discoveries.

Honopū Beach

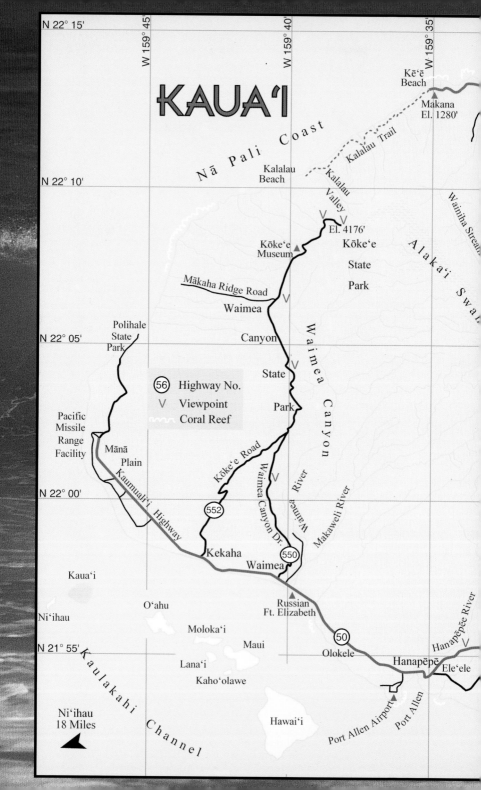

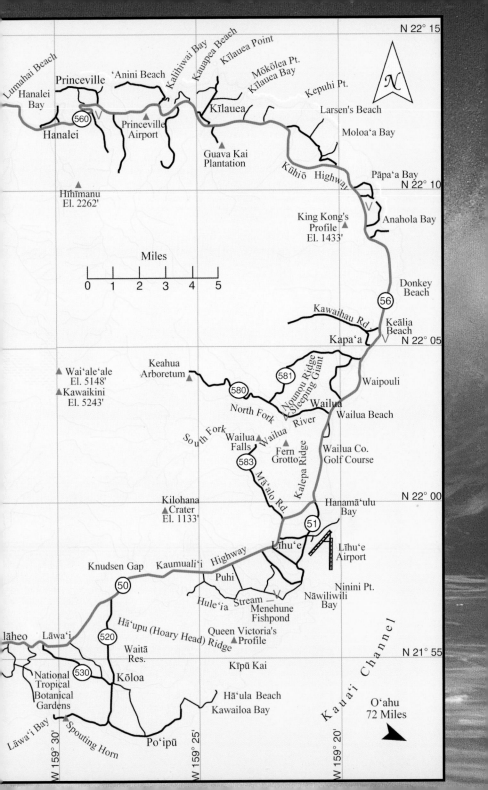

IMPORTANT THINGS FOR TRAVELERS TO KNOW

North American Airlines Serving Kaua'i

All the scheduled airline flights that connect Hawai'i to the U.S. mainland have flights to Honolulu, while some have direct flights to Līhu'e, Kaua'i. Līhu'e's airport runway is not as long as Honolulu's—ruling out nonstop flights to Asia or the Midwest United States. Plans to lengthen the runway have met with opposition from some Kaua'i residents who fear that it may cause environmental damage and the increased visitor traffic would negatively impact island life.

Aloha Airlines and Hawaiian Airlines operate short-hop flights between the Hawaiian Islands. They have aircraft taking off and landing on Kaua'i every few minutes. Passengers can check schedules and book their flights directly on the airline's websites. Kaua'i's main airport is at Līhu'e, airport code LIH. Kaua'i has a small airport at Princeville, but for the time being it has no scheduled flights. The airport code for Honolulu International Airport is HNL.

With airlines recently operating at more than 96 percent capacity on flights from the mainland to Hawai'i, it is prudent to book your flight a few months in advance if possible. During the Christmas season, spring break, Thanksgiving and the summer months, it might be necessary to book several months in advance.

Internet travel services can search for the best flight for you at no charge. They are connected to the airlines' schedules and fares much as a travel agency is. Three of the best ones are Microsoft's Expedia at <www.expedia.com>, Sabre's Travelocity at <www.travelocity.com> and TheTrip at <www.thetrip.com>.

Airplane travel is nature's way of making you look like your passport photo.
—Al Gore

Aloha Airlines
(800) 367-5250, (808) 877-2737
Website: www.alohaair.com
Aloha Airlines controls about 60 percent of Hawai'i's interisland service, flying a fleet of eighteen 737s between Hawai'i's main islands. They also offer service to Oakland and Las Vegas from Honolulu and Maui.

American Airlines
(800) 223-5436
Website: www.americanair.com

Continental Airlines
(800) 525-0280
Website: www.flycontinental.com

Delta Air Lines
(800) 221-1212
Website: www.delta-air.com

Nation of Residence of Visitors to Kaua'i

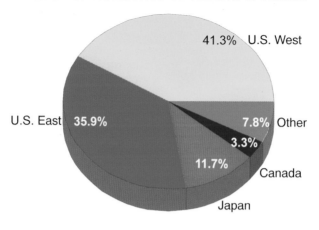

41.3% U.S. West

U.S. East 35.9%

7.8% Other

3.3%

11.7%

Canada

Japan

Hawaiian Airlines

(800) 367-5320

Website: www.hawaiianair.com

Hawaiian Airlines flies their 717s between the main Hawaiian Islands and DC-10s to the mainland.

Northwest Airlines

(800) 225-2525

Website: www.nwa.com

Trans World Airlines

(800) 221-2000

Website: www.twa.com

United Airlines

(800) 241-6522

Website: www.ual.com

United Airlines has daily nonstop flights to Līhu'e from Los Angeles and San Francisco.

Car Rentals

Kaua'i has a limited public transportation system so the best way to get out and about without tour companies is to rent a car. All the major rental companies have outlets on Kaua'i. Car rental agencies based at Līhu'e Airport have shuttle buses to take customers to their car lots. Look for their kiosks across the road outside the baggage claim area. Be ready for a shock when you buy gasoline. Prices are about 25 percent higher than on the mainland.

If you don't have a favorite car rental company and aren't sure which one has the best deal, there are free travel planning services on the Internet that can help. After inputting the dates of your stay and the type of car you want, they will search all the rental companies records and list the rates of available cars by company. Try <www.expedia.com>,

<www.travelocity.com>, or <www.thetrip.com>. Car rental companies, like airlines, like to change their rates, depending upon demand and availability. Often the first rate quoted is not their best rate for a car. Be armed with quotes from other companies and ask if they have any specials for your dates.

Affinity Rent a Car
Reservations (800) 761-7787
Website: www.affinityrentacar.com

Alamo Rent a Car
Reservations (800) 462-5266
Līhu'e (808) 246-0645
Website: www.goalamo.com
The Līhu'e airport location is open 6:00 a.m. to 9:00 p.m.

Avis Rent a Car
Reservations (800) 321-3712
Līhu'e (808) 245-3512
Princeville (808) 826-9773
Hyatt Regency Po'ipū (808) 742-1627
Website: www.avis.com
The hours of business at Līhu'e airport are 6:00 a.m. to 9:00 p.m., at Princeville 7:30 a.m. to 4:00 p.m.; and the Hyatt Regency Po'ipū 8:00 a.m. to 4:00 p.m.

Budget Rent a Car
Reservations (800) 572-0700
Līhu'e (808) 245-1901
Website: www.drivebudget.com

Dollar Rent a Car
Reservations (800) 800-4000
Līhu'e (808) 245-3651
Website: www.dollar.com
The Līhu'e airport location is open 6:00 a.m. to 10:00 p.m.

Hertz Rent a Car
Reservations (800) 654-3011
Līhu'e (808) 245-3356
Marriott Hotel (808) 246-0027
Website: www.hertz.com

National Rent a Car
Reservations U.S. (800) 227-7368
Canada (800) 387-4747
Līhu'e (808) 245-5636
Website: www.nationalcar.com

Thrifty Car Rental
Reservations (800) 367-2277
Līhu'e (808) 246-6252
Website: www.thrifty.com

Driving on Kaua'i

Kaua'i has a simple highway and road system. There is basically one highway that follows the island's perimeter for about three-quarters of its circumference. North of Līhu'e, the Kūhiō Highway (Highway 56) heads up the east coast and the north shore before dead-ending at the Nā Pali coastline. The same road is renamed the Kaumuali'i Highway (Highway 50), where it originates in Līhu'e and transits the south and west coasts. It too, stops dead, this time at the other end of the Nā Pali coast. A road branches south from the Kaumuali'i Highway to Po'ipū and another road carries travelers up the western rim of Waimea Canyon. The speed limit on the highways is 50 m.p.h. with slower limits appearing frequently at intersections and populated areas. Kaua'i has no freeways. Kaua'i County police use radar to enforce speed limits and they do write tickets.

Some of their favorite speed traps are at Wailua Beach for northbound traffic, Po'ipū Road, and the Kōloa-Po'ipū Bypass Road.

Courtesy is the rule of the road here. Drivers will stop to let you enter traffic or turn left onto a busy road. Please return the courtesy when needed. Honking the horn is rude. Most drivers aren't in a hurry, but if you are holding up traffic behind you while taking in the sights, please pull over to allow them to pass.

Directions from locals will include the words: *makai* and *mauka*. On an island, cardinal directions such as north and south mean less than directions that relate to the landscape. *Makai* means "to the sea" and *mauka* means "to the mountain." When told to turn *makai* or *mauka,* it will always be the same direction no matter what direction you came from.

The worst traffic congestion on the island occurs in the corridor between Līhu'e and Kapa'a, especially during the morning and afternoon rush hours. The highway has three lanes—two heading north and one southbound. On weekday mornings, a crew lays down traffic cones to effect a center lane reversal. Traffic is bad all day on Saturdays. The Kapa'a bypass road is an alternate route (see Kapa'a map). Another bypass at Kīpū Road can save time for travelers heading toward Līhu'e from the west. The Kīpū bypass is worthwhile only if congestion is bad and you are heading to the airport or points north.

Highway Mileage

North From Līhuʻe on Highway 56 (The Kūhiō Highway)

	Miles	Minutes
Wailua	7	10
Kapaʻa	10	15
Anahola	15	25
Kīlauea	26	40
Princeville	30	55
Hanalei	32	60
Kēʻē Beach	40	80

South From Līhuʻe on Highway 50 (The Kaumualiʻi Highway)

	Miles	Minutes
Puhi	2	5
Kōloa	11	20
Poʻipū	14	25
Kalāheo	12	20
Hanapēpē	17	30
Waimea	23	40
Kōkeʻe Museum	39	80
Kekaha	26	45
Polihale	38	70

1 mile = 1.6 kilometers

Public Transportation

The Kauaʻi Bus
Phone (808) 241-6410

The Kauaʻi Bus operates a public (fixed route) bus service and a para-transit (door-to-door) bus service from Hanalei to Kekaha daily, except on Sundays and county holidays. Limited service is provided to Kōloa and Poʻipū. Shorter routes branch to Nāwiliwili and to the community college at *Pūhi* from the terminus at Kukui Grove Shopping Center. Buses do not allow bicycles, surfboards, or luggage larger than airline carry-on. There is no service to the airport. Service starts early, with only nine runs made on weekdays and four on Saturdays. All buses are lift-equipped to accommodate persons with mobility aids. Para-transit service requires a 24-hour reservation. Full bus schedules with all bus stops and times are available on the buses or by phoning their office. Fares are $1.50 for adults and $0.75 for seniors and youths.

Miles Per Hour

25	30	35	40	45	50	55
40	50	60	70	80	90	

Kilometers Per Hour

Taxis

A few taxicabs are on hand at the Līhu'e Airport. They park in a holding area away from the terminal and wait for a phone call or a reservation for pickups. One-way fare estimates from the airport are: Princeville, $60; Po'ipū, $40; Marriott, $10. Reservations are recommended for return trips to the airport.

AAA Island Style Taxi
821-7774

Ace Kaua'i Taxi Service
639-4310

Akiko's Taxi
Airport and Kapa'a 822-7588

Al's VIP Limo Taxicab
Po'ipū 742-1390

Bran's Taxi
Island-wide 245-6533

City Cab
Island-wide 245-3227

Kaua'i Cab Service
246-9554

North Shore Cab and Tours
Princeville 826-6189

Po'ipū Taxi
Island-wide 639-2044

Scotty Taxi
245-7888

Southshore Cab
742-1525

Medical Assistance

Wilcox Memorial Hospital
3420 Kūhiō Highway, Līhu'e
245-1100

West Kaua'i Medical Center
4643 Waimea Canyon Dr., Waimea
274-3901

Hyperbaric Center
O'ahu (800) 587-3425

Treatment for divers with decompression sickness, or "the bends."

Poison Control Center
Honolulu (800) 362-3585

Telephone Calls

The area code for all of Hawai'i is 808. Calls made anywhere on the same island are toll-free. Calls made to another Hawaiian island are considered long distance and the area code must be used. A local call on a pay phone costs 50 cents.

Weather Forecasts

For a recorded forecast of weather conditions on all parts of Kaua'i from the National Weather Service, call 245-6001. Call 245-3564 for ocean conditions and high-surf advisories. During emergency weather conditions, call 241-6789 for weather and road conditions.

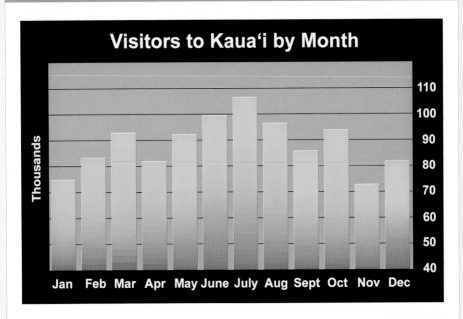

Visitors to Kaua'i by Month

Kaua'i Visitors Bureau

Līhu'e Plaza Building, #207
3016 Umi St., Līhu'e
(808) 245-3971

Stop by to pick up a selection of brochures and advertising materials and talk to a representative of the Visitors Bureau.

Crime

Hawai'i is a reasonably safe place to visit. The state ranks 42nd in the nation in population and ranks 44th in violent crimes. In the United States as a whole, 88 percent of crimes are property offenses, while 12 percent are violent crimes against people. In Hawai'i those numbers are 95 percent property crime and 5 percent violent crime.

Crime on Kaua'i doesn't equal its population percentage of state residents. In the most recently available statistics, 4.8 percent of the state's population resides on Kaua'i, yet it experienced 2.2 percent of the state's violent crimes and 3.7 percent of property crimes.

Criminals mark visitors to Kaua'i as targets for property crimes. Each week, the police report in the *Garden Island* lists the incidents of thefts against visitors. The cases often involve unlocked rooms being entered or watchful culprits lifting unattended purses in public places. Awareness and common sense by potential victims can reduce opportunities for these criminals considerably. A chronic crime problem is theft from rental cars. The shiny, new cars are easily identified, and usually so are the visitors driving them. Don't leave valuables unattended in your car.

Trouble areas are beaches or trailheads, where the car is left unwatched for hours. Placing items in the trunk doesn't help much. In 10 seconds, a thief can break the passenger door window, reach in and pull the trunk release, empty the trunk and take off. Some people suggest leaving items like cameras under the hood. That might help if you aren't being watched when you hide the items. Also, don't forget about your secret hiding place when you return and drive away.

Radio Stations

KFMN FM 97 (96.9)
Popular

KITH (TRAVEL HOST) 98.9 FM
Visitor information and Hawaiian music

KKCR 90.9 FM and **91.9 FM**
Community radio

KQNG (KONG) 570 AM and **93.5 FM**
Popular

KUAI 720 AM
Hawaiian music

KSHK 103.3 FM
Classic rock

KSRF (SURF) 95.9 FM
Hawaiian music

Some AM and FM radio stations based in Honolulu can be heard also on Kaua'i.

Pets

It's not feasible to bring pets along with you on a Hawaiian vacation. Dogs and cats must undergo a 30-day quarantine when entering Hawai'i, even if they are fully vaccinated.

Agricultural Inspection

Before you can leave Hawai'i for the mainland, all your bags are subject to an agricultural inspection at the airport. You will be asked if you have any agricultural products to declare and your luggage will be examined with low level X-ray. Failing to declare an item results in its confiscation and possibly a fine of up to $250. Items that are allowed include: coconuts, unless they are going to Florida; roasted coffee; fresh flowers (excepting maunaloas, gardenias, jade vines or roses); dried or preserved insects; meats; nuts; papayas (only if they have been officially certified); sugar (but not sugar cane). One ounce of beach sand can be taken for decorative purposes, but not soil or potted plants.

Hawai'i at a Glance

Nickname: The Aloha State

Capital: Honolulu

Size: 6,423 sq. miles

Entered Union: August 21, 1959 as 50th State

State Bird: Nēnē

State Tree: Kukui (candlenut)

Yellow Hibiscus

State Flower: Ma'o hau hele (yellow flower hibiscus)

State Fish: Humuhumunukunukuāpua'a

State Mammal: Humpback Whale

State Anthem: Hawai'i Pono'ī

State Gem: Black Coral

State Motto: Ua mau ke ea o ka 'āina i ka pono (The life of the land is perpetuated in righteousness)

State Flag: Designed prior to 1816 for King Kamehameha I, the flag has served the Kingdom, Republic and State of Hawai'i. The Union Jack in the corner honors Hawai'i's early ties with Britain; the eight horizontal stripes represent Hawai'i's eight main islands.

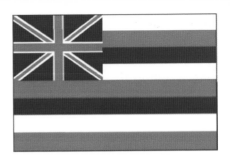

Population: 1,211,537 (42nd in nation)

Life Expectancy: females 82.1 years, males 75.9 years, (highest in nation)

Eight Main Islands: Hawai'i (The Big Island), Maui, O'ahu, Kaua'i, Moloka'i, Lāna'i, Ni'ihau

Five Largest Cities: Honolulu, O'ahu (371,657); Hilo, Hawai'i (40, 759); Kailua, O'ahu (36,513); Kāne'ohe, O'ahu (34,970); Waipahu, O'ahu (33,108).

Most Remote Point From Coast: 28.5 miles—Hawai'i

Miles of Shoreline: 750

Highest Peak: 13, 796 feet, Mauna Kea, Hawai'i

Lowest Temperature: 9°F, Mauna Kea, Hawai'i

Highest Temperature: 100°F, Pahala, Hawai'i

Wettest Place: 460", Mt. Wai'ale'ale, Kaua'i.

Driest Place: 14", Mahukona, Hawai'i.

Average Daily Visitor Population: 159,840

Governor: Ben Cayetano (D)

Lt. Governor: Mazie Hirono (D)

U.S. Senators: Daniel Inouye (D), Daniel Akaka (D)

U.S. Representative: Patsy T. Mink (D)

State Taxes: Excise Tax, 4.167% added to purchases; Transient Accommodations Tax (T.A.T.), 7.25% added to hotel and condo rates in addition to the excise tax.

Kaua'i at a Glance

Nickname: The Garden Island

Island Flower: Mokihana

Island Color: Purple

County Seat: Līhu'e

Size: 552 square miles; 33 miles long and 25 miles wide

Population: 58,303

Average Daily Visitor Population: 16,160

Kaua'i County Historical Censuses

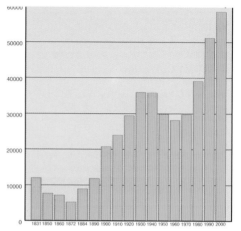

Five Largest Towns: Kapa'a (9,472), Līhu'e (5,674), Wailua Homesteads (4,567), Kalāheo (3,913), Hanamā'ulu (3,272)

Miles of Shoreline: 90

Number of Beaches: 59

Highest Peak: 5,243 feet, Kawaikini

Most Remote Point From Coast: 10.8 miles

Major Industries: Tourism; Sugar, Papaya, Coffee and Guava Agriculture

Number of Hotel Rooms: 3,484

Number of Vacation Condominium Units: 2,869

Lowest Temperature: 29°F, Kōke'e

Highest Temperature: 95°F, Kekaha and Po'ipū

Geographic Opposite: Botswana, Africa

Kaua'i County Mayor: Maryanne Kusaka (R)

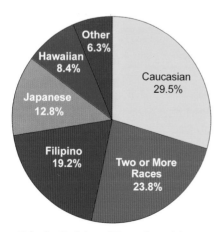

Ethnic Origin of Kaua'i Residents

Other 6.3%
Hawaiian 8.4%
Japanese 12.8%
Filipino 19.2%
Caucasian 29.5%
Two or More Races 23.8%

GEOGRAPHY

The Tropic of Cancer bisects the 132 protuberances of lava and coral that make up the Hawaiian archipelago. At the northwest end, at 28.15° N latitude and rising only 20 feet above the sea is Kure Atoll. Anchoring the chain at the southeast end is the largest island, Hawai'i, which soars to 13,796 feet. With the exception of the five Midway Islands (administered by the U.S. Navy), this chain of shoals, reefs, islets and islands compose the State of Hawai'i. Kaua'i is the oldest and the most northerly of the eight main Hawaiian Islands. A tropical island, Kaua'i lies between 21° 50' N and 22° 15' N latitude. Hong Kong, Mecca and Calcutta share the same latitudes.

The eight main islands clustered at the southeast end of the island chain comprise more than 99 percent of the state's land area of 6,425 square miles. In order of size they are: Hawai'i, Maui, O'ahu, Kaua'i, Moloka'i, Lāna'i, Ni'ihau, and Kaho'olawe. Ni'ihau is privately owned and off-limits to the public. The U.S. Navy until recently used uninhabited Kaho'olawe as a practice target. Hawai'i is the fourth smallest of the United States—larger only than Connecticut, Delaware and Rhode Island.

Sitting alone in the North Pacific, the Hawaiian Islands are the most isolated landmasses on earth. Kaua'i lies 2,300 miles from both California and Alaska and 3,800 miles from Tokyo, Japan. Tahiti is 2,500 miles away and Sidney, Australia, 5,100.

It is two hours earlier in Kaua'i than in North America's Pacific Time Zone, three hours earlier than Mountain Time, four hours before Central Time and five hours earlier than the Eastern Time Zone. In the other direction, Sidney, Australia, is four hours earlier than Kaua'i and Tokyo, Japan, is five hours earlier. Since Hawai'i does not observe daylight-saving time, the differences with most parts of North America become one hour greater during the summer months.

Mana Waipuna Falls was featured in the movie, Jurassic Park

Kaua'i is nearly circular in shape, with its extremes measuring 25 miles by 33 miles. Sixty-five percent of the land is within 5 miles of the coast, with no point being more than 10.8 miles inland. The mean elevation is 1,380 feet with 65 percent of the land above 500 feet and 24 percent above 2,000 feet. Fifty percent of the land has a slope greater than 20 percent.

The high points of the greatly eroded volcano that formed Kaua'i, called Wai'ale'ale, remain at the island's interior. A mile-long ridge joins the peaks of Mt. Wai'ale'ale (5,148 feet) and Kawaikini (5,243 feet) to the south. Extending nearly 10 miles northwest of the summit peaks and covering an area of 30 square miles, the Alaka'i Swamp submerges a cliff-bound plateau. Rainwater is collected and stored in the Alaka'i Swamp at elevations between 4,000 and 5,000 feet. Accessible only by hiking trails, it has the highest elevation of any swamp on the planet. This soggy patch of mire soaks up the near constant rain like a sponge. Broad, shallow valleys traverse the swamp to form drainage lines that carry off the water in a wheel-spoke pattern, feeding seven rivers. Drainage is slow and water stands in pools over shallow depressions. Dense growths of grasses and moss grow over

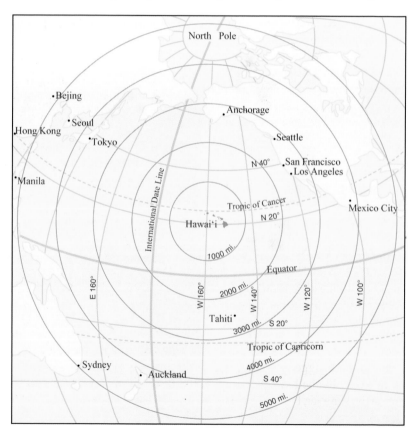

Wai'ale'ale is usually drenched with rain

Nā Pali coast

the nearly still water. Trees, stunted and gnarled by wind, rain and little sunshine, mark a century's passing with growth of a few inches. The Alaka'i Swamp's isolation provides a safe haven for species of rare plants and birds found nowhere else in the world.

The Nā Pali coastline forms a 4,000-foot-high and 15-mile-long bulwark against the North Pacific on Kaua'i's northwest shore. Nā Pali, which means "the cliffs" in Hawaiian, is marked with steep valleys, coastal caves and precipitous ridges. Erosion from rain and wind has carved spires and knife-like serrations in the cliffs. The remote and rugged coastline is accessible only by the Kalalau hiking trail or, in the summer, by zodiac boats and kayaks.

Between the Nā Pali coast and the Alaka'i Swamp, running water continues to carve the Waimea Canyon. Often called "The Grand Canyon of the Pacific," Waimea Canyon presents vistas similar to its namesake, complete with stratified layers of rust, copper, gold and aluminum-colored rock. The two cascades of Waipo'o Falls combine for a total drop of 800 feet in the canyon, producing the highest waterfall on the island. Snaking through the canyon for 19.7 miles is the Waimea River, Kaua'i's longest. The canyon reaches depths of 3,000 feet and forms a 14-mile-long gorge from the island's interior south to the sea. Joined with the Olokele Canyon to the east, the canyons chisel an expanse of rock 10 miles wide.

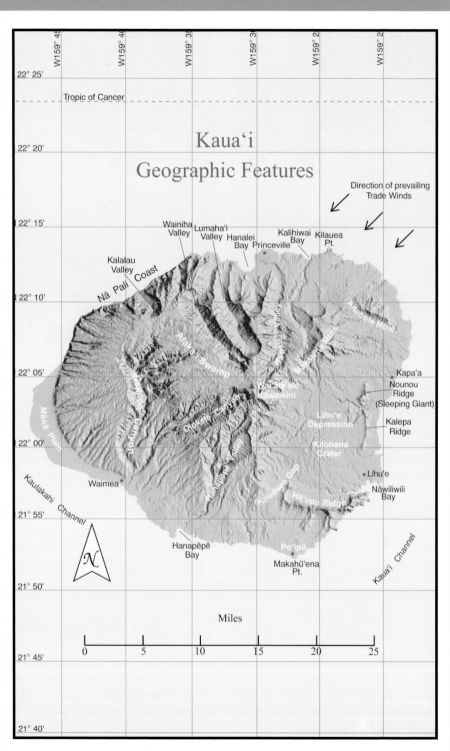

Kaua'i

Geographic Features

Waimea Canyon

Hōkōnui in Hāʻupu Ridge

The southwest and south coast is the leeward side of Kauaʻi and much of its arid acres are planted in sugar cane and coffee. Irrigation of the sugar cane is essential in this hot and sunny area. Waitā Reservoir, built to feed water to the cane fields, covers 424 acres north of Kōloa, making it the largest body of fresh water in Hawaiʻi.

Knudsen Gap separates the Hāʻupu Ridge, which stretches for nine miles in Kauaʻiʻs southeast corner, from the island's mountainous heart.

Also called Hoary Head ridge, the range reaches 2,297 feet at Mt. Hāʻupu, and separates the sugar cane fields and resorts of the south shore from the island's most populated areas along the east coast.

The Wailua River drains the Alakaʻi Swamp to the east. Passenger boats can ease their way upstream for 3 miles—making it the only navigable river in Hawaiʻi. Running at right angles to the river are the small mountain ranges of Kālepa Ridge to

East Kaua'i road, 1905

Hawai'i State Archives

the south and Nounou Ridge to the north. Nounou Ridge is more commonly known as Sleeping Giant.

Another small mountain range, the Anahola Mountains, stand on the northeast corner of the island, marking the start of the North Shore. Here on the windward side, the precipitation is heavier than on the other coasts and, as a result, the vegetation is lush, thick and green. At the heart of the North Shore is Hanalei Bay, the largest bay on Kaua'i. The Hanalei River discharges 140 million gallons of water per day into the bay—the largest average volume from any river on Kaua'i.

There are no large cities on Kaua'i. The most populous towns are the east coast's Kapa'a and Līhu'e.

Līhu'e is the administrative seat of Kaua'i County, which includes the islands of Kaua'i and Ni'ihau. Līhu'e has the only airport with scheduled flights, and nearby Nāwiliwili Bay hosts the busiest seaport.

Kaua'i is the least populated of the four counties in the state. In 2000, the Federal Census counted Kaua'i County's population at 58,463. That was a 14 percent increase over the previous decade's census count of 51,177. The median age of the county's residents increased from 34 in 1990 to 38 in 2000. The nation's mean age in 2000 was 35. Part of the aging phenomenon is explained by Kaua'i's desirability for retirees and the need of many young people to move to the mainland to pursue careers.

Times of Sunrise and Sunset and Hours of Daylight at Līhuʻe

	SUNRISE	SUNSET	HOURS OF DAYLIGHT
January 1	7:17	6:06	10:49
February 1	7:16	6:27	11:11
March 1	6:58	6:42	11:44
April 1	6:30	6:53	12:23
May 1	6:06	7:04	12:58
June 1	5:54	7:17	13:23
July 1	5:58	7:25	13:27
August 1	6:10	7:17	13:07
September 1	6:21	6:54	12:33
October 1	6:29	6:25	11:56
November 1	6:41	6:00	11:19
December 1	7:00	5:53	10:53

ONLY IN HAWAIʻI

Since it occurs only in the tropics, Hawaiʻi is the only state in the nation to experience the phenomenon of Lahaina Noon—the high noon when the sun is exactly overhead. The rest of the nation recognizes the summer solstice as the event when the sun's rays are closest to being direct in the northern hemisphere. Hawaiʻi and other locations south of the Tropic of Cancer receive the sun's direct rays as the apparent path of the sun passes overhead before the solstice and retreats to the south afterwards. At the exact time of Lahaina Noon, which can occur anytime from 12:17 to 12:43 p.m., objects that stand straight up (like flagpoles, telephone poles, etc.) will not cast a shadow. The most southerly points in Hawaiʻi experience Lahaina Noon on earlier and later dates than the northern parts. Hilo on the Big Island encounters the overhead sun around May 18 and July 24; Kahului, Maui on May 24 and July 18; Honolulu, Oʻahu on May 26 and July 15; and Līhuʻe, Kauaʻi on May 31 and July 11. Chosen in a contest sponsored by the Bishop Museum several years ago, Lahaina Noon was the selected appellation because it means "cruel sun," which is what the sun feels like when it is directly overhead.

CLIMATE

It's hard to imagine a climate more agreeable than Kaua'i's. Daytime high temperatures consistently reach the 80s, cooling to the high 60s at night. Sunshine is plentiful and the humidity is moderate. In fact, the climate is a principal reason that Kaua'i attracts more than a million visitors a year.

Kaua'i experiences only two seasons, summer and winter. The warmest months are August and September and the coolest months are January and February, but the average maximum temperature between the warmest and coolest month ranges only 7 degrees. The least precipitation falls from June to September, and the rainiest months are December to February. These are averages and trends however; hot, dry days and cool, wet days will occur in every month.

Kaua'i's equable climate is credited to a number of factors. Its location is tropical; the 22nd latitude north of the equator bisects the island. The vast waters of the Pacific Ocean—which act as a climatic thermostat, warming cool air masses and cooling warm air currents— surround the Hawaiian Islands. Ocean temperatures around Kaua'i range from 76 to 79°F. The trade winds, which regularly blow at 10 to 20 mph, also provide a moderating effect on the temperature and humidity. The average relative humidity at Līhu'e is 75 percent. In fact, after measuring humidity data for 40 years, the average monthly relative humidity there has never varied more than 3.5 percentage points. In the Hawaiian Islands, the trade winds occur well over 50 percent of the time, with this figure exceeding 90 percent in the summer. Sometimes the trade winds are replaced by Kona winds, which can carry rain and uncomfortably humid weather from the southwest.

Despite a lack of strong seasonal variation, Kaua'i is host to an extraordinary diversity of microclimates, from desert to

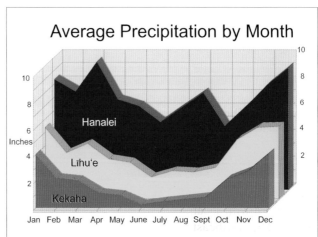

Average Precipitation by Month

Inches

Hanalei

Līhu'e

Kekaha

Jan Feb Mar Apr May June July Aug Sept Oct Nov Dec

Sunrise at Kēʻē

Torrential rain flooded the Hanalei Valley

rainforest. Temperature drops three degrees for every 1,000 feet of altitude. This is a factor you are sure to notice when you drive to the Kalalau Valley lookout and gain more than 4,000 feet of altitude in just 18 miles. Rainfall varies more with location than with season. The northeast shore is the windward side of the island when the

trade winds are blowing. When the winds, laden with moisture, blow over the island, they are forced up by the land. As the temperature of the air drops with altitude, so does its ability to hold moisture. The moisture in the cooler air condenses into rain, mainly in the higher altitudes of the windward side. The air, depleted of much of its moisture, is pushed over the mountains, warming as it descends to the island's leeward side. The sunshine-drenched resort of Poʻipū is in the lee of the Hāʻupu (Hoary Head) Ridge. The extinct volcano that formed Waiʻaleʻale traps most of the moisture headed to the towns of Waimea and Hanapēpē and the sugar cane fields of southwest Kauaʻi. Hanalei, on the windward side of the island, receives four times as much rain as Kekaha.

Some very wet years in the 1960s caused the average annual precipitation measured at the rain gauge at Mt. Waiʻaleʻale to be listed at 460 inches. Since then, every guidebook, brochure and tour guide has called Mt. Waiʻaleʻale the "wettest spot on earth." More recently, Waiʻaleʻale's average precipitation has been between 350 and 400 inches— still voluminous by any standard.

It rains every day somewhere on Kauaʻi. Most rain showers are isolated and of short duration. Severe storms can occur, particularly in the winter. If you plan on hiking in the backcountry, especially the Nā Pali trail, pay heed

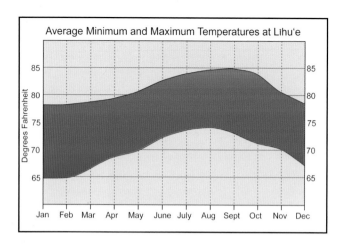

Average Minimum and Maximum Temperatures at Līhu'e

to flash flood warnings given in local weather forecasts.

Winter storms in the north Pacific create swells and large surf on Kaua'i's North Shore. Twenty-foot waves are possible. They are extremely dangerous, but from a safe distance they provide spectacular ocean watching. Hurricanes and tsunamis are possible but rare. Weather forecasts can warn of approaching hurricanes several days in advance. Tsunami warning sirens are positioned throughout the island. They are sounded as a test at 11:45 a.m. on the first government workday of each month.

The hurricanes and tropical storms that affect Hawai'i usually originate off Mexico or Central America. As they head west, they usually travel to the south of Hawai'i or dissipate over cooler ocean water if they turn north. Hurricane season in Hawai'i is July to November. Hawaiian names are given to hurricanes when they pass within 1,000 miles of the Hawaiian Islands. Five named hurricanes have affected Kaua'i in the last half of the twentieth century. Three hurricanes struck Kaua'i in the 1950s, causing two deaths. In 1982, Hurricane Iwa had sustained winds of 81 m.p.h., with gusts up to 117 m.p.h., resulting in one death and more than $200 million in damage. The most devastating hurricane was 'Iniki, which struck in 1992. Its winds and rain took eight lives and caused $1.9 billion in property damage.

In 1957, a major tsunami that originated in the Aleutians hit Kaua'i's north shore. In the town of Hā'ena, the sea rose more than 32 feet above normal. Only four of the 29 homes in the small community were left standing after the waves. The surging water virtually wiped out the villages of Wainiha and Kalihiwai and the North Shore was isolated for days as bridges and roads were destroyed.

Good weather is far more likely to embrace you than bad weather. You can appreciate the weather even more during your visit as you scan the newspaper for temperatures back home.

THE HAWAIIAN LANGUAGE

The prevailing language of Hawai'i today is English, liberally peppered with Hawaiian words and phrases. All of a visitor's requests for services can be understood as well as answered in English. An elementary understanding of the Hawaiian language, however, is the foundation of appreciating all of Hawaiian culture and your attempts to correctly pronounce words will show respect to the people who are your hosts. Hawaiian place names are commonly used, so familiarity will breed less contempt when traveling. Some words such as *aloha*, *lū'au* and *lei*, you already knew before you became a *malihini* (newcomer); other words such as *mahalo* (thank you), you will probably add to your vocabulary of the *'ōlelo Hawai'i* (Hawaiian language) on the first day of your visit.

Hawaiian belongs to the Polynesian family of languages related closely to Tahitian, Marquesan and Māori, and more distantly to Fijian, Malagasy and Malay. The first European to listen to the Hawaiians speak, Captain James Cook, found he was able to communicate with them thanks to his rudimentary grasp of Tahitian. The Hawaiian that Cook heard evolved from the language of the Tahitian voyagers who populated the Hawaiian Islands centuries earlier.

The Hawaiians were rich in unwritten literature that included poems, songs, genealogies and mythologies. Hawaiian existed in only its oral form until the early nineteenth century. Christian missionaries, anxious to have Hawaiians read their teachings, set upon the daunting task of putting the unwritten language to paper. The Hawaiian language, in both oral and written forms, continued as the language of general use for the government, business, and social circles for several decades. As their monarchy died, so did usage of the Hawaiian's language. Hawaiian is no longer spoken as the mother tongue, except on the privately owned island of Ni'ihau and in the homes of a few old Hawaiians. Some local churches hold services in Hawaiian, as well.

Recently, Hawaiian is receiving renewed attention by the state government and the school system. In 1978 Hawaiian was again made an official language by the State of Hawai'i, the only state to officially use a Native American language. The government reestablished schools that teach through Hawaiian in 1987, and the University of Hawai'i offers degree programs in Hawaiian language studies.

Children of Anahola School

Listeners to Hawaiian delight in painting it with such flattering but vague adjectives as: melodious, soft, fluid, gentle and mellifluous. Gushing metaphorically, Hawaiian sways like a palm tree in a gentle wind and slips off the tongue like a love song. There are two unvarnished reasons for Hawaiian sounding this way. First, unlike English, Hawaiian has no consonant clusters, and every syllable ends with a vowel, resulting in a high vowel to consonant ratio. Second, Hawaiian has no sibilants (s-like sounds), an attribute endearing to singers.

The missionaries assigned only twelve letters to the alphabet when they phonetically rendered the Hawaiian language. The consonants are: h, k, l, m, n, p and w. Five vowels are used: a, e, i, o and u. The consonants are pronounced the same as in English, except for the *w*, which is often pronounced as a *v* when it appears in the middle of a word and follows an *e* or an *i*. When *w* follows an *a* it can be pronounced as either *w* or *v*, thus you will hear either Hawai'i or Havai'i. Hawaiian vowels come in both short and long duration forms. Long duration vowels are stressed with a bar above the letter called the *kahakō* in Hawaiian and macron in English. The vowels are pronounced as: *a* as in "father" when stressed and as in "above" when not stressed, *e* as in "they" when stressed and as in "let" when not stressed, *i* as in "marine", *o* as in "boat" and *u* as in "true." As well as the *kahakō*, Hawaiian uses the diacritical mark called an *'okina* and is represented with ' which looks like a backwards apostrophe. The *'okina*

indicates a glottal stop and is used as an additional consonant. In English it would approximate the sound between the vowels in the expression "oh-oh." Use of the *kahakō* and the *'okina* are important to correct pronunciation of the words in which they appear. Their usage has become more prevalent in recent years; in older guidebooks and maps they were sometimes omitted.

There's just one more rule you need to learn. Consonants aren't, but vowels can be clustered into diphthongs. A diphthong is created when two vowels join to form a single sound. The vowels glide together with stress being placed on the first vowel. In English, examples are toil and euphoria. Examples in Hawaiian are *lei* (lay) and *heiau* (hay-ee-ow). The eight vowel pairs that make up Hawaiian diphthongs are: ae, ai, ao, au, ei, eu, oi, ou.

Some words are doubled to emphasize their meaning. *Wiki* means quick, *wikiwiki* means very quick. Hawaiian appears formidable when you are attempting to pronounce many long and similar-looking words. The long words are usually combinations of shorter words and if you segment the long words into their shorter components, pronunciation becomes more easily achievable. Several words begin with *ka*, meaning "the", which is attached to the word itself. Therefore *Kā'anapali*, which means "the rolling precipices," should be broken down to Ka-a-na-pa-li. The name for Hawai'i's state fish is so long it will barely fit on a T-shirt, but when you break down *humuhumunukunukuāpua'a* into humu-humu-nuku-nuku-apu-a-a, it's easy—nearly.

Glossary of Hawaiian Words

a'a rough clinker lava, accepted as the correct geological term

'āina land

ali'i chief, royalty

aloha love, affection, hello, to greet, goodbye

ānuenue rainbow

'apōpō tomorrow

a'u swordfish

hale house

hana bay

haole Caucasian, recently come to mean any foreigner

hapa haole half Caucasian

hau hibiscus tiliaceus

hau'oli happy

hau'oli lā hānau happy birthday

heiau ancient terrace or platform for worship

he mea iki you are welcome

hoaloha friend

hono bay

honu sea turtle

hukilau pull-net fishing

hula Hawaiian dance with chants where a story is told with the hands

'i'iwi scarlet honey-creeper

imu underground earthen oven used in cooking at a lū'au

ka the

kā belonging to, of

kahiko ancient, old

kahuna priest, expert

kai seawater, seaward

kālua to bake in an underground oven, kālua pig is the featured entrée at a lū'au

kama'āina native, literally "child of the land"

kanaka human being, man, person

kānaka human beings, men, persons

kāne male, man, husband, used to indicate a public men's restroom

kapu taboo, forbidden, sacred, keep out if it appears on a sign

keiki child, children

koa a type of hardwood

kōkua to help, assist

Kona leeward or a leeward wind

kukui candlenut tree

kula plain, upland

ku'u ipo my sweetheart

lae point (geographic feature)

lānai porch, terrace, balcony

lani heavenly

lei garland of flowers

liliko'i passion fruit

limu seaweed

lomilomi salt salmon minced with onion and tomato

lū'au traditional feast

mahalo thanks, to thank, admiration

makai toward the sea (used when giving directions)

mahimahi dolphin fish (not a dolphin!)

mai'a banana

maika'i good, fine, beautiful

maka'āinana public, common people, citizen

malihini newcomer, visitor, tourist

mana supernatural power

manō shark

mauka inland (used when giving directions)

mauna mountain

mele song

Mele Kalikimaka Merry Christmas

moana open sea, ocean

moku island

mu'umu'u long loose-fitting dress introduced by the missionaries

nā the (plural), by, for

nani pretty

nēnē Hawaiian goose
niu coconut
nui big, large, important, many, much
'ohana family including extended family
'ono delicious
pāhoehoe smooth and ropey lava, accepted as the correct geological term
pakalōlō marijuana, literally "crazy smoke"
pali cliff, precipice
paniolo cowboy
pau finished, completed
poi starchy paste made from taro roots
poke cubed, marinated and spiced raw fish
pono righteous, honest, moral
pua flower
pua'a pig
puna spring, creek
pūpū hors d'oeuvre
pu'u hill
'ukulele small stringed instrument
wa'a canoe
wahine woman, wife, female, Mrs., used to indicate a public women's restroom
wāhine women
wai fresh water
wailele waterfall
wikiwiki very quick, in a hurry

Meanings of Kaua'i Place Names

'Aliomanu scar made by birds
'Ele'ele black
Hā'ena red hot
Ha'ikū haughty, to speak abruptly
Hanakāpī'ai bay sprinkling food
Hanakoa bay of warriors
Hanalei crescent bay
Hanamā'ulu tired bay
Hanapēpē crushed bay
Honopū conch bay
Kāhili feather standard
Kalāheo proud day
Kalalau the wanderer
Kalapakī double-yolked egg
Kalihiwai water's edge
Kapa'a solid
Keālia salt land
Kekaha dry hot place
Kīlauea spewing of many vapors
Kilohana beautiful view
Kīpū to remain as mist or rain
Kīpūkai Kīpū at the sea
Kōloa tall sugar cane or a native Hawaiian duck
Līhu'e goose flesh
Limahuli turning hand

Makana gift
Moloa'a tangled roots
Miloli'i fine twist
Nā Pali the cliffs
Nāwiliwili grove of wiliwili trees, a member of the legume family
Nu'alolo brains heaped up
Olokele former name of the 'i'iwi or Kaua'i honeycreeper
Pāpa'a secure enclosure
Polihale house blossom
Puhi eel, set on fire
Waiakalua water of the pit
Wai'ale'ale rippling water
Waikea white water
Wailua two waters, spirit of a ghost
Waimea red water
Wainiha hostile waters
Wai'oli joyful water
Waipouli dark water

Pidgin

Pidgin is the spicy Creole tongue that borrows from other languages. Hawaiian pidgin has roots in the plantation days of the nineteenth century, when European and American owners had to communicate with recently arrived Chinese, Japanese and Portuguese laborers. It was designed as a simple language, born of necessity and stripped of dispensable words.

Modern pidgin is a vernacular of mainly Hawaiian and English-derived words with a unique syntax and a rising inflection that can change the meaning of what is being said. It is a colorful, ever-changing dialect as regionally distinct as the speech of Louisiana Cajuns. No longer plantation talk, pidgin is learned at school and on the streets.

Hip young locals are the main pidgin speakers. They choose to speak pidgin as a private "in" language and are perfectly capable of speaking English. Whole conversations can take place in pidgin or one or two words can be dropped into conventional English. You might not be able to understand what the locals are saying in pidgin (that's the idea), but you should get a sense of what is being meant. Pidgin is the mark of the local; newcomers shouldn't attempt to speak it. You won't sound cool—just stupid.

A Sampling of Hawaiian Pidgin

an den? and then?

any kine anything, any kind

ass right that's right, you're correct

beef fight

brah/bruddah friend, brother

broke da mout delicious tasting

buggah guy or thing that is a pest

bumbye later on, after a while

chicken skin bumps on your skin when you get the chills, goose bumps

cockaroach steal, rip off

da kine used as filler when the speaker can't think of the right word to use

garans guaranteed

geevum go for it, try hard

grind to eat

grinds food

Hawaiian time to be late

howzit? how is it going? how are you?

lolo dumb, crazy

Maui wowie particular type of marijuana

mo bettah good stuff, great idea

moke big, tough local guy

pau hana finish work, quitting time

poi dog a mutt, a person of mixed ethnic background

stink eye a dirty look

tita a tough girl

talk story a conversation

shahkbait pale, white-skinned person

yeah yeah yeah yeah yes I know already so shut up

GEOLOGY

The Hawaiian chain of volcanic peaks—consisting of 132 islands, islets, reefs and shoals—stretches 1,523 miles northwest to southeast across the center of the Pacific Ocean. There is more to the Hawaiian Islands than the land you see. If the ocean were drained of its water, this chain would appear as a lofty mountain range. Kaua'i, fourth in size, lies at the northwest end of the eight main islands.

Each volcanic cone is built of dark, iron-rich rock that poured out of vents as highly fluid lava in countless eruptions that spanned millions of years. The result is the tallest mountains in the world, which break the surface of the ocean at about 18,000 feet.

Like most of the world's volcanoes, the Hawaiian cones spawned from a zone of weakness in the earth's crust. Weaknesses occur where giant, slow-moving tectonic plates—segments of the earth's crust—rub and collide as they drift like icebergs atop the mantle. A hot spot is a place where an extraordinary amount of molten rock is generated. Its source is a huge upwelling column of mantle rock. The plume of mantle rock ascends because it is hotter than the surrounding rock, chemically different, or both. When the temperature is high enough, or its pressure has been reduced enough, the rising rock partially melts and pushes through the earth's crust.

The stationary hot spot in the earth's mantle that caused Kaua'i's birth, and later spawned the island of O'ahu and the island cluster of Maui, Moloka'i, Lāna'i and Kaho'olawe, now remains beneath the island of Hawai'i. For 70 million years, a plate of the earth's crust has been moving over that hot spot. Again and again, molten rock has risen from the hot spot to build volcanic islands, and in the seemingly endless procession of geologic time they have drifted away, riding aboard the plate. The oldest volcanoes created by this event are the submerged Emperor Seamounts, which now lie north of the island of Midway. The youngest volcano is a burgeoning seamount named Lo'ihi, 20 miles southeast of the island of Hawai'i. This embryonic island must grow another 3,180 feet before it emerges from the ocean—60,000 years from now.

The volcanoes of the Hawaiian chain are rounded, dome-shaped masses, broad for their height. In profile, they resemble the shields of medieval warriors, hence, they are known as shield volcanoes. These volcanoes build atop vents that effuse highly mobile lava that runs swiftly and spreads widely, accreting a cone of gentle slope.

Around the rim of the Pacific Ocean more viscous lava flows have produced the classic upswept form of a composite volcano. The lava does not flow far before it solidifies, building higher and higher around its vent.

Erosion carved the "Cathedrals" of Nā Pali

Famous composite volcanoes are Fuji in Japan and Rainier, Hood, Shasta and St. Helens in the United States.

Hawaiian volcanoes generally erupt along cracks in the cone's flanks. Movement within the earth's crust tears open a series of fissures, forming a rift zone. Pressing through the cracks, magma fountains onto the land as lava. When an eruption is over, the lava remaining in the fissure hardens into a wall-like mass called a dike. Hundreds of thin dikes may be seen cutting across the west walls of Waimea Canyon on Kaua'i.

Wai'ale'ale, the volcano that formed Kaua'i, had two principal periods of eruptive activity. Between 5 and 6 million years ago, lava flows broke the ocean's surface. Thin flows of lava, each from 5 to 15 feet thick, piled atop each other to eventually build a broad, smooth, dome-shaped mountain. Geologists name rock from this island-building period the Waimea Canyon series. Likely, the neighboring

island of Ni'ihau was linked to Kaua'i and the same volcano consisted of several craters.

Fields of rubble in the ocean floor indicate that massive pieces of the island broke off and slid into the ocean. A slide split the summit of Wai'ale'ale along a north-south line. Part of the island disappeared into the ocean and what remained to the east of present-day Waimea Canyon, dropped in elevation. Another catastrophic slide later broke a large portion off of the north flank of Wai'ale'ale. The towering sea cliff left behind eroded into the Nā Pali coastline. Slides of such magnitude surely must have generated big tsunamis.

Eruptions of lava continued after the slides, building a new volcanic shield in the dropped eastern portion of the island. A caldera formed in the new shield that eventually eroded into the Līhu'e depression, a broad basin five miles northwest of Līhu'e. Some caldera-filling lavas were more

Layers of lava flows are exposed in Waimea Canyon

resistant to erosion and now stand in relief above the eroded flanks. The Hā'upu Range, in the southeast corner, is the remains of a caldera that filled with hard, dense lava, which withstood the ravages of weathering that whittled away the softer lava at its flanks.

Building and rebuilding of the shield that formed Kaua'i continued until 4.3 million years ago. Running water shaped the gentle volcanic slopes into a landscape of jagged ridges and deep valleys. After a time of volcanic quiescence, eruptions began again. This period of renewed volcanism started 3.65 million years ago and lasted until half a million years ago. The lava, cinder cones, and ash beds produced from these more modern eruptions are identified as the Kōloa volcanic series. The largest volcanic vent of the newer series is Kilohana, the 1,133-foot-high mountain west of Līhu'e. Erosion continued relentlessly. Kōloa basalts flowed into valleys, completely filling some of them and diverting streams to erode new channels elsewhere.

Kaua'i, which appeared late in geological history, is doomed to extinction, but on a time-scale of a magnitude that defies comprehension. It will be eroded to a shoal as the plate that carried it past the hot spot of its birth inches inexorably toward the edges of the Pacific. Like a conveyor belt, the plate trundles to the Aleutian Trench, where the sea floor bends into the earth's interior. Kaua'i's cycle will be complete as its remnants are reincorporated into the crust of the earth.

HISTORY

People Come to Kaua'i

People did not rush to settle in the world's most remote place. Humans have inhabited other parts of the Earth 60 times longer than they have lived in Hawai'i. The first migrations to Kaua'i and the other Hawaiian islands likely came from the 11 islands that make up the Marquesas, 2,000 miles to the southeast. The Marquesans were masters at building great double-hulled canoes. The two hulls were fastened together to form a catamaran with a cabin built in the center. At 60 to 80 feet long, these voyaging canoes could carry an extended family of 30 people, as well as all the staples they would need in a new land.

As new evidence comes to light, anthropologists have pushed the date of the first journey to Hawai'i back to about A.D. 400 The Polynesian sailors had neither charts nor navigational instruments, but relied on an internal navigational system programmed by intuition, knowledge, and experience.

The first settlers came prepared. With them they brought useful plants such as taro, ti, sugar cane, ginger, yams, bamboo and the breadfruit tree. They also brought the small pigs of Polynesia, dogs, fowl, and stowaway rats. Native lowland forests were cleared with slash-and-burn techniques to plant crops. The new Hawaiians started to irreversibly and profoundly alter their environment. Habitat loss, competition for food, and predation by the introduced animals wreaked havoc upon the native animals. Many species of birds had already become extinct before the arrival of Europeans.

The Polynesians likely settled the southernmost island of Hawai'i first. To the northwest, they could have easily accessed Maui by crossing the narrow channel and the migration would have continued across the Hawaiian chain. For seven centuries the Marquesans continued their voyages to Hawai'i. They lived peacefully on the new land and the tribes coexisted in relative harmony since there was no competition for land.

Hawai'i State Archives

Man of the Sandwich Islands by John Webber

Hawai'i State Archives

Hawaiian war canoe with masked paddlers by John Webber

In about the twelfth century, an exodus of aggressive Tahitians subjugated the settled Hawaiians. The Tahitian priest Pa'ao introduced the warlike god Kū and replaced basic animistic beliefs with the rigid *kapu* (forbidden) system. Deciding that the Hawaiian blueblood was too diluted, Pa'ao summoned Pili, a Tahitian chief, to establish a new royal lineage. With Pili as ruler and Pa'ao as high priest, a new dynasty was formed. It was to last seven centuries.

Scholars speculate that this second wave of Polynesians drove the former Marquesans farther north in the Hawaiian chain until they were eliminated from the Islands. Conquered Marquesans may have been the Menehune mentioned in early Hawaiian and Tahitian chants. Tahitians bore a similar term, manahune, with honor until warriors from Raiatea conquered their island and the word took on a new context. Manahune became the derisive name for a commoner. When the Tahitians seized the position of leadership in the Hawaiian Islands, they likely labeled the early settlers Menehune, repeating the Raiateans' process of hierarchical demotion.

Legend turned the Menehune into a race of gnome-like, shy, forest dwellers credited as master builders capable of completing major projects in one night. They were regarded as physically small, muscular people who were low on the social scale. The mythical Menehune worked with great diligence, often forming lines miles long, passing stones hand-to-hand. They are credited with such engineering feats on Kaua'i as the construction of the Malae Heiau at Wailua and the Alekoko, or Menehune, fishpond at Nāwiliwili. Remnants of the Menehune Ditch, which was used to divert water from the Waimea River to irrigate taro fields, are still visible. The walls of the ditch were built of cut-and-dressed lava stone, rare in the Hawaiian Islands.

The idea of a physically small race of people caught the imagination of early Westerners. Menehune may have had small importance in the social system of the Tahitians, but of the skeletal remains discovered on Kaua'i, none indicate a race of physically small people. It is not known for certain what became of the Menehune. A story passed down that the king of the Menehune decided that their race had become impure from intermarriage and led his people to seek new lands. Stone structures on the small northwestern islands of Necker and Nihoa indicate that some people stopped there. These tiny islands could have sustained only a very small population. Interestingly, in a census taken in the early 1800s, in an upper section of the Wainiha Valley on the north coast of Kaua'i, 65 persons described their nationality as Menehune.

The Tahitian migration to the Hawaiian Islands lasted for about a century. Their intricate system of beliefs and practices was transformed into a stratified and rigid Hawaiian culture. This caste system placed the *ali'i* (noble class) at the top. Slightly lower in prestige were the *kāhuna*, which included priests, healers and astrologers. Lower down were the *kanakawale*, the craftsmen and artisans who made the canoes, calabashes and lei. Next were the *maka'āinana* (common people) who worked the land and at the bottom were the *kauwā* (untouchables). The noble class had

lower chiefs within it who provided the higher chief with taxes and commoners to serve as soldiers. Land was divided among the chiefs into wedge-shaped plots, called *ahupua'a*, which extended from the ocean inland to the mountain peaks. The tightly circumscribed bloodlines could not be crossed. Most people were at death what they had been at birth.

A man of the Sandwich Islands in a mask by John Webber

Hawai'i State Archives

Life centered on the *kapu*, a complete set of rules that dictated what was sacred or forbidden. A *kapu* forbade women to eat pork, bananas and shark meat; nor could they eat in the company of men. According to the nineteenth century Hawaiian scholar, David Malo, a person could not allow his shadow to fall upon the house of a chief, or pass through that chief's stockade or doorway.

Kapu breakers were believed to be violating the will of the gods and could be executed. While many *kapu* may seem strange, some were founded as conservation measures, such as seasons being established for the gathering or catching of scarce food. The word *kapu* is believed to be the Hawaiian version of the Tahitian *tapu*, from which the word taboo is also derived.

Hawaiians generally worshiped privately at small shrines or in their homes. The focal points of most major religious observances were large open-air temples known as *heiau*. Ruins of these *heiau* can still be found throughout Hawai'i. Today, what remains are usually simple platforms, terraces and walls made of lava stones.

Because ancient Hawaiians did not have a written language, their past was kept alive with the voices of kāhuna who chanted the sacred *mele* (historical record). The most important *mele* was called the Kumulipo and it retold the genealogies of the ali'i. It was by their direct lineage to the progenitor gods Wakea and Papa that the *ali'i* claimed divine right to rule. They believed the union of these gods gave birth to the islands of Maui, Kaho'olawe, Hawai'i, Kaua'i and Ni'ihau. The rest of the Hawaiian Islands were believed to be created when these gods took other mates.

The Kumulipo tells us that Kaua'i enjoyed many decades of peace after the invasion and conquest of a prince called Moikeha. Years of peace had not debilitated the prowess of Kaua'i's warriors. Their courage and battle skills were renowned.

Succeeding Moikeha was Kūkona, who was to become the symbol of the highest ideals of chivalry in battle for all Hawai'i. The *kāhuna* of Kaua'i came before King Kūkona in the mid-fourteenth century to foretell an invasion and a battle in which he would prevail. Across the 90-mile-wide ocean channel the allied forces of all the other Hawaiian islands under the command of Kalaunui-Ohua set sail on an armada of war canoes. Kūkona sent his heir, Mano-Kalanipo, to represent him in battle. The forces of Kaua'i numbered only 500, but in one brief battle the combined armies of the invaders suffered absolute defeat. As was custom, the *ali'i* leading the defeated armies faced being slaughtered and offered as sacrifices to the war god, Kū. Kūkona, however, decided to set the chiefs free providing they took an oath promising that they or their descendants would never again invade Kaua'i. With promises sworn, Kūkona set the conquered chiefs free and gave them and their men provisions. He had their canoes repaired and even gave them more from his own fleet. This was the beginning of a long peace on Kaua'i that lasted until 1795. The chivalry and grace embodied in Kūkona remained throughout centuries of Hawaiian history as the criterion by which all other acts of warfare were measured.

Hawai'i State Archives

An offering before Captain Cook by John Webber

Strangers From a Strange Land

Captain Cook departed Plymouth, England, in 1776. His mission was to find the long-sought Northwest Passage. For more than two centuries, European explorers had tried unsuccessfully to map a link between the Atlantic and Pacific Oceans via a route atop the North American continent. Cook had been instructed by The Earl of Sandwich, First Lord of the British Admiralty, to find the theorized passage from a western approach. The sea passage was officially to be the sole object of his search, but it was Captain James Cook's destiny to turn prosaic instructions into accounts of history.

Cook commanded the 100-foot flagship, HMS *Resolution*, and her companion, the 90-foot HMS *Discovery*. Among Cook's crew were midshipman George Vancouver and William Bligh, who was sailing master on the *Resolution*. Vancouver would go on to captain his own voyages in the Pacific and along the west coast of North America. Ten years later, Bligh became the infamous commander of the HMS *Bounty*.

Captain James Cook

The first Hawaiian island that Cook sighted was O'ahu. Calm winds held his ships offshore during the night while he drifted west until he was in view of Kaua'i. As the ships worked their way closer to Kaua'i's shore, natives paddled canoes out to meet them. The intrepid Englishmen were given a friendly, although timid, reception. Cook found a suitable place to drop anchor at Waimea Bay.

Captain Cook and his crew sailed to Hawai'i on ships similar to this reproduction of HMS Endeavor

Cook went ashore with a guard of armed marines. He was surprised that his presence caused the natives to fall face down to the ground as they would before the highest *ali'i*, rising only with his encouragement. Captain Cook didn't understand that the islanders prostrating themselves in his presence and his reverential treatment resulted from the propitious timing of his arrival. Every year during the winter months a festival called *makahiki* was held throughout the Islands. It was a period of rejoicing and festivity dedicated to honoring Lono, the fertility god of the earth. The islanders celebrated by feasting, dancing, playing games and freely exchanging sex partners. According to legend, Lono was to someday arrive on moving islands. Cook's appearance, commanding ships larger and like none other the natives had seen, was interpreted as the coming of a god.

The *kāhuna* wanted to test the force of this apparition. A real god, they believed, had no want of women; men did. With the approval of the Hawaiian men, throngs of women swarmed the ships to offer their bodies to please Lono and his attendants; whereby the sailors quickly failed their test of divinity. Cook gave strict orders prohibiting sexual relations with the Hawaiians. Of the 112 members of Cook's expedition, 66 showed symptoms of venereal disease. The infected crewmembers were not allowed ashore. The attempt to keep the native population free of this disease, to which they had never been exposed, proved futile. Despite the exhibition of un-godlike behavior from his crew, Cook did not associate with any of the women. Whether this interloper was a deity was something the Hawaiians could ponder in his absence.

The stores of the *Resolution* and the *Discovery* were replenished and on January 23, 1778, five days after first sighting a Hawaiian island, Cook left Kaua'i—the Northwest Passage once again the object of his quest. In honor of his patron in the British Admiralty, Cook christened the islands he came upon by chance the Sandwich Islands.

The next leg of Cook's journey took him through the Bering Strait into the Arctic Ocean. In the middle of summer, at a latitude of N 70° 44', an impenetrable wall of pack ice halted Cook's progress. Disappointed, he decided to return to the warmth of the Sandwich Islands.

On the return trip, winds carried Cook to the east of Kaua'i. At daybreak on November 26, 1778, Cook sighted the island of Maui. Maui's principal chief, Kahekili, paid a visit to Charles Clerke, who captained the *Discovery*, and brought a red feather cloak as a gift. A chief from the island of Hawai'i, Kalaniopu'u, who was battling in the Hāna district of Maui, brought some of his people to stay overnight on the *Resolution*. Some of those who stayed aboard had venereal sores and were given medicine. In less than a year, the infection brought by the English sailors had spread throughout the Islands.

The rocky and exposed north coast of Maui offered no safe anchorage. The English continued sailing to the last and largest island of the chain. For a month Cook sailed along the northern and eastern shores of the island the natives called Hawai'i. He was frustrated in his search for a safe anchorage until he rounded South Point and sailed into the shelter of Kealakekua Bay on January 17, 1779. The two ships anchored in the bay and were received by 10,000 Hawaiians who lined the shore and filled a flotilla of 3,000 canoes.

By an even greater coincidence, Cook's second visit to the Hawaiian Islands was again during *makahiki*, and he happened to choose Kealakekua Bay. According to Hawaiian legend, Kealakekua Bay was considered Lono's private, sacred harbor. Natives from around the island came to pay homage to what they were sure was a returning god.

Congenial relations prevailed for the next two weeks. But the English overstayed their welcome when restocking supplies for another voyage north nearly exhausted the resources of the islanders. On the morning of February 4, the English set sail along the coast to the north, followed by a canoe entourage. After the ships cleared the north point of the island, a violent winter storm broke the foremast of the *Resolution*. Cook's flagship limped back to Kealakekua Bay so that the carpenters could make repairs.

Cook found that the time of the *makahiki* had expired when he returned. The Hawaiians began to share their doubts that a true god would return after the *makahiki*. While repairs to the mast were being made, some natives stole a cutter from the *Discovery*. An infuriated Cook went ashore with Lt. James King and nine marines with the intent of taking Kalaniopu'u hostage in exchange for return of the boat. As Cook and his party searched for the chief, a large crowd of natives gathered around them. When Cook decided to leave, a skirmish erupted at the water's edge. A native menaced Cook with a stone and a long iron spike. Cook fired at the native, but the shot could not penetrate the heavy straw mat that he wore as armor. The native turned triumphantly to the crowd to show them he was unharmed. Emboldened, the crowd of Hawaiians threw stones

Death of Captain Cook by John Webber

at the marines who were lined up against the water. When the crowd surged forward, Cook turned toward his boat and was stabbed in the neck by a native with a dagger. He fell face down in the shallow water where several natives stabbed and clubbed him to death. Four marines were killed as they struggled back to their boat. As the six survivors rowed to safety, they saw their captain's bludgeoned body being dragged away by the Hawaiians.

Charles Clerke succeeded to command the expedition. He made another futile attempt at finding the Northwest Passage, dying of tuberculosis before he reached home. The return of the *Resolution* and the *Discovery* to England caused little fanfare in a nation whose attention was focused on the war with the American colonies. Maps and accounts of their voyages did spawn European and American expeditions of discovery and trade.

George Vancouver returned to Waimea, Kaua'i, in 1792, this time in command of his own expedition. He reported in his journal that the Hawaiians met him with "distant civility." The prince of Kaua'i came to Waimea to meet Vancouver, who agreed to two of his crewmen being exchanged as hostages while the prince came aboard the English flagship. The young prince was Kaumuali'i. Vancouver considered the 12-year-old monarch who was destined to play a significant role in the future of Kaua'i to be cheerful, friendly and bright. The chiefs who came aboard with Kaumuali'i wanted firearms because their enemies on the other islands had traded for them, but Vancouver refused.

Hawai'i State Archives

From Force and Might Come Unity

Kamehameha I at spear practice

Hawai'i State Archives

Captain Cook met his end trying to capture chief Kalaniopu'u. Injured by gunfire in the skirmish was Kamehameha, nephew of the Hawaiian chief. Towering above others at 6 feet, 6 inches, Kamehameha was soon to become Hawai'i's greatest warrior-chief.

Hawai'i became a port of call for the newly opened fur trade between North America and China. In exchange for provisions, the Hawaiians were demanding guns in trade. Kamehameha did well in the Hawaiian arms race. Looting an American ship for its cannons and firearms and kidnapping two skilled seamen to advise him were what he needed to tip the balance of power with competing chiefs in his favor.

After the death of his uncle, Kalaniopu'u, from whom he received his early military training, Kamehameha formed a shaky truce with his cousins. Kamehameha, now with complete control over the island of Hawai'i, invaded and easily conquered Maui and then Moloka'i. When a small civil war broke out on O'ahu, Kamehameha took advantage of the disorder. Landing at Waikīkī in 1795, Kamehameha's warriors steadily drove the defenders back into the surrounding mountains. The beleaguered army from O'ahu made its last stand at Nu'uanu Pali, a great precipice in the mountains behind present day Honolulu. Kamehameha's army claimed final victory by literally pushing the retreating warriors over the top.

Immediately after completing his conquest of O'ahu, Kamehameha prepared for an invasion of Kaua'i. He assembled a fleet of war canoes and an army of soldiers larger than anything the Islands had ever seen. There were between 1,200 and 1,500 canoes and about 10,000 warriors, with perhaps half of them armed with muskets. The armada set sail in the spring of 1796 from the Waianae shore. They departed at midnight, planning on reaching the Wailua area of Kaua'i at daybreak. Strong winds arose during the night as the forces crossed the Kaua'i Channel, capsizing some of the canoes. With canoes sinking and men drowning, Kamehameha ordered the fleet to return to O'ahu. Following his defeat to the forces of nature, Kamehameha returned to Hawai'i to put down a rebellion. He remained there for six years.

Kaumuali'i, the king of Kaua'i, was 16 or 17 at the time of Kamehameha's invasion attempt. He worked hard to secure arms and

Hawai'i State Archives

Feather Helmet of King Kaumuali'i

great kings. In April 1810 Kaumuali'i conceded to Kamehameha that he was the ruler of all Hawaiians and thereby spared his people the ravages of a needless war. Kamehameha undisputedly ruled all the islands—a first in Hawaiian history.

United under Kamehameha's rule, the islanders enjoyed a time of peace unlike any they had ever experienced. Although Kamehameha retained the *kapu* system and readily applied its punishments, he also learned the ways of the foreigners whose ships he supplied with

prepare for the defense of his island, but his resources were not as great as his opponent's.

In 1804, Kamehameha prepared for another invasion of Kaua'i. He assembled an army even more potent than before. While assembling on the eastern shore of O'ahu, disaster once again struck Kamehameha's forces. This time it came in the form of a devastating foreign disease, likely typhoid fever. Kamehameha contracted the illness but was one of the fortunate few who survived. His forces were so decimated that Kamehameha had to scuttle the invasion.

After six years of negotiations, Kaumuali'i agreed to meet with Kamehameha in Honolulu. New England merchant Captain Nathan Winship brokered the meeting. His ulterior motive was establishing a sandalwood trade monopoly with both

Hawai'i State Archives

An officer of the king by Jacques Arago, 1819

provisions. To reap the greatest gain from trading sandalwood with China, the king made the business a government monopoly, requiring all trade to go through him. Realizing that the forests would soon be depleted, he put *kapu* on young trees to protect them. Even so, the depletion that would eventually decimate the sandalwood forests had begun.

The Russian Affair

Georg Anton Schaffer, the Prussian-born son of a miller, was an opinionated, quarrelsome physician with an exalted view of himself. He signed on with the Russian American Company as a ship's surgeon and sailed for Sitka, Alaska, in 1813. There he was given the assignment of sailing to Hawai'i to negotiate the return of Russian cargo confiscated by Kaua'i's King Kaumuali'i, as well as establishing trading relations with Kamehameha.

Schaffer failed in gaining the confidence or trust of Kamehameha. He met with Kaumuali'i only to find that most of the Russian cargo had already been shipped to Sitka with compensation offered for the rest. Instead of a hostile reception, Schaffer met a gracious and conciliatory ruler. The two men immediately wondered how the other could serve his purposes.

In a few days Schaffer became co-monarch of Kaua'i. Kaumuali'i pledged allegiance to the Emperor Alexander I, promised exclusive trade rights on Kaua'i, and granted permission for Russia to establish factories or trading posts anywhere in his domain. In return, Schaffer promised Russian protection of Kaua'i and a ship that would be the beginning of a navy for Kaua'i. The two monarchs paid each other compliments and traded honors. Kaumuali'i bestowed lavish gifts of land upon Schaffer, who in turn appointed Kaumuali'i a Russian naval officer and pinned a silver medal on his uniform. The trouble was that Schaffer did not have the authority to enter into any of these agreements.

In 1816, Schaffer began the construction of a substantial lava-rock fort commanding a view of Waimea Bay. He named it Fort Elizabeth, honoring the consort of Emperor Alexander. On Kaua'i's north shore, Schaffer built two earthen-walled forts. He named the fort on the cliff overlooking Hanalei Bay Fort Alexander, and Fort Barclay, which he named after a Russian general, guarded the mouth of the Hanalei River. Schaffer even renamed the Hanalei Valley, Schafferthal.

By this time, word of Schaffer's ambitions reached the Russian American company. They dispatched orders for Schaffer to cease in his actions and refused to fund his endeavors. At about the same time, the commander of a Russian brig that was anchored at Honolulu reassured Kamehameha that Schaffer was acting without the consent of the Russian emperor.

American traders in H who feared that Schaffe interfere with the sandalwoo on Kaua'i, effected an ingenious plan to rid the Islands of the would-be autocrat. They spread rumors that the U.S. and Russia were having serious disagreements. En route to Kaua'i, the rumors mushroomed the dispute into a war. Kaumuali'i became anxious that he had aligned himself with the weaker of the two powers in the Pacific. Worried Kauaians forced Schaffer to retreat to a leaky ship and leave Kaua'i without even his personal possessions. Eventually, the resilient Schaffer surfaced in Brazil, where he lived the rest of his life with the purchased title, Count von Frankethal. Kaumuali'i, who had in effect committed treason, escaped punishment from Kamehameha—for the time being.

The End of *Kapu*

During his life, Kamehameha had 21 wives. In 1795, he married highborn Keōpūolani, with whom he fathered 11 children. Two of those sons survived to maturity and eventually succeeded him as Hawaiian monarchs. Even though she bore his heirs, Keōpūolani was not the king's favorite wife. That honor belonged to Ka'ahumanu, the only daughter of Maui High Chiefs Ke'eaumoku and Namahana.

Ka'ahumanu was born in a small cave near Hāna, Maui, in about 1773. At 6 feet tall and 200 pounds, she was thought to be a beautiful and desirable woman by the king. On May 8, 1819, when Kamehameha the Great died, Ka'ahumanu was at his bedside. She harged that, with his last breath, he had

named her *kuhina nui*, the person who would run his kingdom and take care of his heir, 20-year-old Liholiho.

Seven days after the bones of Kamehameha had been laid away, the chiefs of the kingdom gathered in a great half circle at the seashore, clothed in feather cloaks and helmets. Ka'ahumanu addressed the assemblage. She proclaimed Liholiho as the "Divine One" and said the will of Kamehameha was that she and Liholiho would jointly rule the kingdom. Liholiho became Kamehameha II and Ka'ahumanu was the powerful Queen Regent.

Immediately, Ka'ahumanu made an incredible demand on the new, young king. She petitioned him to lead the way to the abandonment of the foundation of Hawaiian society's beliefs and conduct—the *kapu* system. It was *kapu* for women of any rank to enter the *luakini heiau*, where political as well as religious decisions were made. Thus, while her relationship to the Kamehamehas, father and son, gave her a position of power, her gender kept her from fully wielding her power. Liholiho hesitated at first, but, after two days of drinking rum, he gave way to her sizable will. He attended a feast arranged by Ka'ahumanu and, by eating with women, he broke the onerous *kapu* forbidding men and women to eat together. When the king ordered *heiau* and religious images throughout the kingdom be destroyed, his subjects learned that he was a monarch of solemn purpose. The Hawaiians, whose belief system had been seriously eroded, were a people adrift in a spiritual vacuum.

Hawai'i State Archives

Grass houses on nineteenth century Kaua'i

Two weeks before Liholiho abolished the kapu system, a ship carrying Protestant missionaries left Boston bound for Hawai'i. They were in search of souls to save.

All God's Children Must Go to Heaven

The attention of the American Board of Commissioners for Foreign Missions was drawn to Hawai'i by a young Hawaiian visitor they called Henry Obookiah. The young Christian convert expressed anguish for his unredeemed countrymen before he died of typhus. This inspired the American Board to organize a missionary company to go to Hawai'i. Six months and 18,000 miles later, the Protestant missionaries landed on the island of Hawai'i and presented themselves to Liholiho. After some deliberation, Liholiho granted permission to the missionaries to stay in his kingdom for one year. Two couples stayed on Hawai'i while the rest of the contingent

sailed on to Honolulu, where they would set up the headquarters of the mission.

In May 1820 the missionaries Samuel Whitney and Samuel Ruggles and their wives arrived in Waimea, Kaua'i. They escorted the son of King Kaumuali'i, Prince George Humehume, who had been in America for nine years. The overjoyed king showered the missionaries with gifts and invited them to stay and teach his people. Such large crowds attended their services that branch stations were set up in Hanalei and Kōloa. On October 19, 1820, Mercy Whitney bore a daughter, the first white baby born in Hawai'i.

Liholiho set forth on a voyage from Honolulu to Kaua'i on July 21, 1821. Kaumuali'i greeted the unexpected guest with kindness. When the subject of the sovereignty of Kaua'i arose, Liholiho averred, "Kaumuali'i, I have not come to take from you your island. I wish not to place any one over it: keep it yourself; take care of it as you have done; and do with the vessels and all your possessions as you please!"

The two kings on their respective brigs took a tour of Kaua'i that lasted 42 days. On September 16 Liholiho invited Kaumuali'i aboard his luxurious vessel, the *Pride of Hawai'i,* while they were anchored at Waimea Bay. At 9:00 p.m. Liholiho secretly ordered the captain to raise anchor and sail for O'ahu. The Reverend Hiram Bingham, who was visiting Waimea at the time, reported that the people of the village were left greatly confused and troubled by the event, fearing they would never see their king again.

Evidently, Liholiho perpetrated the kidnapping according to the wishes of Ka'ahumanu, who then entrusted the guardianship of Kaua'i to her brother, Kahekili Ke'eaumoku. Kaumuali'i's downfall may have been triggered by his overtly friendly reception of the missionaries. Liholiho and Ka'ahumanu no doubt remembered when Kaumuali'i aligned himself with Russia several years earlier and feared that he was about to form an alliance with the American missionaries. The politically astute Ka'ahumanu must have surprised the unsuspecting king from Kaua'i when she made him her husband just four days after he landed on O'ahu. Just to bond Kaua'i even more firmly to the windward islands, Ka'ahumanu then married Kaumuali'i's son, as well.

Queen Regent Ka'ahumanu treated the missionaries with regal haughtiness before she fell gravely ill. Hiram Bingham's wife, Sybil, nursed her back to health, and Ka'ahumanu emerged the unfailing friend of the missionaries, much more receptive to Christian teachings. In April 1824, she publicly announced her conversion to Christianity. Soon many prominent chiefs converted and thousands of commoners listened to the missionaries' preachings.

Wanting the Hawaiians to read the gospel for themselves, the missionaries decided they must reduce the Hawaiian language to written form. Again, they focused on the leaders. By first teaching the chiefs to read and write, the mass of Hawaiians eagerly followed.

In 1841, Father Robert Walsh established the first Roman Catholic mission on Kaua'i at Kōloa. Liholiho had to issue the "Edict of Toleration" in order to end the resistance of some of the Protestant missionaries to Catholic competition. In 1856, Father Walsh built the landmark St. Raphael's church, which is still in use today.

The Whalers Tale

In 1820, Captain Joseph Allen of Nantucket commanded the first whaling vessel to put into Honolulu Harbor. The only two ports in Hawai'i that were suitable anchorages for the whaling ships were Honolulu and Lahaina, Maui. These ships usually stocked provisions in port headed directly for whaling grounds off Japan. In the 1830s, the whaling grounds of the Bering, Arctic and Okhotsk Seas attracted more and more ships. The captains were more likely to stop at Kaua'i, as it was on the way to their northern destinations, and they could find lower prices for produce than at Honolulu. Ships would lay off and on at Kōloa, while crewmen rowed ashore for trading. Kegs of butter, barrels of salt beef, oranges, coffee, potatoes, melons, molasses and wood for stoking the fires under try-pots used to render blubber oil at sea were all available for the whalers. The trade filled a desperate economic need on Kaua'i in the period when the sandalwood forests were depleted and sugar plantations were just taking root.

Crews on whaling ships lived wretched lives. The officers were often brutal men who enjoyed an iron hold on men at sea. After a four-year voyage, a seaman might walk away from his ship with as little as $100 for his labors. To make a voyage more profitable, a ruthless captain might persecute a crewmember to the point where he would jump ship at the next port, reverting his pay to the ship.

Most whale men that came ashore did not behave as sober, law-abiding citizens. They had endured months of bullying and hardships at sea and were inclined to celebrate to excess. The whalers' ports-of-call were rife with drunkenness and prostitution. Kaua'i received fewer benefits in trade with the whalers than Honolulu and Lahaina but escaped its negative influences too.

Whaling's decline began in the 1850s owing to the scarcity of whales. The death knell of the industry rang when the first commercially successful oil well was drilled in Pennsylvania in 1859. Petroleum and its derivative, kerosene, proved to be a better and more cheaply produced fuel than whale oil.

Add Sugar to the Mix

Ladd and Company established the first successful and lasting sugar cane plantation in the Hawaiian Islands in 1835 in the south Kaua'i area of Kōloa. The three partners who founded Ladd and Company could not have been successful without the support of the missionaries. In addition to saving souls, the missionaries desired to raise the desperate condition of the mass of Hawaiians and believed that farming was the way for them to do this. The missionaries arranged for Ladd and Company to lease approximately 1,000 acres of land at Kōloa and the waterfall at Maulili for a period of 50 years at $300 per year. This was the first lease drawn in Hawaiian history and marked a revolutionary change in policy concerning the control of land. Kamehameha III, Governor Kaiki'oewa of Kaua'i and the three partners of Ladd and Company signed the lease. Stipulated in the lease was that the native laborers would be paid a satisfactory wage and be exempted from all taxation. Taxation usually took the form of labor performed for the chiefs. Payment of wages directly to the workers without obligations to their chiefs gave the common Hawaiians more independence—a concept not easily understood by the commoners and feared by the chiefs.

Plans for commercially growing and milling sugar in Līhu'e began in 1849, when Henry A. Peirce of Boston bought between 2,000 and 3,000 acres of land between Nāwiliwili Stream and Hanama'ulu Stream. Partnering with

Līhu'e Plantation, 1905

Hawai'i State Archives

Peirce were Charles Reed Bishop, the founder of Bishop Bank, the forerunner of today's First Hawaiian Bank, and William L. Lee, chief justice of the Supreme Court of the Hawaiian Kingdom. In 1853, the mill ground the first crop of 108 tons of cane. In the early years of the plantation, teams of oxen were used to clear the land, 90 percent of which was covered with a forest of koa, hau, kukui and ahakea trees. The plantation owners built their first mill next to a dam that provided the water power needed to drive the three-ton, ironbound, granite crushers imported from China. By 1854, the mill's capacity increased to three tons per day, while the investors spent five times their original capital to make the operation profitable.

In 1856-57, plantation manager and investor, William Harrison Rice, built the 10-mile Līhu'e Ditch. It was Hawai'i's first large-scale irrigation ditch and was used to bring water down from Kilohana Crater. A young German immigrant, Paul Isenberg, joined the plantation in 1858, and served as its manager from 1862 to 1878. The Līhu'e Plantation's landholdings continued to grow with the acquisition of 17,000 acres at Hanama'ulu in 1872 and the lease of 30,000 acres at Wailua in 1878.

By 1910, the town of Līhu'e was a growing government and commercial center thanks to the income generated by Līhu'e Plantation and the nearby Grove Farm Plantation. The plantation provided land and support for hospitals, schools and churches. To feed its workers and their families, the plantation set up a ranching and dairy farm operation and backed the first general stores in the area. Company lands were sold for the site of the new county building. The plantation greatly expanded again in 1910, when it purchased the Makee Plantation at Keālia and the 6,000-acre Princeville Plantation from the Wilcox family in 1916.

Kaua'i's other important sugar plantation, Kekaha Sugar Co., began when Norwegian immigrant, Valdemar Knudsen, received 30-year leases on Crown lands at Mānā and Kekaha in 1856. Knudsen took over the leases from another Norwegian who tried unsuccessfully to raise tobacco on the land. Feeling that he was too old to build a sugar plantation, Knudsen enticed a group of his nephews to Kaua'i. Part of the land was sublet to a Chinese rice grower, who in turn provided laborers to the fledgling sugar plantation. The Knudsens drained 50 acres of marshy land in the low-lying Mānā Plain and planted the first crop in 1878. In 1880, Paul Isenberg, who prospered as plantation manager at the Līhu'e Plantation, and George Norton Wilcox, from the Grove Farm Plantation, joined forces with the Knudsens to build the first mill at Kekaha. The arid southwest corner of the island receives only 20 inches of rain a year, mainly in winter. Initially the first artesian wells drilled in Hawai'i provided irrigation water. As the plantation grew, work began in 1907 on the 28-mile Waimea-Kekaha ditch. By 1910, Kekaha Sugar had a plantation railroad system with 15 miles of permanent track. Cane floated down the mountains on flumes to the railway loading docks.

A plantation worker victimized the railway in 1920 in the first and only train robbery ever attempted on Kaua'i. Inspired by cowboy movies, the robber made off with the plantation's $10,000 payroll. His trial, where he testified he did it mainly for the thrill, drew overflow crowds at the Līhu'e courthouse.

Sugar plantations were labor intensive and the native population of Kaua'i was in decline, due largely to imported diseases. The population of Kaua'i dropped from an estimated 12,000 in 1831-32 to 7,800 in 1853. The pragmatic islanders who were left saw little value in the backbreaking, low-paying work of harvesting sugar cane, especially when the land and the sea offered them plenty of food staples. To supplement the workforce, plantation owners recruited from overseas workers accustomed to working long days in hot weather. In 1852, the first group of indentured workers arrived from China. In the decades to follow, immigrants from Japan, Portugal, the Philippines, and Korea came to toil in the cane fields and to add to the ethnic mix of the Islands.

KAUA'I TIMELINE

5-6 million years ago: Wai'ale'ale, the volcano that formed Kaua'i, emerges from the sea.

3.65 million years ago: A period of renewed volcanism produces the Kōloa eruptions.

15,000 years ago: The most recent volcanic activity on Kaua'i forms Pu'u Kīlauea.

A.D. 400: The first Polynesians arrive, likely from the Marquesas Islands.

1100: A second wave of settlers arrives from Tahiti.

1350: King Kūkona defeats invading armies and ushers in long era of peace.

1778: Captain James Cook and his crew are the first Europeans to set foot on Hawaiian soil when they land at Waimea.

1780: Kaua'i's last king, Kaumuali'i, is born.

1792: Explorer George Vancouver returns to Kaua'i commanding his own expedition.

1796: An invading army led by Kamehameha is turned back in the Kaua'i Channel by a storm and heavy seas.

1810: Kaumuali'i concedes to Kamehameha as ruler of all Hawaiian Islands.

1816: Georg Schaffer begins construction of a Russian fort at Waimea.

1820: New England missionaries Whitney and Ruggles arrive at Waimea.

1821: Kaumuali'i is taken forcibly to Honolulu and marries Ka'ahumanu, the widow of Kamehameha. Kahekili Ke'eaumoku is installed as governor of Kaua'i.

1835: Hawai'i's sugar industry begins with Ladd and Company establishing a plantation at Kōloa.

1841: Father Robert Walsh establishes the first Roman Catholic mission on Kaua'i.

1849: The Līhu'e Plantation is formed.

1852: The first group of indentured sugar workers arrives from China.

1853: The Līhu'e Plantation mills its first crop of sugar cane.

1856: Valdemar Knudsen receives leases on what becomes the Kekaha Sugar Company.

1868: The first Japanese laborers leave Japan to work in Kaua'i's sugar fields.

1871: Prince Jonah Kūhiō Kalaniana'ole is born near what is now Po'ipū. He served as Hawai'i's delegate to Congress and created the Hawaiian Homes Commission.

1876: Sugar industry benefits greatly when the Reciprocity Treaty is signed allowing sugar into the U.S. duty-free.

1877: The first group of Portuguese contract laborers are recruited in the Azores.

1883: The Government of Hawai'i sets restrictions on the number of Chinese immigrants.

1900: U.S. law prohibits further importation of Chinese workers when Hawai'i is annexed.

1902: The first Korean laborers arrive.

1905: The County of Kaua'i is established and given authority over police, fire control, highways, public works and sanitation.

1906: Laborers from the Philippines arrive.

1911: The Tunnel of Trees is planted north of Kōloa as a community project.

1930: Harbors are built at Port Allen and Nāwiliwili.

1945: The International Longshore Workers Union starts representing sugar workers.

1946: A tsunami hits the north shore on April 1, causing great damage.

1950: Līhu'e airport opens.

1957: A March 3 tsunami slams the north shore.

1959: The U.S. Navy's Pacific Missile Range Facility is built at Barking Sands on Kaua'i's west side.

1960: Kōke'e Tracking Station is installed and used to track early American-manned space flights.

1973: The Kīlauea Plantation closes.

1982: Hurricane Iwa hits the island.

1992: Hurricane 'Iniki, the most powerful Hawaiian hurricane in memory, devastates Kaua'i.

1996: McBryde Co. closes its sugar operations.

2000: Amfac Sugar Kaua'i closes the Kekaha and Līhu'e plantations.

McBryde Sugar Mill, 1905

Hawai'i State Archives

A SUCCESSION OF MONARCHS

Kamehameha I

Kamehameha I, 1795-1819

Towering above others at 6 feet, 6 inches, Kamehameha was to become Hawai'i's greatest warrior-chief. He was royal born in the Kohala district of the island of Hawai'i. Perhaps Halley's comet, which in 1758 marked the year of his birth, foreshadowed his destiny as an unusual and auspicious man. In 1791, Kamehameha became the sole chief of the island of Hawai'i. After conquering Maui and Moloka'i, he invaded O'ahu in 1795 and established his reign there, as well. Stormy seas and an outbreak of disease turned his troops back on two attempts to invade Kaua'i. Accepting the inevitable and wanting to avoid bloodshed, the king of Kaua'i yielded to Kamehameha's rule in 1810. With his grand design of unification completed, he had earned the title, Kamehameha the Great. The first Hawaiian to rule all the islands died in 1819. His bones were buried at a secret location on the island of Hawai'i.

Kamehameha II, 1819-1824

Liholiho bestowed upon himself the title of Kamehameha II, but he did not mirror his father's image of a strong and autocratic ruler. With the overbearing influence of Ka'ahumanu, his father's favorite wife, he disassembled the *kapu* system. During his reign, foreign trade decimated the sandalwood forests and whalers and missionaries strengthened their holds on his kingdom. Seeking the

Kamehameha II, 1824

Hawai'i State Archives

advice of King George IV, Liholiho set sail for England, accompanied by Queen Kamamalu. Before the couple could enjoy an audience with the British monarch, Liholiho and his wife contracted measles and died.

Kamehameha III, 1825-1854

At 30 years, Kauikeaouli, titled Kamehameha III, was Hawai'i's longest-reigning monarch. Ka'ahumanu continued as Queen Regent when the 9-year-old brother of Liholiho became king. The child received a Christian education from Rev. Hiram Bingham, who attempted to instill in him a love for Western values. Kamehameha III grew up, however, to be steadfastly pro-Hawaiian in culture and beliefs. His most significant act was an edict issued in 1848, which became

Kamehameha III and Kalama, 1846

known as the Great Mahele. The act divided Hawai'i's land ownership among the monarchy, the government, and the common people. Hawaiians, who were not used to the concept of land ownership, allowed foreigners to buy two-thirds of all land sold by 1886.

Dr. Gerritt Judd, Prince Alexander Liholiho (Kamehameha IV), Prince Lot (Kamehameha V), 1849

Hawai'i State Archives

Kamehameha IV, 1854-1863

Before his death, Kamehameha III named his nephew and grandson of Kamehameha the Great, Alexander Liholiho, to succeed him. While a prince, Alexander traveled in Europe and America. His experiences in Europe were pleasant and enriching, but he was insulted and humiliated by being ordered off a train in New York City because of his race. During his short reign he tended to shift Hawai'i closer to the British Empire in both spirit and policy. After his son, Prince Albert, died at 4 years, the 29-year-old king, run down by grief, guilt and alcohol, died during an asthmatic attack.

Kamehameha V, 1863-1872

Lot Kamehameha was the older brother of Alexander Liholiho and the last Hawaiian monarch to carry the lineage of Kamehameha the Great. He baptized his strong, autocratic style of leadership by refusing to take an oath to uphold the constitution of 1852, believing it weakened the powers of the monarchy. In its place he offered a new constitution that established a one-chamber legislature for nobles and elected representatives, and required that persons pass literacy tests and own property before being allowed to vote. His determination to strengthen the monarchy sparked resentment among nonroyalists, fueling the forces that would later bring down the monarchy. The "bachelor king" died without leaving a successor. Future kings would be elected.

Lunalilo, 1873-1874

"Whiskey Bill" Lunalilo was a favorite of the Hawaiian commoners and the fact that he was a drunkard did little to diminish his charm. Three of his four cabinet ministers were Americans and were instrumental in paving the way for a treaty of reciprocity whereby the Hawaiian government would lease Pearl Harbor to the United States in return for duty-free access to the American sugar market. Lunalilo died after just 13 months as monarch.

William Lunalilo, 1873

Hawai'i State Archives

David Kalākaua, 1874-1891

After defeating Queen Emma, the widow of Kamehameha IV, in a colorful campaign, David Kalākaua put high priority to reviving Hawaiian heritage. He resuscitated the hula, which had been banned for many years by the missionaries, even contributing his own new dances. He ushered in a renewed appreciation for Hawaiian music and composed "Hawai'i Pono'i", Hawai'i's state song. Because of his jovial style and his love for the performing arts, the *haole* dubbed him "The Merrie Monarch." Kalākaua elevated his critic's rancor by incurring huge debts to build the opulent 'Iolani Palace and treating himself to a lavish coronation ceremony nine years after becoming king. An armed insurrection in 1887 forced Kalākaua to accept a "Bayonet Constitution" that stripped the Chinese of the vote and limited Hawaiian political power, while shifting more power to the land-owning American and British residents. Kalākaua died in San Francisco, leaving his sister to become queen of what was essentially an American-controlled nation.

Lydia Lili'uokalani, 1891-1893

Like her brother, Lydia Lili'uokalani had a talent for music and wrote some of the most beautiful and delicate songs in the Hawaiian language, including "Aloha Oe." Lili'uokalani charged that the constitution of 1887 was illegally forced upon King Kalākaua. She penned a new constitution that promised only true Hawaiians could vote and they would not have to be rich men to cast a ballot or run for office. The Queen, however, could not effect her new constitution. Anti-royalist forces made Lili'uokalani the last Hawaiian monarch and the first to take leave before death.

Above: *Queen Lili'uokalani*

Hawai'i State Archives

Left: *David Kalākaua*

ECONOMY & GOVERNMENT

Kaua'i's economy did not keep pace with the growth generated on the mainland in the 1990s. The sugar industry had been in a steady decline with plantations closing and workers being laid off. The visitor industry took several years to rebound from the devastation of Hurricane 'Iniki in 1992.

Visitor arrivals are again topping the 1 million-per-year mark. The numbers have yet to duplicate the pre-'Iniki record of 1,267,620, but not many people on this small island yearn for a repeat of that lofty mark. Trends indicating growth in the visitor industry reflect marketing efforts made by the Department of Business, Economic Development and Tourism, as well as the healthy mainland economy. Traditionally, Kaua'i receives fewer Japanese visitors than the other islands, and the fallback of visitor counts from Japan has been more than made up in increased visits from the U.S. Hotels on Kaua'i enjoy an occupancy rate of 73.5 percent, with an average daily rate of $154. Just 34 percent of visitors to Kaua'i made it their only destination— a rate lower than all the other major Hawaiian Islands.

For close to two centuries, agriculture on Kaua'i has meant sugar cane production. With sugar plantations closing permanently due to depressed world prices and high production costs, serious attempts to diversify agricultural production are being attempted. McBryde continues to expand its coffee acreage after closing sugar operations in 1996. Agricultural parks have been set up, allowing former sugar workers to grow vegetables and fruit for local markets. Among the most promising agricultural products are: seed corn, fruit for export, and tropical flowers. There are four seed corn companies in operation on the west side, where weather conditions allow for four crops a year.

The potential for tree farming on Kaua'i has been bolstered by a bill that exempts landowners with ten or more acres planted in tree crops from paying real property taxes until the trees are harvested. With the island's favorable growing conditions, forestry analysts predict exotic hardwoods could be harvested in 10 to 13 years. Critics claim that without marketing commitments or contracts in place for the forestry products, the primary motive for tree farming is as a tax-sheltered parking lot for agricultural lands.

Military presence on Kaua'i amounts to the Pacific Missile Range Facility, which occupies about 2,000 acres at Barking Sands on the island's west side. The facility employs 435 civilian contract workers, 126 military personnel and 136 civil service workers. A family housing area containing 69 units provides accommodations for workers not living on the west and south sides. The range collects scientific and

Land Ownership on Kaua'i

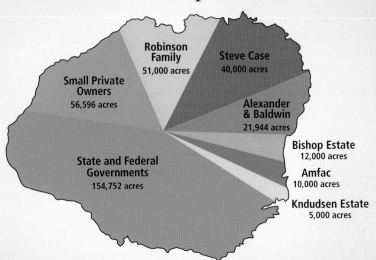

Robinson Family
51,000 acres

Steve Case
40,000 acres

Small Private Owners
56,596 acres

Alexander & Baldwin
21,944 acres

Bishop Estate
12,000 acres

Amfac
10,000 acres

State and Federal Governments
154,752 acres

Kndudsen Estate
5,000 acres

Ownership of Kaua'i's usable land area is highly concentrated among governments and a small, powerful group of people and enterprises. The federal, state (including Hawaiian Home Lands) and county governments own 44 percent. The remaining 56 percent is privately owned, and three quarters of that is controlled by six owners.

Robinson Family - The Robinson predecessors started buying land on Kaua'i in 1865, when Frances Sinclair purchased the *ahupua'a* (ancient land division) of Makaweli from Victoria Kamamalu, granddaughter of Kamehameha I. In addition, the family owns the entire neighboring island of Ni'ihau. The family partnership leases nearly all of its land to Gay & Robinson Inc., the last remaining sugar operation on the island.

Steve Case - In 2000, Steve Case, chairman of America Online, purchased the shares of Grove Farm. Among its assets are Kukui Grove Shopping Center and Puakea Golf Course. The following year, case bought former Amfac land that ranges from Hanama'ulu to Puhi.

Alexander & Baldwin - A&B's land holdings include conservation land on the north shore and the former McBryde Plantation near Kalāheo. Since ceasing sugar production in 1996, the company has become the state's largest coffee producer. A&B is investing in a large real estate development on the south shore and also owns the Matson Shipping Line.

Bishop Estate - These lands were part of the trust granted by Bernice Pauahi Bishop's will to establish and support the Kamehameha Schools. Primarily the lands are in agricultural or conservation areas located at Waipā and Lumaha'i on the north shore.

Amfac - Amfac began servicing the sugar industry in 1853. In 2000, the company closed its sugar operations and listed its property for sale. Steve Case added to his Kaua'i landholding by purchasing a substantial portion of Amfac land.

Knudsen Estate - The estate of the adventurous Norwegian named Valdemar Knudsen, who came to Kaua'i in search of a climate favorable to his failing health, stretches from Mt. Kāhili, across Knudsen's Gap and Kōloa, to the sea.

operational data regarding fleet operations and training. Six helicopters and two radar surveillance and electronic warfare planes operate from the airfield and its 6,000-foot runway.

Kaua'i has put on a pretty face for more than 50 films over the past 60 years—usually playing the role of somewhere else. The Kaua'i Institute for Communications Media is seeking to turn the island into a mecca for professionals involved in the new technologies being used in film, television, computer software, publishing and other communications arts. The County's Film Office continues to attract media productions of all types, including film, television, commercials, documentaries, travel segments, and still photo shoots.

County Building, Līhu'e, 1920s

The Kaua'i Economic Development Board has successfully attracted digital technology businesses to its new facility at Waimea. This project, as well as other high tech possibilities, are supported by island-wide fiber optic capabilities and a highly advanced digital cellular telephone network.

Government

Hawai'i has three levels of government: federal, state and county. Hawai'i residents are represented in Washington, D.C., by two senators and two representatives. Honolulu is the state capital. The state's executive power is vested in a popularly elected governor who serves a four-year term, as do the lieutenant governor, state legislators and county mayors. The State Legislature is comprised of a 25-member Senate and a House of Representatives with 51 members. Kaua'i and Ni'ihau send one senator and two representatives to the State Legislature, which meets in regular session each year. Kaua'i's North Shore also shares a state senator and state representative with sections of Maui. For several decades the dominant political party at all levels has been the Democratic Party.

Hawai'i is divided into four county governments, but, unlike mainland states, it has no municipal government. Kaua'i County is governed by a mayor and a seven-person county council and provides the services such as police and fire protection that are usually assigned to cities. The mayor reports to the council and submits her operating and capital budget to them for approval, but she has no vote on the council. The council passes ordinances and resolutions for the government of the county, and these go to the mayor for approval. County revenues include a portion of the state excise tax, all the real property tax, the county liquid fuel tax, motor vehicle weight taxes, local license fees, and court fines.

Hawai'i Sugar Co. Train, 1905

FACTS ABOUT SUGAR CANE

- Polynesian settlers brought sugar cane to Hawai'i more than 1,000 years ago.

- Sugar cane is a giant grass that can produce stalks that range from 8 to 30 feet tall.

- Hawaiians chewed on the stalks for the sweet juice but did not make sugar.

- Fields of sugar cane start as 12-inch slips cut from a stalk of cane.

- Machines cut furrows into the ground, drop in the seed cane, insert drip tubing, and cover the furrows in one operation.

- Young plants are constantly watered with drip irrigation pipes. This more efficient irrigation system has reduced the water needed to produce a ton of sugar cane to one ton.

- In some fields, stands remaining after harvest are used to grow a new crop. This is called ratooning.

- It takes 24 months for the young plants to grow to harvest height but crops can be planted at any time of the year.

- By harvest time, cane stalks can be 30 feet long and form a thick, twisted mat.

- Cane fields are set afire to clear excess leaves from the cane before harvesting. The high water content of the stalks prevents them from burning.

- Cane burning is scheduled to take advantage of favorable winds and weather conditions.

- Do not stop your car near a cane burn.

- An acre of land yields 90 tons of cane, or 12.5 tons of raw sugar.

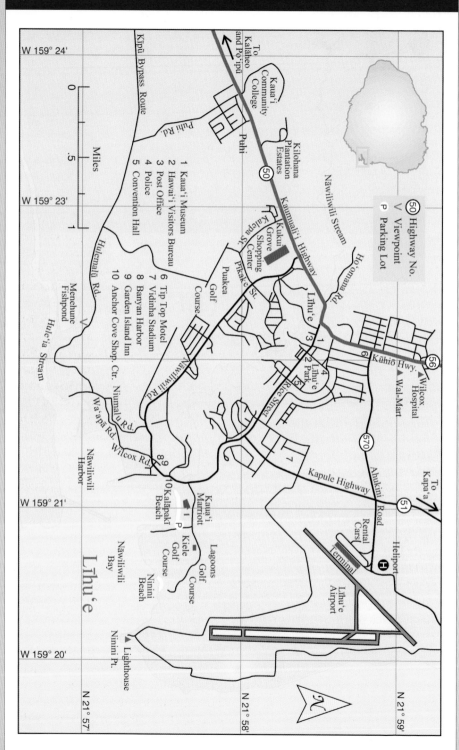

EAST SIDE SIGHTS

K Kaua'i's east coast is where most of the island's people live. The two main towns of Līhu'e and Kapa'a are here, as well as populated and developed areas such as Wailua and Anahola. The area is, however, by no means densely populated. Līhu'e and Kapa'a each have a population of less than 10,000 inhabitants. Līhu'e is the seat of county government for Kaua'i County, which includes the islands of Kaua'i and Ni'ihau. Kapa'a is just a few miles up the highway from Līhu'e. Commuter traffic clogs the three-lane highway connecting the towns each weekday morning and afternoon. Highway 50, the Kaumuali'i Highway, which began at the southern extent of the Nā Pali shoreline, enters Līhu'e from the south. The Kūhiō Highway (Highway 56) begins its route at Līhu'e, passing through east Kaua'i to the north shore and coming to a dead stop at Kē'ē Beach, the north end of the Nā Pali coastline.

Mauka (inland) of the east coast are Kilohana Crater behind Līhu'e, and Kālepa Ridge and Nounou Ridge (Sleeping Giant) behind Wailua. The land in the valleys that slice into the ridges is utilized principally for growing sugar cane. Small farms and acreages dot the landscape, as well. Fine beaches and resorts line the east coast. Many visitors choose to stay here when visiting Kaua'i because of its central location to the north and south shores, as well as its proximity to the airport at Līhu'e.

Līhu'e

Līhu'e is the island's commercial center and the arrival point of nearly all visitors. Līhu'e Airport is located on the coast, a mile east of the town center. It was opened in 1950 and has been modernized and expanded several times since. With only a 6,500-foot-long runway, the airport is limited mostly to jets commuting to the other Hawaiian Islands. Plans to lengthen the runway have been shelved by Governor Cayetano. This pleases the residents, who are concerned about the increase in visitor traffic and introduction of alien plant and animal species associated with direct flights to Asia and mainland America. Proponents of a longer runway are business operators who would benefit from expanded visitor traffic and farmers who could deliver fresh produce to a larger market.

Along with being the county seat, Līhu'e houses offices for the state and federal governments. The Kaua'i Community College is situated in nearby Puhi. Workers and students from all over the island converge on, and then leave Līhu'e each day.

Līhu'e did not figure in the island's history until 1837, when Kaua'i Governor Kaiki'oewa chose it as a site to plant sugar cane. He moved his capital there from Waimea and built

Līhu'e

a residence and church. The ancient name for this area was Kala'iamea, which means, "calm reddish brown place." Kaiki'oewa named his new home, Līhu'e, which means "goose flesh," after his homeland on O'ahu. The local sugar industry grew as the Līhu'e Plantation was founded in 1849 and a mill was started in 1851.

Līhu'e Museum

Nāwiliwili Harbor opened in 1930. That, with the opening of a modern airport in 1950, started the transformation of Līhu'e from a plantation town to a commercial center. In the 1960s, Līhu'e Plantation began converting some of its cane land to commercial and residential developments. Office buildings and the Līhu'e Shopping Center were built near the town center. Residential subdivisions gave plantation workers their first opportunity for home ownership.

The downtown section, on Rice Street, has a few architecturally interesting buildings that house government offices. Definitely worth visiting is the **Kaua'i Museum**—the best Hawaiian museum outside of O'ahu. The museum's collections are displayed in two buildings. The museum entrance is in the Wilcox Building, which was built by the missionary family's Emma Wilcox on 1924 as the first public library in Kaua'i. The two-story structure, built with lava rock walls and a blue tile roof, was added to the museum in 1970. Next door, the Rice Building (also named after a missionary family) was the original home to the museum when it was established in 1960.

The displays begin with murals and dioramas depicting Kaua'i's volcanic birth under the ocean floor.

Kalapakī Bay

Exhibits move on to cover the arrival of Polynesians, the landing of Captain Cook, the missionary influence and the early days of the sugar cane industry. Important artifacts from Hawai'i's monarchy period and a beautiful, hand-carved koa canoe grace the exhibit halls. The museum is augmented with a bookstore and gift shop stocked with quality, Hawaiian-made products.

The Kaua'i Museum is located at 4428 Rice St. Its phone number is 245-6931. Hours of operation are 9:00 a.m. to 4:00 p.m., Monday to Friday, and 9:00 a.m. to 1:00 p.m. on Saturdays. Admission is $5 for adults, $4 for students and $1 for children.

Nāwiliwili Bay, the deep-water port and commercial harbor on the southern edge of Līhu'e, is Kaua'i's principal port. The bay was well known for its grove of wiliwili trees, a member of the legume family that has red and orange pea-like flowers clustered near the ends of its branches. The harbor accommodates oceangoing freighters, interisland barges, fishing boats and cruise liners, which have made Hawai'i ports increasingly popular destinations. A long breakwater protects the harbor from surf and wind.

On the north side of the bay is **Nāwiliwili Park**. The seaward edge of the park is a concrete retaining wall facing **Kalapakī Bay**. The park is popular for picnicking and fishing. Beyond Nāwiliwili Stream, which flows through the north end of the park, are Kalapakī Beach and the Marriott resort (see Beaches chapter).

One and a half miles along Nāwiliwili Road from Nāwiliwili Park is the **Grove Farm Homestead Plantation Museum**. A small sign on the north side of the road marks it. The museum is the two-story plantation period house, built in 1864 by George Wilcox, son of missionaries Abner and Lucy Wilcox, and several other buildings dispersed throughout the 80-acre estate. The house's salons, libraries, music room, bedrooms, morning room, formal dining room, and kitchens are filled with furniture of the period and beautiful Hawaiian quilts. Small groups are escorted around the house and grounds for two hours. Tours are given three times a week and cost $5. Reservations are required and can be made by calling 245-3202.

Up the hill from Nāwiliwili Park on Nāwiliwili Road is the south turnoff to **Menehune Fishpond**. The viewpoint over the fishpond is a mile up Niumalu and then Hulemalū Roads. Across a large bend in the Hule'ia Stream is a 900-yard-long dirt levee faced with stone. Trees grow on top of the dam now and it has a gap near the middle. Originally there were three gaps in the dam before two of them were filled in the 1800s by nearby Chinese farmers who raised mullet in the fishpond. Ancient Hawaiians built wooden fences across the gaps to trap fish in the pond. Slats in the fences were built close enough to trap large fish but would let smaller fish swim freely through them.

Menehune Fishpond

Hawaiian legend says that the race of people called Menehune placed the stones on the facing of the dam at the request of Chief 'Alekoko and Chiefess Kalālālehua. The Menehune would not do this job unless the chief and his wife agreed to remain in their house and not peek at their work. Throughout the night the Menehune passed the stones hand to hand from the plains of Wahiawa. Chief 'Alekoko listened to the voices of the workers and the sounds of stone falling on stone until he couldn't stand it any more and peered out from his grass house. Immediately, the Menehune chief ordered his people to stop work on the wall. The Menehune workers, who had been handling rough stones all night, washed their bleeding hands in the almost completed fishpond and left. The unfinished fishpond stood as a reminder to Chief 'Alekoko of a promise broken. To this day, the fishpond bears the name 'Alekoko, which means, "rippling blood."

Rather than turning around on Hulemalū Road and returning to Līhu'e, you can continue and make your way back to Highway 50 at Puhi, across from the Kaua'i Community College. This area is called Kīpū, which means, "to remain as mist or rain." William Hyde Rice, who bought 1,800 acres of land from O'ahu ali'i, founded the Kīpū Ranch in 1912. Magnificent rows of Norfolk pine trees mark the entrance to the cattle ranch. Shipbuilders prized these tall, straight trees to use as their masts. You can take the side road to the ranch entrance gate and see a monument dedicated to Mr. Rice by his Japanese workers.

At the highway, in front of the college is a marker indicating the scene of **Queen Victoria's Profile**. Nature has formed a resemblance of the British monarch in the east slope of Mount Hā'upu in the Hoary Head Ridge to the south. With some imagination you can make out the queen's crown, her noble profile facing left and an erect finger. Local wits, such as tour bus drivers, like to say she is pointing her finger at her grandson, William II, and admonishing him with the words, "Now Willy Willy" (she's facing Nāwiliwili Bay).

On the north side of the highway, between the community college and Līhu'e's Kukui Grove Shopping Center is **Kilohana Plantation Estates**. Once, sugar was king on Kaua'i and the prosperity it grew for plantation owners is captured and preserved here at Kilohana. Built is 1935, the manor house of Gaylord Parke Wilcox, once head of Grove Farm Plantation, was to become the most expensive and most beautiful home ever built on Kaua'i.

Steamer Likelike *at Ahukini Landing, 1910*

Ninini Pt. Lighthouse

Visitors are free to wander through the halls and great room filled with artwork, antique furniture, and crafts. Display cases show off stone poi pounders and Hawaiian artifacts. Most of the smaller rooms are leased to art and Hawaiian crafts shops. Gaylord's restaurant is in the U-shaped courtyard looking out onto the estate's gardens. Clydesdale horses draw riders aboard century-old carriages about the 35-acre grounds and gardens. The shops and galleries at Kilohana are open 9:30 a.m. to 9:30 p.m., Monday to Saturday, and 9:30 a.m. to 5:00 p.m. on Sundays. Carriage rides are available 11:00 a.m. to 6:30 p.m., Monday to Saturday, and 11:00 a.m. to 5:00 p.m. on Sundays. They are available on a first-come, first-served basis and cost $8 for adults and $4 for children under 12. Reservations for a horse-drawn tour through a sugar cane field may be made by calling 246-9529.

When you are at Nāwiliwili Bay, you can look out to the open water and see **Ninini Point** and a lighthouse marking the north side of the bay's entrance. It's possible to drive to the point to see the lighthouse as well as a spectacular view of the bay and Hoary Head Ridge. In Līhu'e, turn off Kapule Highway (Highway 51) across from Vidinha Stadium, halfway between Ahukini Road (the airport entrance road) and Rice Street. Drive past a guardhouse as the road turns left and then makes two gentle right turns. The road goes around the golf course and gives you a very close look at the airport's main runway. In two miles, the road turns to dirt and ends at **Ninini Point Lighthouse**. The lighthouse, which was built in 1932, stands 118 feet above the water and its light is visible for 17 miles. A couple of picnic tables stand next to the foundation of what was once the lightkeeper's quarters. As a bonus to the views of the coastline, you will be treated to close-up looks of the underside of roaring jets coming in to land at the airport.

You can take an alternate route when you leave Ninini Point. Just past the parking area, at the runway fence, take the dirt road that forks to the right. This will lead you around the other side of the airport and end at **Ahukini Recreation Pier State Park** on the south side of Hanamā'ulu Bay. The old pier and the breakwater were built in the 1920s to facilitate the shipping needs of the sugar plantations. It was used extensively until 1945, when shipping operations were relocated to Nāwiliwili Harbor. The pier was dismantled, and in 1978 the landing was converted to a park that has become a prime locale for pole fishing. Ahukini Road crosses abandoned narrow gauge railway tracks and returns to the airport and then Kapule Highway.

Wailua

The valley of the Wailua River was considered one of the most sacred areas in all of ancient Hawai'i. Kings chose Wailua as their capital, and it was also the home of the high chiefs of Kaua'i. Legends tell of sailors who journeyed to Wailua from Tahiti and returned to spread the word of this sacred place. Before the thirteenth century, Wailua was famous throughout Hawai'i, as well as parts of Central Polynesia. The heart of this area was called Wailua Nui Hoano, or Great Sacred Wailua. It extended from the mouth of the Wailua River for 2 miles along the south bank and for 3 miles along the northern section. This area was reserved for the *ali'i* of Kaua'i. A commoner was allowed in this exalted area only with the permission of an *ali'i*.

Wailua River

Wailua Falls

It was no wonder that Wailua was such a desirable place to live in ancient Hawai'i, for it was a garden of plenty. The Wailua River supplied fresh water in abundance and the fertile soil was ideal for growing taro, yams and bananas. The ocean offered fish and the coconut trees were a source of food, utensils and fibers.

Wailua means "two waters" because the river splits into a north fork and a south fork, 2 miles from the ocean. The Wailua River is 12 miles long from its source at Mount Wai'ale'ale, in the heart of the island, to the ocean. It is claimed to be the only navigable waterway in Hawai'i.

On the river's south fork is the 80-foot drop of **Wailua Falls**. The waterfalls usually split into a double cascade of water at the upper lip, but can gush into a single torrent when water flow is high. The falls used to be called Wai'ehu, "spraying water." Kaumuali'i, the last king of Kaua'i, was said to jump off the falls into the pool below for sport. While dangerous then, it would be even more so now, as over half the water flow is diverted for sugar cane irrigation. Turn off Highway 56, between Hanamā'ulu and Līhu'e, onto Mā'alo Road and follow it for 3-1/2 miles to the falls viewpoint.

Between mile markers four and five on the Kūhiō Highway you will

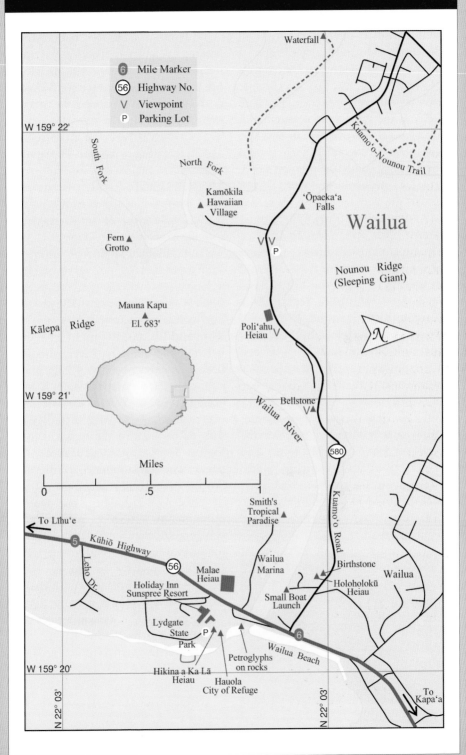

Waterfall

6 Mile Marker
56 Highway No.
V Viewpoint
P Parking Lot

W 159° 22'

South Fork

North Fork

Kuamo'o-Nounou Trail

Kamōkila
Hawaiian
Village

'Ōpaeka'a
Falls

Wailua

Fern
Grotto

V V
P

Nounou Ridge
(Sleeping Giant)

Mauna Kapu
El. 683'

Kālepa   Ridge

Poli'ahu
Heiau
V

N

W 159° 21'

Wailua River

Bellstone
V

580

Miles
0   .5   1

Smith's
Tropical
Paradise

Kuamo'o Road

To Līhu'e

5   Kūhiō Highway

56

Wailua
Marina

Birthstone

Wailua

Malae
Heiau

Holoholokū
Heiau

Holiday Inn
Sunspree Resort

Small Boat
Launch

Leho Dr.

Lydgate
State
Park
P

6

Wailua Beach

W 159° 20'

N 22° 03'

Hikina a Ka Lā
Heiau

Hauola
City of Refuge

Petroglyphs
on rocks

N 22° 03'

To
Kapa'a

see the Wailua County Golf Course on the *makai* side and Kālepa Ridge on the *mauka* side. The ridge is a remnant of older lava flows that stood while new lava flowed around it. The bare sides of the ridge were covered with sandalwood forests 200 years ago. The trees were cut down and sold to foreign markets that valued the fragrant wood.

At mile marker five, a sign directs the way onto Leho Drive and to **Lydgate State Park**. The park is named after Rev. John Lydgate, a Protestant minister who was a founder of the Kaua'i Historical Society and an advocate of preserving historic sites on Kaua'i. The park features the **Kamalani Playground**, which was designed by architect Bob Leathers and built by community volunteers. *Keiki* (children) are free to walk into a play lava tube and crawl up the inside of a 20-foot-high volcano. Then they can ride down on a curving slide. Adults and children can gather at the pavilion built of lava stones and sheltering dozens of picnic tables. Highlighting the park is a beach and rock-enclosed swimming area in the ocean (see Beaches chapter).

East Kaua'i shoreline

North of Lydgate State Park's parking lot, under a coconut grove, are the remains of the *heiau*, **Hikina a ka Lā**, meaning "rising of the sun." Here on Kaua'i's eastern shore, the sun's rays would first hit the large structure, 395 feet long, 80 feet wide at the front, and 56 feet wide at the rear. The stone walls of the enclosure measured 8 to 11 feet thick and 6 feet high. Centuries later, the remains appear mostly as a loose collection of large stones forming a rough outline. Originally, the walls of Hikina a ka Lā were formed from great slabs of rock set on end in a double row, with the space between filled with smaller stones. The paved interior was divided into three sections. The middle section held graves belonging to a family that reportedly desecrated the place by living and cultivating land within the walls of the sacred structure. Part of the interior was a *pu'uhonua* (place of refuge). This *pu'uhonua*, on the banks of the Wailua River, was called **Hauola**. A person who had committed a crime or broken a *kapu* and reached the place of refuge would be safe from punishment within its walls. The person would then remain at the refuge for several days and perform certain rites prescribed by the priests. The expunged *kapu* breaker could then return to society, free from retribution. Along the shore, at the south edge of the mouth of the Wailua River, are **boulders with petroglyphs** carved on them. Depending on the flow of the river, they may be exposed or they may be covered with sand.

Petroglyphs at the mouth of the Wailua River

Malae Heiau

Another *heiau* stands a few hundred yards to the west of Hikina a ka Lā, on the other side of the Holiday Inn Sunspree Resort and the highway. The **Malae Heiau** stands about 50 feet west of the highway. At 273 feet by 324 feet in size, Malae is the largest *heiau* on Kaua'i. Its outer walls were 7 to 10 feet high and 13 feet thick. Back in its day of use, there was an altar in the middle of the enclosure. All around the inside of the wall was a ledge 6 feet wide and 2 feet above the ground on which people could sit during ceremonies. After being converted to Christianity in 1830, Debora Kapule, wife of Kaua'i's King Kaumuali'i, used the high walls of the enclosure as a cattle pen to signify that it was no longer a holy place. The jungle swallowed the *heiau* when maintenance was halted after the queen's death. Builders of the sugar plantations in the late 1800s and early 1900s pillaged the *heiau's* rock walls for construction materials. This prompted the Rev. John Lydgate and other civic leaders to found the Kaua'i Historical Society in 1914 to protect the Malae Heiau and others. Recently, 400 volunteers worked to rid the *heiau* of the guava trees, java plum and weeds that overran it. Plans of the state Department of Land and Natural Resources call for an additional seven acres around the *heiau* to be cleared for a cultural park with interpretive signs.

Turning *mauka* at the road on the south bank of the Wailua River takes you to the Wailua marina. The Parks Division of the state Department of Land and Natural Resources built the marina to accommodate the great volume of visitors who take the riverboat excursion upriver to the state park at the **Fern Grotto**. Besides the visitors staying on Kaua'i, the visitors on one-day tours of Kaua'i from other islands invariably take the cruise to see the famous grotto. That totals more than a million visitors a year, more than any other state park on Kaua'i. The marina's main building houses ticket offices for the river cruises, gift shops and restrooms. A restaurant is next door, conveniently close to the high volume of visitor traffic. Two companies operate boat tours to the Fern Grotto. Both Wai'ale'ale Boat Tours (822-4908) and Smith's Motorboats (821-6892) start the one and a half-hour tour every half-hour from 9:00 a.m. to 3:00 p.m., skipping a run at noon. Their rates are $15 for adults, $7.50 for children, and $14 for seniors. Reservations are not needed, just arrive 15 minutes before departure. The scenery along the river and the Fern

Fern Grotto

Grotto are beautiful, but the boat tours can best be described as touristy. Amplified 'ukulele music and travelogues intrude on an otherwise peaceful setting. When you dock at the Fern Grotto, your group walks up to the grotto while entertainers serenade you in the natural amphitheater. This is a popular place for weddings. Tropical ferns hang from the ceiling of the cavern like green stalactites. When the Wailua River was higher, it carved the cave from a flow of Nā Pali basalt, which was weaker than the flow of Kōloa lava that forms the roof. The only way to reach the Fern Grotto is by boat. You can also visit the grotto by renting a kayak and paddling up the river for 2 miles (see Activities chapter). One advantage of doing that is you can have the grotto to yourself for a few minutes between tour boat landings.

West of the Wailua marina is the theme gardens of **Smith's Tropical Paradise**. You can stroll along a mile-long meandering pathway or ride a tram through the 30 acres of gardens, lagoons and re-created ethnic villages. Admission to the gardens and a tour is $5 for adults and $2 for children. The gates open at 5:00 p.m. and the tram tour starts at 5:30. On Monday, Wednesday and Friday, Smith's presents a lū'au at 6:30 p.m. Cost of the lū'au is $52 for adults and $27 for children. You can skip the feast and check in for the pageant and music for $14, adults, and $7, children. Call 821-6895 for reservations.

Immediately north of Wailua River is Kuamo'o Road. In ancient times, the "path of chiefs" originated at the river's mouth and passed by several *heiau* before ending at Wai'ale'ale at the center of the island. The second road going towards the river off Kuamo'o Road leads a few yards to a small boat-launching ramp. It's here that the people renting kayaks can park their cars and start their paddle up the river. Shortly after that, on the south side of the road, is **Holoholokū**, the oldest *heiau* on Kaua'i. Situated below a ridge and only 24 by 40 feet, it held a place of great significance. It is believed that this was a place where priests offered human sacrifices to the gods. A tower of 'ōhia wood was erected over the large stone on the southwest corner of the *heiau*. Each month on a designated night, an unfortunate victim, usually a war captive, was chosen for sacrifice. The *kahuna* (priest) would stand atop the tower and commune with the gods. The victim, who had been strangled by the *kahuna's* executioner the night before, was hung from the tower. In the morning, the body was placed on the sacrificial stone and left there until its flesh fell away from its bones.

To the right and slightly beyond Holoholokū's enclosure are the **Royal Birthstones**. The birthstones are two large pieces of smooth stone—one supported the woman's back and the second was a brace for her feet. A grass house adjacent to the stones was where the expectant mother would stay until the moment of birth drew near. It was essential for women of royalty to come to the royal birthstones in order to insure the royal status of the newborn infant. After the birth of a royal infant, the umbilical cord was cut and wedged into the wall of the stone bluff rising behind the birthstones and covered with rocks and hala seeds to keep rats away. If the umbilical cord of an infant were to be eaten by rats, it was believed that the child would grow up to be a thief.

Kuamoʻo Road begins an incline onto a ridge. Kuamoʻo means "spine of a lizard" and the Wailua River represents the fluid running through the spine. A dirt road appears to the left just after mile marker one. The dirt road angles behind so it is easier to approach from the other direction. About 200 hundred yards along the dirt road two upright boulders stand at the edge of the bluff. One of these, no one is sure which, is the **Bellstone**. One legend states that the newborn child of a chief was carried up the hill from the Royal Birthstones to a boulder on the ridge overlooking the valley. The *kāhuna* would strike the Bellstone with a rock in a way that would bring forth a sonorous sound that carried up and down the Wailua Valley, announcing to everyone that a new chief was among them. Both of the stones have chips in them, probably from the curious trying to make a rock sound like a bell. You may try, too. A petroglyph is carved onto one of the stones. Its design is too perfect and its archaeological importance is suspect.

Two hundred yards up the road is the **Poliʻahu Heiau**. It is a relatively well-preserved *heiau* with a grand view of the Wailua River meandering 683 feet below Mauna Kapu, the last peak of the Kālepa Ridge. You can follow the river's path to the ocean, a little more than a mile to the east. The large Malae Heiau is visible from here. It is believed that besides announcing royal births, the Bellstone may have been used to communicate with the *heiau* of the lower elevation, possibly warning of war canoes invading from the sea. Poliʻahu Heiau was a paved enclosure with walls 242 feet long and 165 feet wide. A wooden oracle tower containing three stories rose above the floor. It was *kapu* to all but the *aliʻi nui* (ruling chief) and the *kahuna nui* (head priest).

A few yards up the road from Poliʻahu Heiau and on the opposite side is the parking lot for the **ʻŌpaekaʻa Falls** viewpoint. From the parking lot, which has restrooms, walk the short path to the viewpoint of the 200-foot-high twin cascades. ʻŌpaekaʻa, meaning "rolling shrimp," was named for the shrimp that once gathered at the pools formed at the base of the falls.

ʻŌpaekaʻa Falls

Directly across the road from the falls viewpoint is another viewpoint of the Wailua River valley. To the right, you can see where the river splits into a north and a south fork. Both forks narrow shortly after the split and even kayakers will have to turn around. The Fern Grotto is on the south fork and Wailua Falls is two miles upstream of that.

Below the viewpoint, on the north bank of the river, are the thatched huts of **Kamūkila Hawaiian Village** (823-0559). The reconstructed Polynesian village features demonstrations of native craft making. A guided tour of the village takes 30 to 45 minutes and costs $5. Their hours are 8:30 a.m. to 4:30 p.m., Monday to Saturday. A side road just above the viewpoint leads down to Kamūkila. The village is named after a legendary lizard that gathered all the precious stones of Kaua'i and left with them, which is why no precious stones are ever found on the island.

Kuamo'o Road (Highway 580) continues west towards the heart of the island. The air cools as you pass through the residential neighborhoods of Wailua Heights and then on to the Homesteads. This area of cattle ranches, vegetable farms and poultry ranches was settled by homesteaders awarded land grants after Hawai'i became a territory of the United States in 1900. The road becomes a rough 4WD trail at a stream crossing, 6.7 miles from the Kūhiō Highway intersection. On the other side of the stream is **Keahua Arboretum**. If the stream is low, you can drive across, or you can park and walk the few yards to the arboretum trail. The trail begins at a stand of painted eucalyptus trees. Unfortunately, many of the trees are not labeled. The short trail carries over a knoll, where picnic tables look over a valley to the west. If you are lucky and clouds don't obscure the view, you can see the volcanic center of Kaua'i and the highest point of the island. The peak on the south end of the steep ridge is Kawaikini, which rises to 5, 243 feet. Follow the ridge a mile to the north to see Wai'ale'ale, with an altitude of 5,148 feet.

Nounou Ridge stretches north for 2 miles from 'Ōpaeka'a Falls. The ridge reaches its highest elevation of 1,241 feet in its middle. The east side of the ridge slopes gradually to the coast—evidence of the original slope of Wai'ale'ale. Erosion has erased nearly every other remnant of the slope on the island. More colorfully, the elongated mountain is called **Sleeping Giant**. When viewed from the east, Nounou offers a profile vaguely resembling a giant in repose, its feet to the right, its head on the left and the high point in the middle being its chest. A sign on the highway points to a Sleeping Giant viewpoint behind the Waipouli Complex.

Legend says the giant, named Puni, was sleeping when a fleet of war canoes from O'ahu attacked. The Menehune, who were friends of Puni, tried to wake him, but to no avail. When their pushes and prods didn't work, they lit huge bonfires around Puni, but he didn't waken. In desperation the Menehune threw large rocks on Puni's stomach, which bounced off and into the sea near the

Kaua'i's highest point, Kawaikini, peaks at the left end of the ridge and Wai'ale'ale is at the center

The head of the Sleeping Giant of Nounou Ridge is at the center of the ridge. His chest and feet lie to the right.

canoes. When the invading forces saw boulders dropping around them and the illuminated outline of a giant on land, they turned and fled for home. The next morning, the Menehune tried to wake Puni to thank him, but their friendly giant would not stir. Sadly, some of the rocks bouncing off his stomach landed in his mouth and choked him to death.

Kapa'a

The Kūhiō Highway between Līhu'e and Kapa'a can become congested, especially during morning and afternoon commutes. To help alleviate the traffic problem, the Kapa'a Bypass Road is utilized every day from 5:00 a.m. to 9:00 p.m. The road runs through private land and is gated during off hours. The south end of the bypass connects with the highway between mile markers six and seven. It runs

mauka of Waipouli and reconnects with the highway at Kapa'a's town center, at the traffic lights next to the ABC store. The bypass is designated as a temporary road pending renegotiation of the lease with the property owner. Interestingly, the property owner of the 1,400-acre estate planted in sugar cane is entertainer Bette Midler, who has expressed interest in growing timber on the land and has no plans to develop it.

The area north of the bypass turnoff is called the **Royal Coconut Coast**. Rows of planted coconut trees tower and sway above both sides of the highway. This area has been developed with four resort hotels, a condominium complex, and the Coconut Marketplace shopping center.

Kapa'a is a charming small town, with false front stores painted in bright colors and second-story balconies that give it the feel of a nineteenth century plantation town—which it once was. It was home to Hawaiian Pineapple Canneries and Hawaiian Fruit Packers until they closed in the 1970s. The town

The Royal Coconut Coast in the early morning

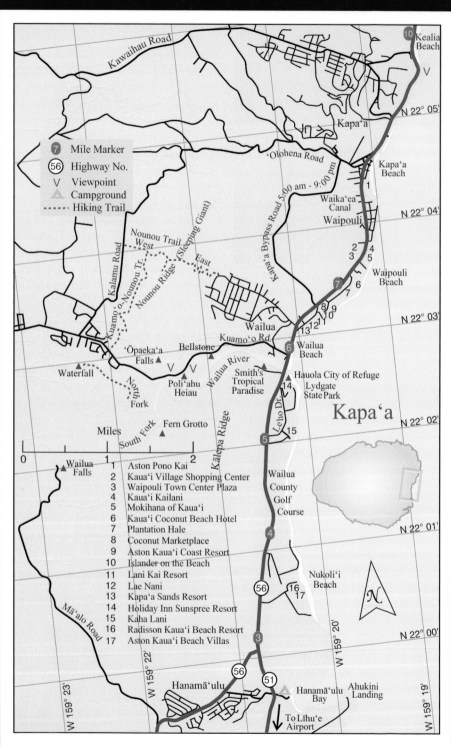

Kawaihau Road

Kealia Beach

Kapa'a

Kapa'a Beach

'Olohena Road

Mile Marker
Highway No.
Viewpoint
Campground
Hiking Trail

Waika'ea Canal

Waipouli

Nounou Trail West

East

Nounou Ridge (Sleeping Giant)

Kalamu Road

Kuamo'o-Nounou Tr.

Waipouli Beach

Wailua

Kuamo'o Rd.

Wailua Beach

'Ōpaeka'a Falls

Bellstone

Wailua River

North Fork

Poli'ahu Heiau

Smith's Tropical Paradise

Hauola City of Refuge Lydgate State Park

Kapa'a

Miles

South Fork

Fern Grotto

Kālepa Ridge

Leho Dr.

Wailua County Golf Course

0

1

2

Wailua Falls

1 Aston Pono Kai
2 Kaua'i Village Shopping Center
3 Waipouli Town Center Plaza
4 Kaua'i Kailani
5 Mokihana of Kaua'i
6 Kaua'i Coconut Beach Hotel
7 Plantation Hale
8 Coconut Marketplace
9 Aston Kaua'i Coast Resort
10 Islander on the Beach
11 Lani Kai Resort
12 Lae Nani
13 Kapa'a Sands Resort
14 Holiday Inn Sunspree Resort
15 Kaha Lani
16 Radisson Kaua'i Beach Resort
17 Aston Kaua'i Beach Villas

Nukoli'i Beach

Mā'alo Road

N

Hanamā'ulu

Hanamā'ulu Bay

Ahukini Landing

To Līhu'e Airport

declined but has rebounded. Shops and restaurants catering to the visitor traffic line the highway, which is the town's main street. Businesses and strip malls on side roads serve the community that works and lives there. The highway has a viewpoint on the north end of Kapa'a, which is a good place to watch the sun rise over the ocean and light up the east coast.

Anahola

North of Kapa'a, the Kūhiō Highway crosses over Kapa'a Stream and runs along the length of Keālia Beach. Hawaiians used to collect seawater to dry into salt along this coast. Salt was needed to preserve fish and flavor poi. Little is left of the plantation town that later developed in this area. Keālia had a sugar mill, a train depot, and a steamer landing.

The spread-out village of Anahola straddles the highway at mile markers 13 and 14. Almost a hundred years ago it was designated as a settlement where Hawaiian people could live and acquire land with long-term leases. Later, the Hawaiian Homes Project assisted Hawaiians in financing their homes on land once leased to sugar and pineapple companies. The only commercial developments in the community are a general store, a post office, and a hamburger stand.

Behind Anahola stand the beautifully rugged Kalalea Mountains, at the east end of the Anahola Range. The peak on the left is Hōkū'alele, which means "shooting star." Atop this peak was a *heiau* with three terraces. Next to Hōkū'alele is Kalalea, which means "prominent." Commonly, the peak is called **King Kong's Profile**. Before the famous ape debuted on movie screens, Hawaiians thought the mountain's sharp outline resembled the dorsal fin of a shark as it cleaved the surface of the sea.

Near the top of the ridge to the right of King Kong's Profile is **Hole In The Mountain**. Erosion and landslides on both sides of the ridge have exposed a lava tube that once ran from the volcanic center of the island to the sea. In the early 1980s, more landslides filled the hole until it nearly disappeared. Erosion is again opening the hole, so that a small amount of daylight is visible through the mountain. There are many legends to account for the hole.

King Kong's Profile

Several involve a spear being hurled through the mountain. There is a viewpoint for King Kong's Profile between mile markers 14 and 15. Hole In The Mountain can be seen between mile markers 15 and 16.

The Kūhiō Highway reaches farther inland as it heads north and west and approaches the north shore. Ko'olau Road connects with the highway at mile marker 16 and again in 3 miles. It's an alternate route you can take for a change of pace and scenery. Side roads lead off Ko'olau Road to Moloa'a Bay and Larsen's Beach (see Beaches chapter).

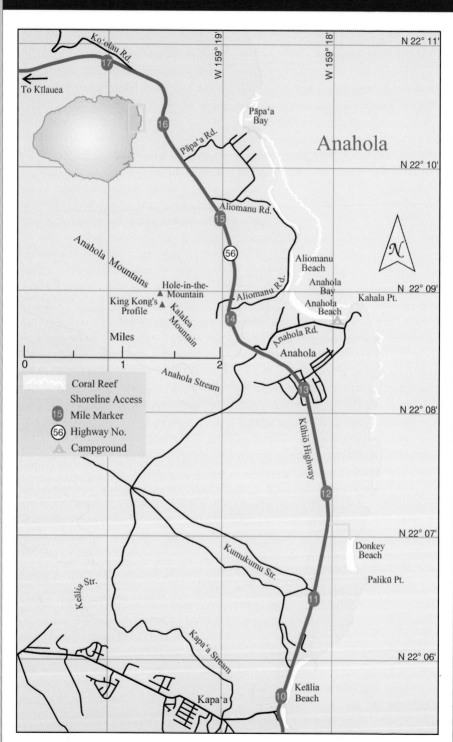

NORTH SHORE SIGHTS

The 20-mile stretch of shoreline from Kīlauea to the sea cliffs of Nā Pali is considered the North Shore. It is a luxuriant ribbon of tropical vegetation, lava cliffs, sandy beaches and scenic coves, backdropped by primordial peaks that carve a mystical silhouette. Nurtured by the prevailing trade winds, the North Shore receives more rainfall than other parts of the island. The rain brings rainbows and feeds the vegetation, causing it to be even more lush and green than the rest of the island. On rainy days, the mountains robed in rain forest, present an ethereal quality as clouds alternately shroud their peaks then drift and lift, revealing waterfalls spilling back to the sea.

The Kūhiō Highway winds its way through the North Shore, labeled as Highway 56 until it reaches Princeville, where it becomes Highway 560. From here the pace of traffic and life slows, as the road rolls through the quaint village of Hanalei and snakes along the coastline. Ten miles from Princeville, the road ends and the Nā Pali coastline begins.

Kīlauea

At Mile Marker 20, the Kūhiō Highway turns west and soon the prominent hill of Pu'u Kīlauea projecting from the shoreline becomes visible. The eruption that caused the 568-foot volcanic cone occurred between 13,000 and 15,000 years ago and probably represents the most recent volcanic activity on Kaua'i.

In the lush land east of Pu'u Kīlauea, **Na ʻĀina Kai Botanical Garden** recently opened to public tours. The stunningly beautiful estate built by Ed and Joyce Doty operates as a public trust and welcomes visitors to its 12 acres of formal gardens, 45 acres of exotic fruit trees, and 110 acres of tropical hardwood forests. Tour guides take visitors along meandering paths that pass by arbors, waterfalls, gazebos, topiary, and koi-filled ponds. More than 65 bronze statues of people and animals designed in Americana style highlight the natural splendor. The botanical garden is sectioned into 12 theme gardens. In the Shower Tree Park the guide will lead you past a rose arbor to serene Ka'ula Lagoon, where a Japanese teahouse sits by a waterfall. An arched bridge leads to an island in the lagoon and the statue of a dancing hula girl. A large maze sculpted from mock orange hedges into the design of a flowering plant rewards the

Statues highlight the natural beauty of Na ʻĀina Kai Botanical Garden

Na 'Āina Kai Botanical Garden

adventurous with whimsical statuary hidden in its confines. Stunning cacti and succulents stand in contrast to the surrounding tropical foliage in the Desert Garden. Juxtaposed to the desert, the Palm Garden shades you with green and silvery-gray fronds. Your guide will open a cast iron security gate to allow you to enter the Carnivorous Plant House (the gate keeps chickens out). A bog environment is created in the house that harbors Venus fly traps, butterworts, and tropical pitcher plants. Tours take visitors through a plantation of hardwood trees, grown to hopefully become commercially viable. Rows of teak and mahogany trees give way to less familiar sounding names like cocobolo, rainbowbark, mangosteen and pau ferro, used as a sound wood by violin makers. All tours of Na 'Āina Kai are guided and are given Tuesdays, Wednesdays and Thursdays. Participants ride on trams between the garden areas. A tour of the Formal Gardens starts at 8:30 a.m., takes 1.5 hours and costs $25 per person. A tour of the Wild Forest Garden leaves at 1:00 p.m., takes 1.5 hours and costs $25 per person. A 2.5-hour Nature Walk Tour is given Thursdays at 9:00 a.m. at a cost of $35. An Evening Stroll takes place each Wednesday at 3:00 p.m. It lasts 3.5 hours and costs $35. Twice each month the physically fit are taken on a five-hour Full Tour. The cost is $70, with lunch included. Children under the age of 13 are not allowed on the tours. Additional tours may be added as demand warrants. Reservations are necessary and can be made by phoning (808) 828-0525. Wailapa Road is the entrance road to

Na 'Āina Kai. Turn *makai* onto Wailapa between mile markers 21 and 22 of the Kūhiō Highway and follow it to the end.

The former plantation town of **Kīlauea** is generally considered the gateway to Kaua'i's North Shore. The Kīlauea Sugar Company was incorporated in 1880 and was half-owned each by British and American interests. Princess Lili'uokalani visited Kīlauea in the early 1880s to dedicate the first sugar cane train line constructed on Kaua'i. The 24-inch gauge railway had a small engine, 3 miles of portable track and 24, cars that were used to haul cane and bags of sugar.

Workers for the plantation were brought in from China, Japan, Portugal, Germany, and even the Gilbert Islands. Most immigrants came to work on a four-year contract. At first the ethnic groups were segregated into their own camps. However, as the decades passed, the system changed and bachelor workers lived in one camp, families in another, with better homes being allocated according to job rank.

In 1883, some of the newly arrived workers went on strike. They claimed that the plantation failed to provide suitable housing and the use of plots of land as was promised to them. Those who weren't jailed for striking carried the matter to court in Honolulu. As a result, some of the laborers were released from their contracts.

C. Brewer and Company took over management of Kīlauea Plantation in 1922. L.D. Larsen, who has a namesake beach at Moloa'a, became its manager. Larsen was instrumental in the building of the numerous stone-walled houses and buildings in Kīlauea. Both quarried stone and stones cleared from cane fields were used. The sturdy structures replaced run-down wooden plantation homes.

The plantation closed in 1971 due in part to mill waste running off into the ocean in violation of newly enacted Environmental Protection Agency regulations. Predictions that Kīlauea would soon fold didn't materialize. Today Kīlauea is a well-maintained residential community, with residents who work mainly in the visitor industry in Princeville or commute to jobs in Līhu'e. When it closed, the plantation gave its workers still living in Kīlauea an opportunity to buy lots, with choices based on seniority. Rank and file workers were housed along the edge of hillsides overlooking the Kīlauea River, above the plantation dump. Today the dump is covered over and the lots are the most valuable in town because of their excellent views.

The entrance to Kīlauea is Kolo Road, just past the 23-mile marker at the Shell service station. Where Kolo Road intersects with Kīlauea Road is **Christ Memorial Episcopal Church**. The present church of cut lava stone walls and stained glass windows from England was built in 1941. Adjoining the church is a cemetery with headstones dating back to the 1880s, when the original Hawaiian Congregational Church stood here.

A short distance farther along Kolo Road is the octagonal-shaped **St. Sylvester Catholic Church**. This church-in-the-round has pews nearly circling the altar. Above the altar, the Stations of the Cross are frescos painted by the late Jean Charlot, one of Hawai'i's most important artists.

Drive north on Kīlauea Road and stop at the **Kong Lung Store** on the right. Originally, this handsome stone building held the Kīlauea Plantation's store. Plantation workers would have depended on this store for life's necessities and paid with deductions from their next paycheck. Now the store beautifully showcases clothing, art, fragrances and gift items from Asia and Hawai'i.

A mile north on Kīlauea Road is the most northerly point on Kaua'i and the **Kīlauea Point National Wildlife Refuge**. The refuge encompasses 160 acres of rugged sea

Kīlauea Point historic lighthouse

cliffs, a peninsula jutting into the waves and the rocky islet of Moku'ae'ae. Standing proud at Kīlauea Point is the **historic lighthouse**, erected in 1913 to aid commercial shipping between Hawai'i and Asia. The Coast Guard deactivated the lighthouse, which contains the largest clamshell lens in the world, in 1976 and replaced it with a high intensity beacon. The view from the point is truly grand. Surf crashes on the rocky cliffs 200 feet below, and to the west is a sweeping view of Secret Beach and the North Shore.

The Wildlife Refuge, a sanctuary to five species of sea birds, can turn a casual observer into an ardent bird watcher. The mostly black great frigate birds soar effortlessly on pointed wings that may span seven feet and have a distinctive forked tail. Great frigate birds nest in the Northwestern Hawaiian Islands and visit Kaua'i to feed. The Hawaiian name for the species is 'iwa, which means "thief." The great frigate bird likes to harass other sea birds that have just caught a fish. If its victim releases its catch, the avian pirate swoops down to nab the fish in mid-air. Red-footed boobies claim the entire cliffside to the east of Kīlauea Point in the spring and summer months. Boobies have long pointed wings, long tails, pointed bills and brightly colored feet. Sometimes called gannets, the term booby apparently arose because the nesting birds acted so boldly and fearlessly towards people that they were considered stupid. Boobies plunge-dive to catch their prey of fish and

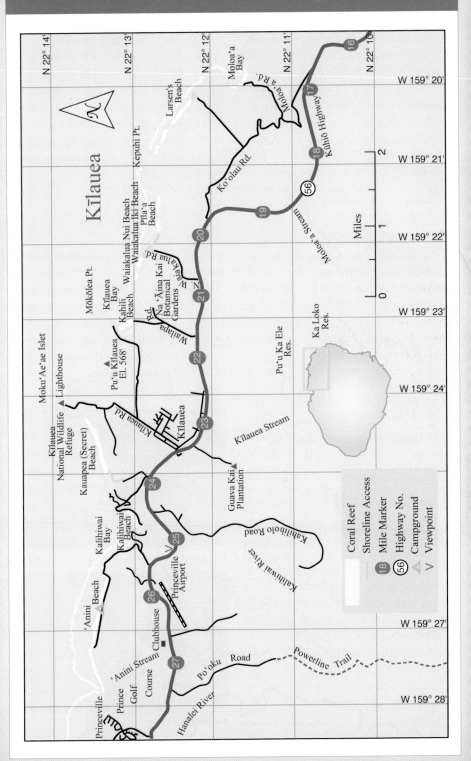

squid underwater. Unlike most other birds, the boobies have nostrils that close to prevent water rushing into their lungs as they hit the ocean. Tropic birds present a striking silhouette when they fly with two very long, thin tail feathers, called streamers. These white or white-and-black birds have short legs unsuited for walking on land and webbed feet. Tropic birds breed in nests they build in rock cavities on the adjacent cliffs. Both parents incubate a single egg. The other two species of sea birds at the refuge, the wedge-tailed shearwater and the Laysan albatross, are members of the same family of sea birds called tubenoses. They are so called because their nostrils emerge through tubes on their distinctly hooked upper bills. A gland between their eyes permits them to drink seawater by filtering salt from the water and concentrating it. This concentrated salt solution is excreted in drops from the base of the bill and directed to the end of the bill by the nostril tubes. The wedge-tailed shearwater breeds in burrows and cavities on hillsides. They can be easily seen sitting on their nests from the pathways on Kīlauea Point. Both parents will incubate the single egg for six to nine weeks and take turns in feeding the chick. The burrow or cavity is reused each year by the same pair. Laysan albatrosses began using the Kīlauea Refuge for breeding in the 1970s. Albatrosses use a type of non-flapping flight known as dynamic soaring. They use their long narrow wings to take advantage of strong winds blowing across the ocean's surface. Their soaring flight takes them in huge loops from high above the ocean, where the wind is fastest, to down toward the surface, where friction slows the wind, and then up into the faster wind again, never having to flap their wings. To take off from the sea they face the wind to get maximum lift just as an airplane does. If the wind is strong enough, just extending its wings out will get the albatross airborne. Otherwise, the large bird must run across the surface of the water or land to take off. Albatrosses are sometimes called gooney birds because of their awkwardness moving on land and their clumsiness during takeoffs and landings (crashing into beach shrubbery and taking nose-dives are common occurrences). The albatross mates for life and may live for 40 years.

Nesting wedge-tailed shearwater

Laysan albatrosses

A project by Wake Forest University and funded by Kīlauea Point Natural History Association has fitted satellite transmitters to some of Hawai'i's albatrosses. The purpose is to track Laysan albatrosses on their voyages across the Northwestern Hawaiian Islands. The transmitters have shown that these birds can cover thousands of miles in several days. The project has an internet site that keeps track of the tagged birds. At the site, students in grades four through nine can sign up to receive e-mail notification of the bird's location every 24 hours. The address of the internet site is: www.wfu.edu/albatross.

Besides the sea birds, watch for a recently introduced mating pair of nēnē close to the lighthouse. In the sea you may see green sea turtles and dolphins and, during the winter months, watch for humpback whales.

Displays and dioramas about native Hawaiian habitats, endangered native plants and wildlife are placed on pathways about the peninsula and in the interpretive building. A guided hike to Crater Hill leaves the interpretive center at 10:15 a.m. Reservations may be made by calling 828-0168, or arrive at departure time and you will be included if they have openings. There is no charge for the guided hike, but participants must pay the entrance fee to the refuge. The walk is approximately one mile long and takes two hours. Native and introduced plants and wildlife encountered will be identified, and the geological features of Crater Hill will be pointed out. The refuge is open daily from 10:00 a.m.

to 4:00 p.m. and an entrance fee of $3 is collected. Volunteer docents are often on hand to answer visitors' questions and lend binoculars.

Across from Kīlauea, just north of mile marker 23, is the entrance road to the **Guava Kai Plantation**. Two very large guavas wearing sunglasses mark the spot. The plantation has 480 acres of guava orchard under commercial cultivation. The mile-long access road to the visitor center passes neat rows of hybrid guava trees bearing exceptionally large fruit. Here, you can learn how Kaua'i guava is grown and processed. The processing plant is in operation from August to December and is open for viewing. Free juice and jam samples are available at the gift shop, which sells all kinds of guava-based products. Visitors are welcome to stroll into the orchard and pick some guava fruit. A small botanical garden waits on the other side of an archway next to the parking lot. A pathway crosses a stream and leads past many labeled tropical trees and plants to a gazebo and picnic benches next to a pond. The visitor center and garden are open daily, 9:00 a.m. to 5:00 p.m. No admission fee is charged.

At mile marker 24 of the highway is the first of two intersections with Kalihiwai Road. This is the turnoff for access to both Secret Beach and Kalihiwai Beach (see Beaches chapter). A devastating tsunami washed out the bridge over Kalihiwai Stream on April 1, 1946, and yet another tsunami hit here on March 3, 1957. Remnants of the bridge supports still stand in the stream, but Kalihiwai

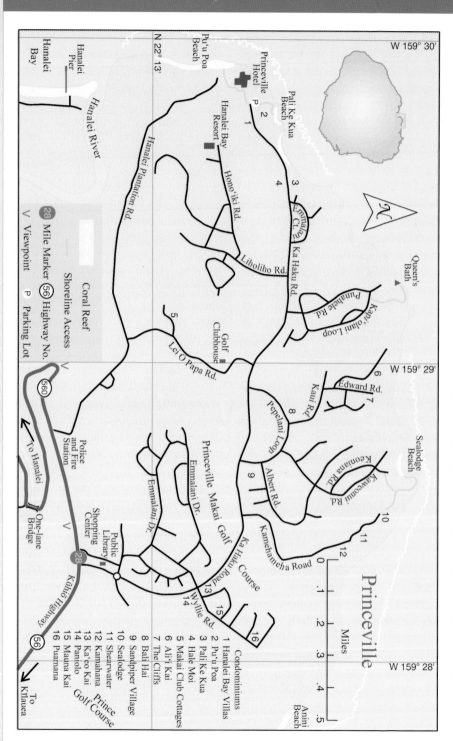

Princeville

Miles
0   .1   .2   .3   .4   .5

Condominiums
1 Hanalei Bay Villas
2 Pu'u Poa
3 Pali Ke Kua
4 Hale Moi
5 Makai Club Cottages
6 Ali'i Kai
7 The Cliffs
8 Bali Hai
9 Sandpiper Village
10 Sealodge
11 Shearwater
12 Kamahana
13 Ka'eo Kai
14 Paniolo
15 Mauna Kai
16 Puamana

Legend:
Coral Reef
Shoreline Access
28 Mile Marker   56 Highway No.
V Viewpoint   P Parking Lot

N 22° 13'
W 159° 30'   W 159° 29'   W 159° 28'

Hanalei Bay
Hanalei Pier
Hanalei River
Hanalei Bay Resort
Pu'u Poa Beach
Princeville Hotel
Pali Ke Kua Beach
Hanalei Plantation Rd.
Hono'iki Rd.
Emmalani Ct.
Ka Haku Rd.
Liholiho Rd.
Queen's Bath
Punahele Rd.
Kapi'olani Loop
Kaui Rd.
Edward Rd.
Sealodge Beach
Lei O Papa Rd.
Golf Clubhouse
Pepelani Loop
Keoniana Rd.
Kawaouni Rd.
Albert Rd.
Princeville Makai Golf
Emmalani Dr.
Police and Fire Station
Shopping Center
Public Library
Kamehameha Road
Ka Haku Road
Wyllie Rd.
Anini Beach
Kūhiō Highway
To Hanalei
One-lane Bridge
To Kīlauea
Prince Golf Course

Road is permanently bisected. A bridge on the Kūhiō Highway now crosses Kalihiwai Stream at higher ground. There was a parking area for a viewpoint of the **Kalihiwai Valley** next to the bridge, just past mile marker 25, but the county installed a barricade, believing pedestrians were endangered. By walking onto the bridge you can usually see a waterfall a half mile up the valley, cascading towards Kalihiwai Stream from the right. On the *mauka* side of the highway and a few yards up the hill from the barricade is another waterfall.

Prince Albert

Kalihiwai Valley

At mile marker 24 is the second intersection with Kalihiwai Road. This part of the road leads to ʻAnini Beach (see Beaches chapter). The Princeville Airport appears next on the *mauka* side of the highway. Presently it is only being used as a heliport for Heli USA's sightseeing tours. In the past, small airplanes used Princeville Airport for scheduled flights.

Princeville

After passing the Prince Golf Course clubhouse, you approach the entrance to the resort community of Princeville. Princeville is a carefully planned development spread over 11,000 acres on a 200-foot-high lava shelf between ʻAnini Beach and Hanalei Bay. An elegant, old-world-style fountain and statue greets visitors and residents at the entrance to this manicured enclave of two luxury resort hotels, 16 condominium and time-share complexes, several private homes, and two renowned golf courses.

Robert Chrichton Wyllie

The plateau overlooking Hanalei Bay was once a plantation owned by Scotsman Robert Crichton Wyllie. Wyllie served as foreign minister for the kingdom of Hawai'i under Kamehamehas IV and V. To honor the visit of Kamehameha IV and Queen Emma in 1860, Wyllie named his estate, Barony de Princeville, in honor of the royal couple's young son, Prince Albert. Sadly, the boy-prince died shortly afterwards at the age of four. Every year in May, a festival is held in Princeville in his memory. The festival is marked by concerts of Hawaiian and classical music and a children's hula recital. In his capacity as foreign minister, Wyllie sought and received recognition of Hawai'i as an independent nation by countries around the world. He was less successful in his business endeavors. Upon his death in 1865, Wyllie's estate was sold to pay off his sizable debts.

When attempts to grow and mill sugar by landowners A.S. Wilcox, and later, the Līhu'e Plantation, proved unsuccessful, the property at Princeville became a cattle ranch. In 1968, the land was sold to a Denver-based oil and gas company for development. Today, Princeville Resort is a private corporation owned by a corporation owned by a consortium of Japanese companies.

The main road in Princeville meanders for two miles, past condominiums and the Makai Golf Course, ending at the **Princeville Hotel**. The multitiered edifice cascades down its perch overlooking Hanalei Bay. Built in 1985, the hotel and its 252 rooms underwent major remodeling in 1989. The lobby exudes elegance on a grand scale. Gold-crowned Corinthian columns draw the eye up to ethereal ceilings painted with wandering clouds. A central skylight brightens bountiful floral arrangements. Gurgling reflective pools mirror the panorama that unfolds beyond the floor-to-ceiling windows. Even this elegance and beauty can't overshadow the wonderful view of nature at its best. Below the verdant ridges and towering waterfalls of Nāmolokama Mountain, Hanalei Bay carves a perfect arc of blue ocean and white sand. Beyond the bay, rain-carved ridges repeat to the west. Silhouetting the setting sun, the mystical peak of Bali Hai defines what seems to be the farthest edge of paradise.

In 1951, Princeville was a cattle ranch.

Hawaiʻi State Archives

On the front lawn of the Princeville Hotel the vestiges of earthen walls vaguely outline the perimeter of what was **Fort Alexander**. An ambitious agent of the Russian-American company, Georg Schaffer, built the fort in 1816 to have a commanding view of the entrance of Hanalei Bay. Acting without the authority of the Russian government, Schaffer made an alliance with Kaumualiʻi, the king of Kauaʻi. In return for land and trading rights, Schaffer promised Russia's help in overthrowing Kamehameha's rule of the island. Schaffer couldn't deliver on his promises and was chased off the island in 1817. In 1973, archaeologists from the Bernice Pauahi Bishop Museum mapped and excavated the remnants of the fort. The walls were constructed entirely of clay and topsoil. They discovered foundations for two small structures within the fort. All that remains of the foundations are a few stone pilings. Interpretive signs at the fort tell the story of the brief, unofficial Russian interlude on Kauaʻi.

Below Princeville, on a north-facing lava shelf, the ocean's waves have worn a depression into the lava rock. Waves splashing over the shelf fill the depression, creating a salt-water swimming pool called **Queen's Bath**. High winter surf may, however, make swimming in the pool dangerous. Watch for green sea turtles bobbing in the surf along the lava shelf. To find Queen's Bath, turn *makai* from Ka Haku Road, Princeville's main road, onto Punahele Road. The end of Punahele Road intersects with Kapiʻolani Loop. A small parking area here is the start of the trail to the lava shelf. At the bottom of the steep trail turn left and make your way over the rocks to the pool.

Queen's Bath

The view of the Hanalei Valley is pretty enough for a postcard

Returning to the highway, the 2,487-foot-high twin peaks of the mountain Hīhīmanu appears behind Princeville's water fountain. Hīhīmanu means "manta ray" and is so named because the peaks resemble the fin tips of the manta ray.

Princeville's shopping center caters to both local residents and tourists. Tenants include a supermarket, a hardware store, a medical clinic, restaurants, banks, and the last gas station along the north shore. Across the highway from the shopping center is the **Hanalei Valley Overlook**. Laid out before you is the sweeping vista of the valley and flatland drained by the Hanalei River and a green curtain of mountains. The patchwork of shimmering taro fields that fill the valley's floor is split down the middle by the river, visible for 4 miles from your vantage point. Every postcard rack on the island stocks a picture of this scene. The ridge along the east (left) side of the valley was once a canyon almost 2,000 feet deep. Thick flows of lava from the later-occurring Kōloa eruption filled the canyon to the brim and, in so doing, displaced the canyon's stream to the west. There, the stream

eroded the weaker Nā Pali basalt flows to a depth of about 1,000 feet, creating the modern Hanalei Valley.

In 1972, the U.S. Fish and Wildlife Service designated 917 acres of Hanalei Valley as Hanalei National Wildlife Refuge. Taro, which is used to make poi, has been cultivated here for 1,200 years, and the refuge helps ensure its survival by maintaining the main irrigation ditches. The taro farmers in turn maintain their own dikes, ditches and crops, creating the diverse habitats of marshy land, shallow standing water and ponds needed by native waterbirds. In the last 200 years, sugar cultivation and urban developments have reduced Hawai'i's natural wetlands and taro ponds to 5 percent of their original acreage. As these lands were drained, native waterbird populations declined. Birds like Hawaiian coots, Hawaiian gallinules, Hawaiian ducks, and Hawaiian black-necked stilts were placed on the federal endangered species list. These birds, as well as such migrating birds as the northern pintail, northern shoveler, golden plover and the sanderling, are represented in the Hanalei Refuge.

From here, Highway 56 changes to Highway 560 and the mileage markers start at zero. Half a mile along Highway 560 is another viewpoint, this time on the right side of the road. Visible from this vantage point are the town of Hanalei, Hanalei Bay, and the north shore mountains to the west. Around a couple of sharp curves in the highway is the historic Hanalei Bridge, built in 1912. The rusted steel trusses above the bridge are no longer needed for support.

Sunlight breaks through the clouds over Hanalei Bay

Reinforcements added to the structure under the road deck now support the entire structure. The Hanalei Bridge is the first of seven one-lane bridges on Highway 560. All of the one-lane bridges have yield signs from both approaches. Whoever enters the bridge first has the right-of-way. All vehicles behind that vehicle proceed, as well. So, if the vehicle in front of you goes, you go, too. When the line of vehicles has cleared, then the traffic from the other direction takes its turn.

At the other end of the bridge, Ōhiki Road branches to the left. You may follow this narrow road into the refuge for 1.8 miles. You will get a close look at the heart-shaped leaves of the taro plant, and there is an abandoned rice mill that is being restored. You are not allowed to walk into the refuge, however. That privilege is restricted to the farmers and the birds.

Hanalei

Beyond the Hanalei Bridge, the highway runs between the river and the taro fields for a mile of pastoral scenes before reaching the town of Hanalei. This small community blends an eclectic mix of farmers, artists, surfers, hippies, and tourists into comfortable co-existence. Along the main street are several good

Hawai'i State Archives

Hanalei Liquor Store, 1951

Canoe paddlers train on Hanalei Bay

Hawaiians have grown taro in the Hanalei Valley for centuries.

Ultralight aircraft flies over Hanalei Bay at sunset

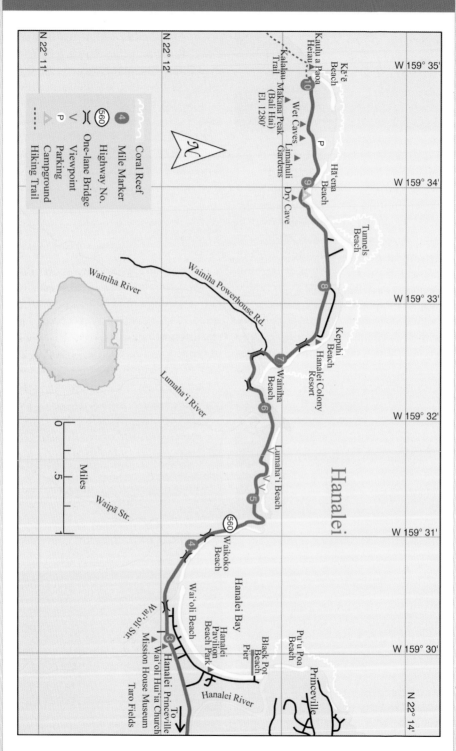

restaurants and two shopping centers, the Ching Young Village and the Old Hanalei School Center. *Mauka* of the main street are more taro fields and the towering green wall that is **Nāmolokama Mountain**. After heavy rains, as many as 23 waterfalls flow down its face. The middle massif is **Māmalahoa**, 3,745 feet high and named after the wife of Kāne, the supreme god of ancient Kaua'i.

One block *makai* is Weke Road, which follows the curve of Hanalei Bay. Turn right onto Weke Road from any of the connecting roads (all named after Hawaiian fish) and you are headed towards the **Hanalei Pier** and the mouth of the Hanalei River. On the way to the Pier there is a large brown house with a wraparound porch to the right. This is the old Wilcox estate, home to descendants of early Hanalei missionaries Abner and Lucy Wilcox. The concrete pier is a great place to view the bay and mountains. It was rebuilt in the early 1990s as a replica of the original pier that was used to load rice and taro onto ships. Remnants of narrow-gauge railway tracks can still be seen in the parking lot in front of the pier.

An historic incident occurred in 1824 in the middle of the bay, where the Wai'oli Stream flows out. Kamehameha II bartered $90,000 worth of the kingdom's sandalwood to buy the fastest and finest yacht in the world. Officially named *Pride of Hawai'i*, it was popularly known as *Cleopatra's Barge*. While the king was visiting England, the reputedly inexperienced and irresponsible crew took the king's yacht to Hanalei Bay, where they ran aground on a reef. Hawaiians from all over the island gathered at Hanalei Bay to try to save the royal craft. They strung cables of hau bark to the masts and, at a given signal, everyone on land heaved and pulled. The crew pulled the yacht onto its side, where it lay until it broke up in the waves. In 1995, researchers from the Smithsonian Institution began a search for the long-lost wreck. They were successful and over three years recovered about a thousand rare artifacts that helped tell the story of what life was like in the early days of the Hawaiian Kingdom.

Standing predominantly next to the highway in the center of town is the **Wai'oli Hui'ia Church**. The green wooden church retains an airy Pacific Islands feel, with large windows that open outward and a high, sharply pitched roof. The bell tower houses the original mission church bell brought from Boston in 1843. Built in 1912, the quaint structure is on the National Register of historic places and is a favorite subject of artists. The church doors are left open and you are

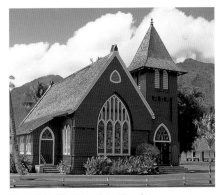
Wai'oli Hui'ia Church in Hanalei

welcome to look inside. Services in both English and Hawaiian are held at 10:00 a.m. on Sundays.

Hanalei's first missionaries, the Reverend and Mrs. William Alexander, arrived aboard a double-hulled canoe in 1834 to establish the Wai'oli Mission. They built the **Wai'oli Mission Hall** in 1841, which stands next to the church. The timber frame building is the oldest surviving church building on Kaua'i. The Mission Hall is distinguished by its wraparound lanai and high, double-pitched roof, which provides for shade and ventilation. It is a notable example of the adaptation of New England building traditions to Hawaiian culture and climate. The Alexanders lived in a grass hut for three years before they built a New England-style house. In 1846, Abner and Lucy Wilcox took residence in the house and it has been associated with the preeminent Kaua'i family ever since. The missionaries' home is now the **Wai'oli Mission House Museum** and is open to public tours. The two-story, white clapboard house is large and simple. Wood moldings adorn windows and doorways. The original koa wood floor, long ago destroyed by termites, was replaced with Douglas fir boards 12 inches wide. A separate cookhouse was built and subsequently attached to the main house to serve as the kitchen and pantry. Daguerreotype photographs of Lucy and Abner Wilcox adorn the walls of the parlor. Lucy had a friendly and sympathetic face; Abner resembled Henry Fonda. A bookcase is full of the leather-bound books read by the family 150 years ago. Upstairs, the guest

Wai'oli Mission House Museum

bedroom housed visiting missionaries and was dubbed the "room of the traveling prophet." Looking through the wavy glass of the windowpanes, you'll view spacious grounds and gardens. Taro grows in plots behind the house in the Wai'oli Valley. Take away the power lines and the scene is the same as the time the house was built. Around the house are china and artifacts such as a butter churn, spinning wheel, and a pie safe built from zinc tiles recycled when the roof was re-covered with wood shakes. Guided tours are given on Tuesdays, Thursdays and Saturdays from 9:00 a.m. to 3:00 p.m. There is no admission charge, but donations are accepted. The parking area is reached by turning *mauka* onto the gravel driveway between the Mission Hall and Hanalei School.

End of the Road

As you leave Hanalei, the road follows the curve of the bay, crossing three more one-lane bridges and the Wai'oli and Waipā Streams. Just after leaving sight of Hanalei Bay, the road takes a sharp bend to the left and several cars will likely be parked along

Pastoral North Shore scene

Wainiha Bridges

A reef calms the water at Hā'ena's Tunnels Beach

the side of the road. This is the start of the trail down to Lumaha'i Beach (see Beaches chapter). Right at mile marker five there are two viewpoints of **Lumaha'i Beach**. You'll get a better view from the second, as trees have grown to obscure much of the beach from the first viewpoint. Yet another viewpoint is a short distance ahead. This one looks over the west end of Lumaha'i Beach. The Lumaha'i Valley contains the largest landholding on Kaua'i of the Bishop Estate.

The **Wainiha Valley** is the longest valley on Kaua'i, extending 14 miles from its headland at the Alaka'i Swamp to the sea. Wainiha means "hostile waters" and its name warns of the floods that occur in the narrow, steep-sided valley during torrential rains. At the Wainiha River, you are treated to the most scenic of the narrow bridges. Two white wooden bridges cross the river, offering a terrific photo opportunity. The two bridges should be treated as one when waiting for traffic to clear. Immediately after the bridges is a side road that travels 1.8 miles up the valley to the Wainiha hydroelectric station. The waterfalls of Wainiha Valley have been generating electrical power since the McBryde Sugar Company built the station in 1906. Power lines from the plant climb the cliff of the valley's headland and cross the island to 'Ele'ele and Waimea. Wainiha has a very small roadside general store. It is the last place on the north shore that you can buy beverages, food, snacks and shave ice.

Next along the road is the idyllic region of **Hā'ena**. Everyone's expectations of a South Seas' tropical paradise is fulfilled here. The narrow road slowly cuts through artists' scenes of curving beaches shaded by coconut palms and jagged mountains clothed in lush foliage and veiled in mist and mystery.

The last resort (literally) on the north shore is the recently renovated Hanalei Colony Resort. The reason many of the houses here are built on stilts is for protection from tsunamis. The great tsunami of 1946 slammed against this low-lying coast, destroying every building and tree in its path with a wave that crested at 45 feet.

Boogie boarder takes a ride at Hā'ena Beach

Hā'ena Beach County Park just before mile marker nine has parking, bathrooms, showers, picnic tables, and grills. Camping is allowed by permit. The campground is cleared every Monday for maintenance and to prevent campers from taking up

residence. A lunch wagon is usually parked at the park and sells fresh fruit, sandwiches and beverages.

Thousands of years ago when sea level was higher, waves carved three caves, one dry and two wet, into the cliffs between Hā'ena and Kē'ē. The dry cave is directly across the road from Hā'ena Park. **Maniniholo Dry Cave** has a wide entrance and broad ceiling. Water drips sporadically onto the dirt floor. It is called Maniniholo, after the head fisherman of the Menehune people.

A Hawaiian legend tells of two brothers and a sister who traveled throughout the world in the form of rocks. They came to the reef at Hā'ena, where the sister remained. The rock could be seen on the reef until the tsunami of 1946 washed it away. The two brothers continued their journey onto land, where one brother decided to stop and rest near the puhala trees. That rock is called **Pōhakuloa** and lies prominently next to the road around the bend from mile marker nine. The other brother attempted to climb the steep cliff to the mountain peak, but, because of his round shape, he kept rolling back. The god Kāne saw his struggle and reached down and lifted the rock onto the peak. This rock is called **Pōhakuokāne** and can be seen sitting on the mountain peak, 1,800 feet above its brother rock. Should Pōhakuokāne ever fall from its perch, it is said the sea will rise to the height of Kāne.

As you drive through a couple of more curves in the road, the unmistakably prominent, triangular peak of **Makana** comes into view. The sharply rising faces, jagged spires and pointed peak gave it the mystical qualities the makers of *South Pacific* were looking for when they portrayed it as the fictitious South Seas mountain called **Bali Hai**. Through special effects, advanced for the 1950s, Makana Peak was lifted from its Hā'ena location to an offshore vista. The name of Bali Hai stuck and is used locally, especially with commercial concerns. Ancient Hawaiians used Makana Peak as the setting for their version of a light show. They would climb the precipitous ridges of Makana carrying firebrands, which were pieces of dried hau or pāpala wood whose core was soft and thus burned before the outer layers. At the summit, they would hurl the burning firebrands off the mountain. If conditions were right, the wind would carry the flaming torches and their trail of embers out to sea. People crowded the beach below and waited in canoes to watch the spectacle.

Makana Peak looms over the Limahuli Valley

The last valley before the Nā Pali coast is Limahuli. An interesting visit here is the **Limahuli Garden**, one of the three National Tropical Botanical Gardens (NTBG) on Kaua'i. Mrs. Juliet Rice Wichman, who wanted this valley preserved as a vestige of ancient Hawai'i, donated the land and garden to the NTBG in 1976. In 1994, her grandson, Charles Wichman, established the Limahuli Reserve with his gift of the adjoining 985 acres in the valley. The garden is built around a Hawaiian terrace system estimated to be at least 700 years old. Water from Limahuli Stream is diverted to sustain plantings of rare native and introduced plants and trees. Besides appreciating their beauty, Hawaiians utilized the plants for their medicinal and nutritional qualities. The American Horticulture Society bestowed Limahuli Garden with its award for the best natural botanical garden in the United States. Guided and self-guided tours are available by reservation only. Phone 826-1053 well in advance. The garden is open Tuesday to Friday and again on Sunday from 9:30 a.m. to 3:00 p.m.

After you cross Limahuli Stream, there is a parking lot on State Park land. If the parking area at Kē'ē Beach is full, it is used as the overflow lot. On the other side of the road from the parking lot is a small clearing where about four cars can park and is the start of a 150-yard trail to the first of two wet caves along this road. The first is called **Waikapala'e Wet Cave** and the second is **Waikanaloa Wet Cave**. Swimmers in Waikapala'e will find the water deep and cold. At the back wall of the cave, on the right side, is the entrance to a hidden chamber. The entrance is about 10 feet long and the chamber is about 8 feet across. With a low ceiling and no good handholds, the hidden chamber is not for those with an aversion to close spaces. Look above the cave's entrance at the sheer cliff wall for a good example of a volcanic dike. Rising vertically across the horizontal layers is lava rock between a foot and 3 feet wide. Movement within the earth's crust split the hardened lava into a vertical fissure. Later, lava flows filled the fissure and hardened into a wall-like mass. The Waikanaloa Wet Cave is a tenth of a mile further ahead and is right next to the road.

A short distance from the wet caves is the end of the road and Kē'ē Beach. A path covered by almond trees at the left side of the beach leads to two of Hawai'i's most celebrated *heiau* dedicated to teaching hula. An overgrown section of flat land formed by the remains of a stone wall are what is left of the **Kaulu a Laka Heiau**, dedicated to Laka, the goddess of the hula. Fifty yards beyond where the sand turns to boulders is the **Kaulu a Paoa Heiau**. Stone terraces rise above the shoreline. The *hālau* (long hall) in which the hula was performed was built on the upper terrace. A rock trail ascends the mountainside for 150 yards to the upper terrace. Here, with a commanding view of the sea and Kē'ē Beach and with the green and black peak of Makana towering above, aspiring students came from all of the

islands to learn the hula. Young people were taught the traditions, chants and dances that told the stories of their ancestors. They were subjected to strict rules and kapu during their time of training. At graduation, the students were required to swim from the lagoon at Kē'ē, through the channel, and come ashore in the cove behind the *heiau* called Nāhiki, where waves surge against the rocks on even the calmest day. To survive, the test required that the shark, which was fed by a chiefess, spare them. It was said that students who broke any of the strict *kapu* were devoured and those without fault came ashore and climbed the rocks back to the *heiau*. The *hālau hula* at this site was used until the 1920s.

On the rocky shoreline at the bottom of the trail that leads up to the terraces is a deeply furrowed rock named **Kilioe**. The basalt boulder is still used as a *pōhaku piko* (a place for umbilical cords). An infant's umbilical cord is wrapped in a leaf and wedged under the rock or in a crack. The fate of the cord is supposed to foretell the events of the child's life.

Sunset at Kē'ē and the Nā Pali coast

Kēʻē Beach at Kaʻīlio Point at sunrise

Kalalau Beach and "Cathedrals," Nā Pali coast

NĀ PALI SIGHTS

Nā Pali coast

In Hawaiian, Nā Pali means simply "the cliffs." The Nā Pali coast is a rugged 15-mile stretch of cliffs, valleys, and beaches between the end of the road at Kē'ē Beach at the northeast, and the opposite end of the road at Polihale State Park in the southwest. Remote and nearly inaccessible, Nā Pali showcases nature at its rawest and most beautiful extremes. It is one of the most dramatic engagements of land and water anywhere. Emerald vegetation blankets seven major valleys; each barricaded from the other by sheer cliffs. Razor-sharp ridges top cliffs rising 4,000 feet to the clouds. Some valleys overhang the sea, their streams cascading from low cliffs. Beaches front four valleys. One beach has a fronting reef and another beach is swept away by winter surf, only to return each summer. The high cliffs of the northern section of Nā Pali wring much of the moisture out of the trade winds, leaving arid conditions on the southern coast. Miloli'i Valley receives only half as much rainfall as the lush Hanakāpī'ai Valley.

Geologists believe that a large block of the original north side of Kaua'i broke off and slid into the ocean millions of years ago. Left behind at the headwall of the slide was a sheer cliff thousands of feet high. The unstoppable force of erosion began to cut deep valleys and canyons into the sea cliff. Only 3 miles inland from the cliff, thick layers of lava had formed the Olokele Plateau. The composition of the plateau is a harder basalt that resists erosion better than the surrounding Nā Pali flows. This enabled the top of the plateau to stand high, while running water cut steep slopes to the sea. Extending from the plateau are tendrils of vertical dikes where the erosion-resistant lava flowed. Like the plateau, these dikes persisted to form the high ridges running from the island's interior to the sea.

The rugged and isolated Nā Pali coast once hosted a sizable Hawaiian population. Each valley had a system of irrigated taro fields. Nu'alolo 'Āina Valley taro growers terraced their land completely—down to the ocean end of its hanging valley. Houses were built on stone platforms, utilizing land that was useless for agriculture. Stories abound

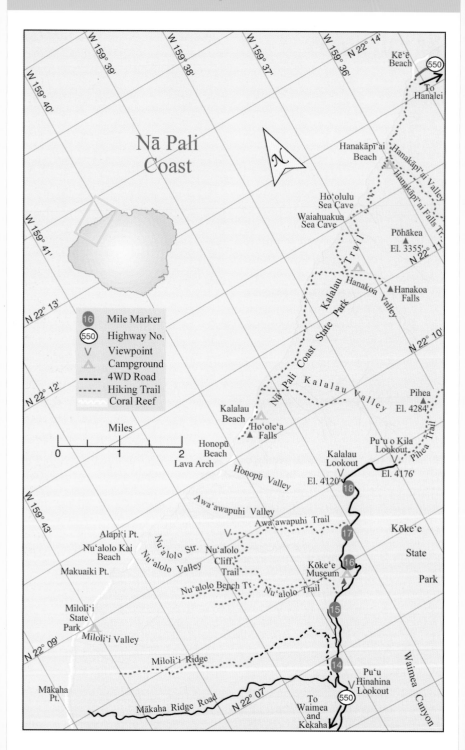

Honopū Valley

Now uninhabited, Hawaiians once lived in Nuʻalolo Valley and built terraces to grow taro

of the missing people who lived in the "Valley of the Lost Tribe." Although considered fact by some accounts, the tale was concocted by Oʻahu school students who explored the valleys of Nuʻalolo and Honopū during a summertime excursion in the 1920s. Their account was lent credence when it was published in a Honolulu newspaper. The largest population of Nā Pali was in the Kalalau Valley, but by 1920 the last residents had moved to Hāʻena and Hanalei.

The Kalalau Trail connects the North Shore with the Hanakāpīʻai, Hanakoa, and Kalalau Valleys. In more ancient times trails crisscrossed the upland regions. Hawaiians could cross the back of the valleys to travel to Hāʻena, as well as take the oceanfront route of the Kalalau Trail. Parts of the

Kalalau Trail were widened with dynamite blasts in 1860. The Controller of Roads, Gottfried Wundenberg, supervised more than 400 blasts along the coast so that coffee and oranges grown commercially in the three valleys could be hauled out by heavily laden donkeys.

Experiencing the sights of Nā Pali takes more effort than on other parts of Kauaʻi. A road will never transit its wilderness. By driving to the last lookout at the top of Kōkeʻe Road, motorists have a spectacular view down into the Kalalau Valley. The modes of transportation that take you to Nā Pali are hiking, boat tours, or helicopter tours. Hiking the 11-mile long Kalalau Trail takes adventurers into the first three valleys of Nā Pali, ending at a campground next to Kalalau Beach. The trail is very strenuous, somewhat hazardous, and requires two days to hike in each direction. State permits are required for the hike and to camp at Kalalau (See Hiking chapter). The first 2 miles of Kalalau Trail lead to Hanakāpīʻai Beach from the trailhead at Kēʻē Beach and can be hiked without obtaining permits. The Nā Pali coastline is the premier attraction on helicopter tours. Pilots take their aircraft into the valleys, treating passengers to heavenly views. Powerboat tours leaving from the south coast ply the coastline, with some offering landings at Nuʻalolo Kai Beach. In the summer, guided kayak trips leave from the north shore. Aided by a tail wind and a favoring current, the trip ends later the same day at Polihale Beach (see Activities chapter).

Honopū Beach

SOUTH SIDE SIGHTS

The landscape on Kaua'i's south side lifts from the bluffs, ledges, and beaches of the shoreline through tilted sugar cane and agricultural country to peak in sharp-ribbed ridges that began as molten lava more than 5 million years ago. Wai'ale'ale, at the heart of the island, and the Hā'upu Ridge, running to the southeast corner, capture moisture from the predominant trade winds. The result is arid agricultural land that needs irrigation to produce crops and a warm and sunny climate to attract vacationers. Forty percent of the visitors to Kaua'i choose the sunny south side as the home base for their Kaua'i vacation. According to a recent survey by the Po'ipū Beach Resort Association, visitors' biggest complaint when they leave is that they didn't allocate enough vacation time to enjoy all that the region has to offer.

You approach the south side from Līhu'e by following the Kaumuali'i Highway (Highway 50) through **Knudsen Gap**. This is the gateway between the Hā'upu Ridge, or Hoary Head Ridge, and Mt. Kāhili, the 3,089-foot peak ending a ridge running from island's center. The gap is named after Valdemar Knudsen, a Norwegian immigrant and sugar planter who owned the property in the area. An ancient trail led journeying Hawaiians from Kalalau through the gap and north along an inland route, crossing

Tunnel of Trees

the gap above Anahola. Today, the electric company runs power lines from hydro stations in the north shore's Wainiha Valley along the trail.

A sign for Highway 520 indicates the path south to Kōloa and Po'ipū. Highway 520, or Maluhia Road, begins with the **Tunnel of Trees**. Over the two-lane road the branches of a double row of towering eucalyptus trees, also called swamp mahogany, grow into a dense, green Gothic arch. Alexander McBryde directed the planting of the nearly mile-long grove of trees in 1911 as a community project.

Kōloa

Maluhia Road leads to the old town of Kōloa, which in Hawaiian means, "tall sugar cane." Original Polynesian settlers brought sugar cane to Hawai'i. Kaua'i farmers had names for at least 40 varieties of sugar cane.

The tallest variety, kō, grew up to 30 feet in height. It was perhaps not a coincidence then that the first sugar cane to be successfully grown and harvested commercially in Hawai'i was at the Kōloa Plantation. Started in 1835 by Ladd and Company, the Kōloa Plantation continued under a string of owners until McBryde Sugar Co. shut down in 1996.

Kōloa was also busy as an early missionary center. The Gulick family started the first station in 1835. Thomas Lafon M.D. joined the station two years later and was the first medical doctor on Kaua'i. Where the Kōloa Mortuary now stands was the site of the missionary school for white children run by Daniel Dole. Attending the Kōloa School in the 1850s was Daniel's son, Sanford, who went on to become instrumental in the overthrow of the Hawaiian monarchy and who served as president of the short-lived Republic of Hawai'i.

Standing at Kōloa's main intersection is a brick chimney; a relic of what was the plantation's third sugar mill, dating back to 1841. In the center of the park, a monument immortalizes the many ethnic groups that worked the sugar plantation. Chinese, Korean, Japanese, Portuguese, Filipino, and Puerto Rican workers wearing native field dress are sculpted in bronze. The Hawaiian worker wears a loincloth called a *malo* and has a poi dog by his side. A plaque on the wall gives reference to a *haole* overseer. Finding the image of a Caucasian boss seated on a high horse unacceptable, local people caused the politically incorrect depiction to be omitted from the statuary at the last minute.

Kōloa's main street is lined with false-front businesses that give it an Old West feel. While its history is rooted in sugar, its present is unmistakably focused on tourism. Souvenir shops, boutiques, art galleries, and restaurants cater to visitors' tastes and encourage a walking tour of the town. The former Yamamoto General Store now houses a Crazy Shirts outlet, with a lifelike statue of a craggy mechanic standing next to an antique Texaco gas pump. A huge monkey pod tree, planted by Walter Yamamato in 1925, shades the store and sidewalk. Behind the building is a square and history center with displays of artifacts and interpretive signs recalling the town's history.

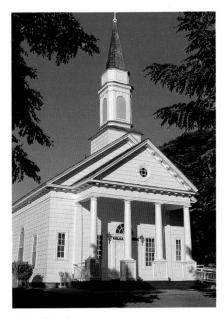

Kōloa Church

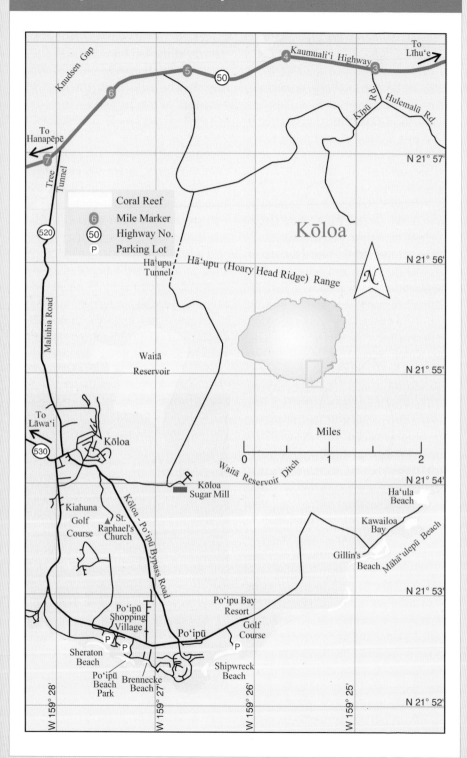

From Kōloa's main street, you have two choices in routes to Po'ipū. One is to turn south at the Chevron station and follow Highway 530. The other is to turn south onto Weliweli Road and follow it to the new Po'ipū Bypass Road. Signs from Weliweli Road also mark Hapa Road, which leads half a mile to **St. Raphael's Church**, the oldest Catholic church on Kaua'i. Buried in its adjoining cemetery are some of the first Portuguese immigrants to settle on Kaua'i.

Rising above the fields to the east of the bypass road, just before reaching Po'ipū, is a volcanic cinder cone called **Pu'u Wanawana**. The symmetrical cone was breached on one side when a lava flow erupting from its base floated part of the cone away.

Po'ipū

Weather and ocean conditions spurred the resort development of the south shore area of Po'ipū. So reliable and consistent is the sunshine that it has earned the often-used nickname of Sunny Po'ipū. There is no traditional town in the area, rather a collection of exclusive resorts, time-share developments, condo complexes, multi-million-dollar homes, and a shopping center. Probably nowhere else on Kaua'i do homes and hotels encroach so closely to the ocean. That fact slammed home when Hurricane 'Iniki struck in 1992, hitting the south shore first and hardest. Buildings and beaches were devastated. The buildings have been rebuilt and nature has healed its wounds.

Resort development at Po'ipū began in the early 1960s, when the Wai'ohai Hotel was constructed as a branch of the exclusive Halekulani Hotel at Waikīkī. The Wai'ohai sat empty and damaged for many years after 'Iniki until Marriott bought the property and developed it into time-share units. The Sheraton Kaua'i became the island's first hotel managed by a national hotel chain when it was built next door in the mid-1960s. Hyatt Regency added its luxury resort and golf course to the east, in front of Shipwreck Beach. Development continues to the west of the Sheraton. A subsidiary company of Alexander & Baldwin is building a sprawling resort and residential complex on its property near Kukui'ula Bay.

In 1938, when Po'ipū was part of a sugar plantation, manager Hector Moir and his wife started a garden of cacti and exotic flowers and plants. Over the years, the gardens grew larger and more lavish. Now the **Moir Gardens** are surrounded by the Kiahuna Plantation Resort (across from Po'ipū Shopping Village) and are maintained by two dozen gardeners. Thousands of varieties of flora and a lagoon adorn the 35-acre gardens, which also act as landscaped grounds for the Plantation Gardens Restaurant.

When Po'ipū Road passes the Hyatt Regency, it turns into a dirt cane road. If you follow the dirt road for 1.8 miles to a stop sign and turn right, you will end up at the wildly beautiful **Māhā'ulepū coastline**. The coastline, marked with three beaches (see Beaches chapter), features lithified

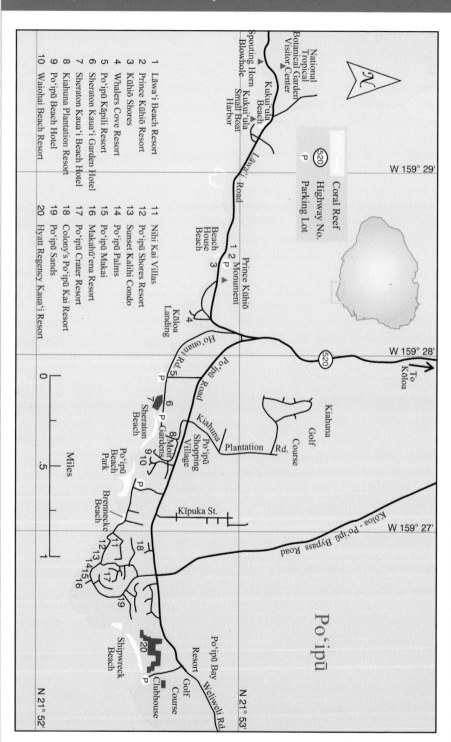

1 Lāwa'i Beach Resort
2 Prince Kūhiō Resort
3 Kūhiō Shores
4 Whalers Cove Resort
5 Po'ipū Kapili Resort
6 Sheraton Kaua'i Garden Hotel
7 Sheraton Kaua'i Beach Hotel
8 Kiahuna Plantation Resort
9 Po'ipū Beach Hotel
10 Waiohai Beach Resort

11 Nihi Kai Villas
12 Po'ipū Shores Resort
13 Sunset Kalihi Condo
14 Po'ipū Palms
15 Po'ipū Makai
16 Makahū'ena Resort
17 Po'ipū Crater Resort
18 Colony's Po'ipū Kai Resort
19 Po'ipū Sands
20 Hyatt Regency Kaua'i Resort

National Tropical Botanical Garden Visitor Center
Kukui'ula Beach
Spouting Horn Blowhole
Kukui'ula Small Boat Harbor

Coral Reef
520 Highway No.
P Parking Lot

Lāwa'i Road

Beach House Beach

Prince Kūhiō Monument

Kōloa Landing

Ho'onani Rd.

Po'ipū Road

520

To Kōloa

Kiahuna Golf Course

Kiahuna Plantation Rd.

Po'ipū Shopping Village

Po'ipū Beach Park

Sheraton Beach

Moir Gardens

Brennecke Beach

Kīpuka St.

Kōloa - Po'ipū Bypass Road

Po'ipū Bay Resort Golf Course

Shipwreck Beach

Clubhouse

Weliweli Rd.

Po'ipū

0 .5 1
Miles

W 159° 29'
W 159° 28'
W 159° 27'

N 21° 53'
N 21° 52'

Ancient sand dunes lithified into strange and beautiful formations

Waves undercut the beach rock on Māhāʻulepū coast

beach rock and cliffs. A group of sand dunes were probably actively moving here until sea level rose rapidly at the end of the last great ice age, about 11,000 years ago. The sea submerged the dunes and cemented the sand into solid limestone. Centuries of wear from waves and rain have twisted and channeled the stones. Hawaiian monk seals frequently come ashore at Māhāʻulepū.

A walk along the Māhāʻulepū coastline provides interesting, up-close views of the lithified beach rock. Walk east from the Hyatt Regency parking lot, where a trail leads to the top of Makawehi Point, the bluff at the end of Shipwreck Beach. Follow the trail as it winds a path between the golf course and the uniquely eroded beach rock. The trail will take you to Gillin's Beach, Kawailoa Bay, and Haʻula Beach (described in Beaches chapter). If you follow the beach trail about 100 yards east of Kawailoa Bay, you will come across a small blowhole just 6 feet *mauka* of the trail. The trail you are walking on is on a shelf undercut by the sea waves. Waves rolling into the shelf forces air through a small crack in the shelf, causing a whoosh of air and spray that is sure to surprise unsuspecting hikers.

According to legend, Māhāʻulepū was the scene of a fierce battle in 1796 between local inhabitants and an invading squadron of Kamehameha's war canoes. The king, who was attempting to unify the Hawaiian Islands by force, led the attacking fleet that was launched from Oʻahu. While crossing the treacherous Kauaʻi Channel, the canoes were swamped by strong winds and high seas. Reluctantly, Kamehameha ordered his warriors back to Oʻahu. Some of the squadron didn't receive the order to return and continued on to Kauaʻi, landing at Māhāʻulepū Beach, exhausted from fighting the storm all night. While they slept on the beach, waiting for their comrades, armed men from Māhāʻulepū attacked, clubbing most of the invading force to death. A few of Kamehameha's men managed to escape in their canoes. Ashamed of their defeat and afraid of facing their king's wrath, the men headed directly to the Big Island of Hawaiʻi to hide out with their families. The ruse worked, as Kamehameha historians mention only that the fleet returned to Oʻahu or perished at sea.

An interesting geological feature, a sandstone sinkhole, is close to Gillin's Beach, the first of the three

Māhā'ulepū coastline

Prince Kūhiō Monument

beaches at Māhā'ulepū. A small stream empties into the ocean at the west end of the beach. Cross the stream and head uphill along the trail for about 100 yards. To the right of the trail is the large sinkhole. The hole is about 50 feet deep and wide. It has sheer walls and openings to caves on its floor.

Māhā'ulepū's future as an undeveloped, natural area is threatened. As early as 1974, Grove Farm officials, who owned the land, proposed a residential community that included four hotels, four golf courses, and thousands of homes. The State Land Use Commission denied permit application. When the golf course was built adjacent to the planned Hyatt Regency Resort in 1988, an environmental group sued on the grounds that it was an illegal use of zoned agricultural land. The Hawai'i Supreme Court ruled in favor of the developer. Shortly after AOL's founder,

Steve Case, bought the Grove Farm property, the Kaua'i County Council passed a resolution committing Kaua'i County to work with state officials on a plan to preserve the 2,900-acre *ahupua'a* (Hawaiian land division).

At the intersection of Po'ipū Road and Highway 530, the road also branches west to become Lāwa'i Road. Half a mile from the intersection is **Prince Kūhiō Park**. A monument in the park marks the birthplace of Prince Jonah Kūhiō Kalaniana'ole. Kūhiō was a great grandson of King Kaumuali'i and nephew of Queen Kapi'olani, who adopted him. Prince Kūhiō took an active part in the attempt to restore the monarchy in 1895 and was imprisoned for his actions. Later he was elected as the Territory of Hawai'i's delegate to Congress—a position he held for 20 years. Although he didn't have voting power in Congress, Kūhiō worked hard to benefit the Hawaiian people. He spearheaded the Hawaiian Homes Commission Act, which provided homesteads for Native Hawaiians. The

Spouting Horn blowhole

through the blowhole. Spouting Horn is most spectacular in the summer when the surf is highest on the south coast. At any time it is usually more impressive than the blowhole at Koko Head on O'ahu. Spouting Horn is one of the most-visited sights on Kaua'i. Tour buses bring loads of visitors and a shopping bazaar is set up next to the parking lot. Signs warn viewers not to leave the elevated viewpoint and go down to the lava shelf for a closer look. Occasionally a large wave will pour over the top of the shelf and retreat down the blowhole. Deaths have resulted when people have been swept into the hole and down into the crashing waves below. Hawaiian legend attributes the moaning sound of the blowhole to the mourning of a sacred lizard, mo'o, over the death of his two sisters on the island of Ni'ihau.

three-acre park has terraced lava rock walls and a pond. Also on the park are an ancient Hawaiian house platform and the **Ho'ai Heiau**.

A short distance farther down Lāwa'i Road is **Spouting Horn blowhole**. Ocean waves created the blowhole by cutting under a flat lava shelf. Waves surging under the shelf are forced through a lava tube, escaping as a geyser of water and air, sometimes 30 feet high. Depending on the force of the south swell, the water and air can emit a plaintive groan or make a loud "whoosh" as it erupts

Across the road from Spouting Horn is the visitor center for the **National Tropical Botanical Garden**. Converted from a 1920s plantation-style cottage, the visitor center offers information about tropical plant conservation, research, new discoveries, and the garden's efforts to save Hawai'i's endangered

Lāwa'i Stream and Kāhili Mountain

Dracaena

Allerton Garden's Water Garden

species. The center also serves as the departure point for tours of the **Allerton Garden** and the **McBryde Garden**. The visitor center's gift shop is stocked with handcrafted items made of natural materials and made by Kaua'i artists, such as feather leis and hatbands, wood carvings and jewelry.

Of the five gardens that make up the National Tropical Botanical Garden, three are on Kaua'i, two of which are here, adjacent to each other on the banks of the Lāwa'i Stream. The NTBG has assembled what is believed to be the largest collection of federally listed endangered plant species anywhere, including the largest collection of native Hawaiian flora in existence. They have pioneered propagation techniques and established growing protocols for more than 45 percent of the existing Hawaiian flora.

A guided tour of the Allerton Garden or the McBryde Garden begins with a bus ride along an old railroad grade overlooking the once private estate and Lāwa'i Bay. Those on the Allerton Garden tour leave the bus and follow the direction of expert volunteer guides on a leisurely mile-long walk through the 100 acres. Queen Emma started the garden in the 1870s and built a summer cottage there. Later, Chicago industrialist Robert Allerton bought the property and expanded the garden. Allerton Garden has landscaped features, fountains and statues to set off its natural splendor. Guides will point out plants brought to Hawai'i by voyaging Polynesians 1,500 years ago. The breadfruit tree provided a staple food and the rough underside of its leaves was used to provide a sandpaper finish to wooden boats and bowls. Ti plants of many

Angracum Sesquipedae orchid in McBryde Garden

Orchids abound in the McBryde Garden

The cycad is the oldest seed-bearing plant in the world

The Moreton Bay fig tree

varieties were used to wrap foods and build homes. When the small red globule of the miracle berry is eaten, your taste buds are altered for hours, so that a lemon tastes sweet. The massive buttress roots of the Moreton Bay fig trees, a member of the ficus family, suggest prehistory. Guided tours of the Allerton Garden begin four times a day, Tuesday through Saturday, and last 2-1/2 hours. The cost is $30; reservations may be made by calling 742-2623.

Since the McBryde Garden is spread over 252 acres, guided tours use a bus to transport visitors between sections. The McBryde Garden doesn't have buildings or sculptures, as does the Allerton, giving it the feel of a wild preserve. It is home to the largest *ex situ* collection of native Hawaiian flora in existence. Extensive plantings of palms, flowering trees, heliconias, orchids, and many other plants have been wild-collected from other tropical regions of the world. The tour takes you down to beautiful Lāwaʻi Bay, where green sea turtles return to lay their eggs. Guided tours of the McBryde Garden are given at two times, only on Mondays, and cost $30. Reservations are essential and may be made at 742-2623.

Kalāheo

Travelers leaving Po'ipū have two choices when returning to Kōloa. If you are headed to Līhu'e, then Highway 520 is the route to take. Those heading west can turn left at the Chevron station and take Highway 530, or Kōloa Road, to Highway 50 and the village of Lāwa'i. Farmers in the rolling hills of this area and west to Kalāheo raise cattle, poultry, fruit, and coffee. In 1860, a Scotsman by the name of Duncan McBryde leased land in the Kalāheo countryside to start a cattle ranch. He married Elizabeth Moxley that same year and together they had six children. When Duncan McBryde died in 1878, his widow and his son, Walter, took over operations and added sugar cane to their ventures. In 1899 his property was incorporated into the McBryde Sugar Company. Walter turned over a large tract of land to the territorial government with the agreement that it would be used for homesteading. Between 1906 and 1914, families were able to buy land near Kalāheo for between one and five dollars an acre. To qualify for ownership, the homesteaders had to live on the land, cultivate small crops and plant trees. Today, many of the residents of Kalāheo are descendants of Portuguese immigrants who came to homestead and work for the McBryde Sugar Company. In its early years, Kalāheo was called "Homestead." By 1918, the Postal Service was having difficulty directing mail because other communities went by the same name, so the name was changed to Kalāheo, which means "proud day."

88 Holy Places of Kobo Daishi

Immediately west of the intersection with Highway 540 at Lāwa'i, Kaumuali'i Highway is crossed by Wawae Road, the entrance to the **88 Holy Places of Kobo Daishi**, a Buddhist shrine. Follow Wawae Road, *makai* of the highway past a few houses to the hillside shrine, or follow a short footpath from the highway, 200 yards west of Wawae Road, next to utility pole #344. The setting for 88 miniature cement shrines, a steep, rocky hillside under the shade of eucalyptus trees, reflects the traditional aesthetic sense of the Japanese worshippers. Each shrine is named for a Buddhist saint and in each are small offerings. Under the shrines are buried the sacred sands brought from the original 88 Holy Places that was erected by Kobo Daishi, a great teacher

Sea water evaporating from this rock produced salt.

The stone, Pohakuloa, symbolized the fish god.

of the Shingon sect of Buddhism in Japan more than a thousand years ago. The number of shrines signifies the 88 sins committed by man. Buddhist pilgrims believe worshiping here will release them from the 88 sins.

Kukuiolono Park, once the estate of Walter McBryde, is one of the oldest gardens and golf courses on Kaua'i. It is situated on the crest of a broad hill to the south of Kalāheo. To find it, turn left at Kalāheo's only signal light and follow Papalina Road for three quarters of a mile. Walter McBryde built an elegant park on his hilltop, laying out trees, shrubs, flowering plants, and expanses of lawn open to the superb views. A Japanese garden, with its carefully selected and placed rocks, is a key feature. Nearby lies Walter McBryde's grave. McBryde gathered legendary stones significant to early Hawaiians from around the island and assembled them into an interesting collection of Hawaiiana. Among them is Pōhaku Awa, or the fish stone. Fish being taken from Nōmilo Pond near the coast to pools in higher land were kept overnight in cool water in the bowl-shaped stone. A flat-topped rock with raised edges was used to obtain salt by evaporating seawater on it. Tree moulds were formed when lava poured over trees in the Lāwa'i Valley about 2 million years ago. There are rocks that were used in games similar to shot-putting and bowling and a stone shaped like a map of Kaua'i. Tallest among the stones is Pōhakuloa, which symbolized the fish god. Surrounding the park is the Kukuiolono Golf Course. McBryde, an enthusiast of the game invented by his father's countrymen, built a nine-hole course that he and his workers could enjoy (see Activities chapter).

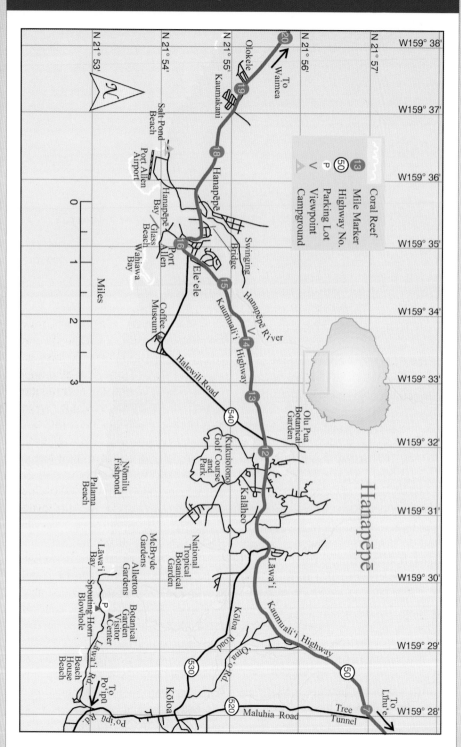

WEST SIDE SIGHTS

Coffee tree

As the Kaumuali'i Highway heads west from Kalāheo, the green rolling hills of the countryside give way to flat coastal lowlands. In the rainshadow of Wai'ale'ale, Kaua'i's west side is arid, sunny and hot—more so than any part of the island. Sugar cane still grows on the west side, thanks to an elaborate irrigation system that collects Wai'ale'ale's watershed.

When the McBryde Sugar Company shut down its sugar production in the mid-nineties, it switched much of its acreage to coffee. Now it has 3,400 acres of former sugar land planted with row upon row of coffee trees. You will drive through the Kaua'i Coffee Company estate as you follow the highway west from Kalāheo. The Kaua'i Coffee Company has built a **coffee museum and visitor center** (335-0831) near its production facility at the former sugar camp of Numila. The visitor center is off the Kaumuali'i Highway on Highway 540. It may be easier to stop on your way back from the west side. In that case, turn onto Highway 540 at Ele'ele. The visitors center is housed in two renovated plantation workers houses. One structure houses exhibits about coffee production and a coffee roasting area. In here are freshly brewed free samples of the dozen or so varieties of coffee they produce. The coffee company converted the other plantation house into a gift shop where you can buy their coffee, of course, as well as souvenirs related to all things coffee. A continuous video shows the process by which the coffee is grown and harvested, through its milling and sorting process, and ending with the product being cupped, or taste-tested for quality. Kaua'i coffee is 100 percent Hawaiian arabica. Wholesalers and roasters buy most of the beans with the best beans sold as Kaua'i Coffee on the specialty market.

An **overlook of the Hanapēpē River Valley** at mile marker 14 of Kaumuali'i Highway offers a choice view of the green river valley trimmed with red cliffs. Hanapēpē Valley marks the eastern limit of the Makaweli Depression, where a great wedge of land slumped down from the volcano's caldera. Lava flowed out of the caldera into the depression to form high walls of Nā Pali basalt. After a long period

Upper reaches of the Olokele Canyon

Hanapēpē

Hanapēpē bills itself as "the biggest little town on Kaua'i," and it might also include "bougainvillea capital of the world" in its boasts. Cascades of red and purple bougainvillea spill onto the roadside and hang from the bluff overlooking the town. Hanapēpē's historic district looks as if dilapidation battled renewal to a draw. Hanapēpē Road, the town's main street, is lined with refurbished storefronts, art galleries, and restaurants painted in tropical pastels. Interspersed are abandoned, run-down buildings—vestiges of a successful past.

In 1923, a riot between police and striking sugar cane workers took place in Hanapēpē. Six people died in the clash. Hanapēpē was a bustling town during the 1930s and World War II, with movie theaters, roller rinks and other businesses flourishing. As Līhu'e developed and transportation improved, business on the westside fell off. Many of the old wooden buildings could not withstand the force of Hurricane 'Iniki in 1992. Some of their ramshackle remains hang on.

Each Friday from 6:00 to 9:00 p.m., Hanapēpē galleries celebrate **Friday Art Night** festivities. Galleries open their doors to the public, inviting folks to browse the studios and workshops and meet Kaua'i artists. Refreshments and entertainment add to the informal atmosphere.

A suspension footbridge, called the **Hanapēpē Swinging Bridge**, crosses the river from the town center. You can cross the photogenic bridge,

of erosion, eruptions of Kōloa basalt covered the valley. Hanapēpē River has cut this valley repeatedly; first through the collapsed flow of the shield volcano, and again in the period of rejuvenated volcanism. The cycles of lava flows and erosion have exposed layer upon layer of red rock in the valley walls.

Across the highway from the overlook, in fields now planted in coffee, is the scene of the **last battle fought on Kaua'i**. In 1824, George Humehume Kaumuali'i, son of the last king of Kaua'i, led an unsuccessful revolt against the kingdom of Hawai'i, ruled by Kamehameha II, son of Kamehameha the Great. The forces of Kamehameha II destroyed the Kaua'i army. For two weeks, before amnesty was declared, the Kaua'i *ali'i* suffered terrible retributions.

Hanapēpē's historic district

Some houses in Hanapēpē have seen better days

Hanapēpē Swinging Bridge

Bougainvillea grow everywhere in Hanapēpē

At the east end of Hanapēpē Road, where it turns to the highway, is a staircase with a metal pipe railing leading up the bluff that stands over the town. A short climb will give you a good view of the bougainvillea growing on the hillside and the river curving around the town as it empties into Hanapēpē Bay.

Across the highway from Hanapēpē is **Port Allen**, where many sightseeing and whale-watching cruises depart. The four towers near the dock are exhaust stacks for Kauaʻi Electric Company's main generating plant.

On the west side of Hanapēpē, a sign indicates the Route 543 turnoff to the Port Allen airport and Salt Pond Beach. The airport is used by one helicopter tour company and by ultralight aircraft enthusiasts. Between the airport and the Salt Pond Beach

which will swing and bounce as you do, and walk along a trail on the river levee. Residents here, on the other side of the river, live in small wooden houses and goats live in the yards. Chickens live wherever they please. Fruit trees abound and taro is grown in small plots. The scene harks to bygone days of rural Hawaiʻi.

Park are the old **Salt Ponds**. For centuries, Hawaiians have evaporated seawater for salt to use for seasoning and preserving fish. Sailors would stop to trade for the valuable commodity. Here, shallow ponds, sealed with a clay-rich soil, allowed the sun to evaporate seawater into salt crystals. The soil imparts a red tinge and special flavor to the sea salt. Salt is no longer produced here commercially, but in the spring and summer months locals manufacture salt for their own use.

Bougainvillea at the Robinson estate

Two miles west of Hanapēpē, at mile marker 19, are the old sugar camps of Kaumakani and Olokele. Here, in a former field office, is the office of the **Gay and Robinson Sugar Plantation Tour**. Now the last working plantation on Kauaʻi, Gay and Robinson runs guided tours to plantation fields and mill factories that have been off-limits to visitors. The focus of the tour is on the history of the plantation, its operation, sugar processing and astounding irrigation system. Tours run year-round, but during the months of April through October you will see the mill in operation. During the off-season, the mill is down for repairs. Participants

of the bus and walking tour will come away with an understanding of the industry that has contributed to Hawaiʻi's economy for more that 170 years. They can also expect to come away with a layer of red dust. Plan on wearing old or dark clothes, as the bus, plantation vehicles and the factory kick up a lot of the west side's famous red dirt. Closed shoes are necessary for the factory tour; hard hats and safety glasses are provided. Small children are not encouraged to join in the tour. The tour office is open 8:00 a.m. to 4:00 p.m., five days a week. Knowledgeable guides lead two-hour tours twice a day. Reservations are required and can be made by calling 335-2824.

Gay and Robinson Co. conducts an **Olokele Canyon Tour** beginning at their tour office. Popular with both visitors and residents, the informal tour takes a group of no more than four on a ride in an extended-cab pickup truck. The three and a half-hour tour follows the old carriage road on Gay and Robinson land. It begins in slanted sugar fields and moves into the Gay and Robinson Makaweli Ranch, which still raises the Durham Shorthorn breed of cattle that the Sinclair family brought to the island in 1865. The tour ends at the overlook of the Olokele Canyon and the eastern rim of Waimea Canyon. A helicopter tour is the only other way to see these sights. Lunch is provided on the tour, which departs the visitor center at 8:30 a.m. The tour cost is $60 for passengers older than 12 and $45 for children 12 and under. To make a reservation, call (808) 335-2824.

Waterfall in Olokele Canyon

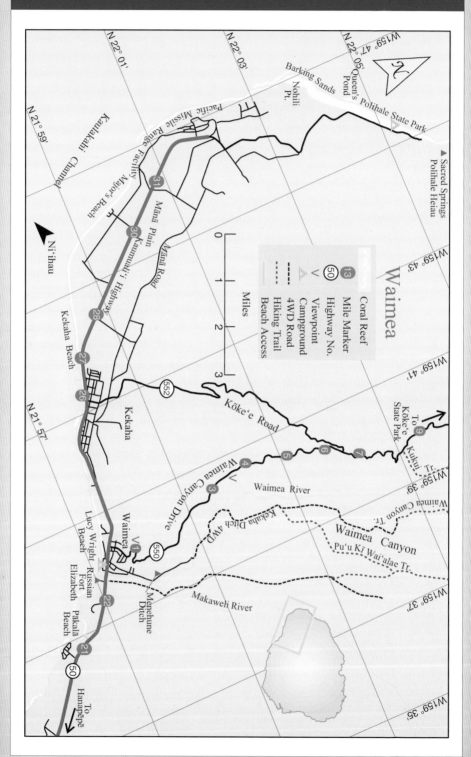

Waimea

Captain Cook Monument

Waimea has figured prominently in Kaua'i's history. It was an ancient capital and major population center. Captain James Cook and his crew were the first Westerners to ever set foot on Hawaiian soil when they landed at Waimea on January 19, 1778. The site of the famous explorer's landing is noted with a simple plaque at Lucy Wright Park, on the west bank of the Waimea River. A statue of Cook's likeness stands in the town square, next to the highway. It is a replica of the original statue by Sir John Tweed that stands in Cook's hometown of Whitby, England. In the 1820s, shortly after an odd episode of Russian intervention, Waimea was the base for missionaries who came to Kaua'i to spread the word. In 1850, Waimea became a port of entry for foreign ships. Japanese, Chinese, and Portuguese immigrants landed at Waimea to begin

Waimea is in the heart of Kaua'i's sugar-producing area

their fulfillment of work contracts with sugar plantations. And before any of them, the Menehune settled the Waimea area, building *heiaus* and ditches to convey water.

Fort Elizabeth State Park commands a sweeping view of Waimea Bay from a bluff on the east side of the Waimea River. Named after the Russian czarina, Hawaiian and Aleut laborers began construction of Fort Elizabeth in 1816. Georg Schaffer, who posed as an emissary of the Russian American Company of Alaska, promised Kaua'i's King Kaumuali'i that the czar would assist him in vanquishing Kamehameha and thus return sole rule of Kaua'i to Kaumuali'i. The star-shaped fort, built with 38 cannons trained on the important landing of Waimea Bay, was part of the plan enthusiastically supported by Kaumuali'i. Schaffer's demise came when he was exposed as an imposter. Kaumuali'i banished Schaffer and ordered the Russian flag removed from the fort just as it was completed in 1817. The cannons of the fort are long gone, and parts of the stone walls have been dismantled. It takes some imagination now to picture the piled stones overgrown with yellow-flowered 'ilima as a strategic military outpost. An interpretive walking trail leads through the remains of the fort. There are restrooms and a pay phone in the parking lot.

About a mile and a quarter along Menehune Road from Waimea, next to a suspension footbridge, is an archaeological site called the **Menehune Ditch**. The earliest settlers

How the Menehune cut and dressed the stones in their irrigation ditch is unknown

Roadside scene near Waimea

Gold trees in Waimea flower in April and May

of Hawai'i are credited with building an aqueduct to carry water several miles from the upper reaches of the Waimea River to taro fields in the lower valley. In a manner unseen elsewhere in Hawai'i, the stones of the Menehune Ditch were cut and dressed to fit together closely and present a smooth, flat surface. The ditch's walls were estimated to be 24 feet high, with a footpath along the top. Unfortunately, all that remains of the ditch is a section about 2 feet high and 50 feet long next to the road. Construction of Menehune Road destroyed parts of the ditch and stones were removed to use in buildings such as the Protestant church in Waimea.

The people of Waimea are pushing to revitalize the sleepy town and take economic advantage of the nearly one million people that pass through each year. A 110-seat brewpub has opened at the Waimea Plantation Cottages. The historic Waimea Theatre, built in 1938 at the height of the Art Deco period, has been beautifully restored and is showing movies again after a 30-year hiatus. It was the first theater on the island to have a marquee with electric lights.

The **West Kaua'i Visitor and Technology Center** (338-1332) features interactive displays about Kaua'i's culture and technological abilities. It's open seven days a week and is located where Waimea Canyon Drive intersects with the highway.

If you plan on driving up to Waimea Canyon, watch for the sign pointing to Highway 550, Waimea Canyon Drive. A highway sign indicates that Waimea Canyon is straight ahead, but you have two choices. Another access to the canyon begins at Kekaha, on Kōke'e Road. You could drive up to the canyon on one road and down on the other. Before venturing up the canyon or west to Polihale, check your fuel gauge, as there are no gas stations beyond Waimea. If you are about to explore Waimea Canyon, see the following chapter on Kōke'e Sights.

West Kaua'i sugar cane

Kekaha

The highway skirts the outside edge of Kekaha, the last town on the west side. A block inland, the town's main street parallels the highway, passing a limited number of shops and restaurants. The sugar mill in Kekaha is closed. Idle heavy equipment rusts in the mill yard, awaiting its final disposition. Former sugar workers also are unsure of their future.

Barking sands were a curiosity in the 1930s

Hawai'i State Archives

Kekaha Beach drifts up to the highway, elevated just a few feet higher than the waves. An uninterrupted strip of sand covers the coastline for 15 miles to the start of the cliffs at Polihale, making it the longest beach in Hawai'i (see Beaches chapter). In Hawaiian, Kekaha means "dry hot place" and you're experiencing a rare day at Kekaha if the sun isn't blazing from a clear sky. The neighboring island of Ni'ihau and the attendant islet of Lehua are plainly visible across the Kaulakahi Channel.

The broad, flat platform of land from Waimea River to the cliffs of Nā Pali is called the Mānā coastal plain. Fertile land that grew sugar cane for generations now sprouts alternative crops such as seed corn and sunflower. Rising behind the plain are numerous valleys and gulches separated by steep ridges. Once the slopes were covered with pili, the dry, yellow grass used to thatch houses, innumerable shrubs and bushes, and groves of koa, sandalwood and 'ōhia lehua trees. Perennial streams flowed from the valleys to feed a huge marsh and complex of ponds that lay below

the level of the sea behind high sand dunes. Large populations of birds lived in the marsh and fish were grown in the ponds—providing an ample supply of protein for Hawaiians living in settlements tucked between the cliffs and the swamp. It was possible to paddle a canoe across the marsh from Waimea to the *heiau* at Polihale during the rainy season.

After western contact, cattle and goats were introduced and left to forage freely in the valleys, where they ate the grass down to the roots. Trees were cut to provide firewood for the trading vessels that anchored at Waimea. Chiefs ordered sandalwood trees on their land cut to feed the demand for the fragrant wood in China. The barren land of the ridges eroded and blew into the Mānā Plain, destroying its beauty. Norwegian settler Valdemar Knudsen established a large cattle ranch on the plain in 1856. Knudsen built a ditch to drain the marsh and planted sugar cane on the land. By the 1880s, several planters were raising cane in the area. They consolidated in 1898, forming the Kekaha Sugar Company.

From Kekaha, the highway cuts a straight line across the Mānā Plain, emphasizing its size and flatness. *Makai* of the highway are the installations of the U.S. Navy's **Pacific Missile Range Facility (PMRF)** and its underwater range. The naval, civil service, technical and scientific staff at the PMRF track everything that sails, flies or orbits the central Pacific. The facility has a huge impact on the economy of West Kaua'i. Next to state and county government and the visitor industry, the military presence on the west side is the largest single source of jobs and revenues on Kaua'i. There are nearly 1,000 civilian employees on the base, not counting those working for civilian contractors, while the actual number of active-duty military stationed at the PMRF is closer to one-tenth of the civilian workforce.

Clear skies and limited light pollution on the west side lends itself to excellent star-gazing opportunities. In 1989, amateur astronomers established the **Kaua'i Educational Association for Science and Astronomy** (KEASA) to provide astronomical education to the public. KEASA operates an observatory on the Pacific Missile Range Facility. The group uses a 14-inch Celestron telescope, which is housed permanently at the observatory. KEASA (245-8250) meets monthly for stargazing on the closest Saturday to the New Moon and welcomes the public to join them at sunset. To reach the observatory, turn *makai* onto Tartar Road at mile marker 30.

Shortly after passing the main entrance to the missile range, the paved highway ends. A pot-holed cane haul road continues through the plain and ends in 5 miles at **Polihale State Park**. Wind has drifted deep sand into high and wide dunes that sometimes spill over to the road. Campgrounds and picnic tables are part of the park (see Beaches chapter). In spite of its isolated location, the park is frequented by surfers and polefishers. They drive along the wide beach in four-wheel-drive vehicles with oversize tires. The beach that began in Kekaha ends at the far end of Polihale, where the Nā Pali cliffs begin. Kayakers who paddled the length of Nā Pali are picked up by drivers of the outfitting companies here. **Sacred Springs heiau** is located about 200 yards inland on the cliffs. This was where the Hawaiians believed the spirits of the dead escaped their mortal shells. Brush grows over the *heiau*, making it hard to find and difficult to discern its shape if you do find it.

At Polihale, the longest beach in Hawai'i ends where the Nā Pali coast begins

KAUA'I'S NEIGHBORS: NI'IHAU, LEHUA AND KA'ULA

Ni'ihau is Kaua'i's closest island neighbor

Seventeen miles across the Kaulakahi Channel lies Kaua'i's nearest island neighbor, **Ni'ihau**. It is nicknamed the Forbidden Island because the entire island is owned by the Robinson family of Kaua'i and visitors are not allowed unless specifically invited. The Robinson family descends from the Sinclairs, who originally purchased the island in 1864. About 160 people live on Ni'ihau, the majority of whom are pure Hawaiian. Most men work on the Robinson sheep ranch. Traditional practices such as making shell jewelry and exporting yams and kiawe charcoal also provide them with income. Hawaiian is the primary spoken language of Ni'ihau's residents, although English is taught in its school. Children must travel to Kaua'i to continue their high school education. Ni'ihau families are free to travel off the island whenever they please and are allowed to invite guests to visit them. Should they choose to live elsewhere, they are not permitted to live on Ni'ihau again. People and goods are shuttled to Kaua'i by a WWII vintage Navy landing craft. Electricity is available only from small generators. Ni'ihau has no telephones, paved roads, medical clinic and no police force. Its principal settlement is a loose collection of houses, a church and a school at Pu'uwai. With its long isolation and patriarchal overseer, Ni'ihau is a sociological curiosity.

Ni'ihau is the seventh-largest Hawaiian Island. Its area covers 73 square miles and its highest point, Pani'aū, rises to 1,281 feet. Because it lies in the lee of the high mountains of Kaua'i, Ni'ihau is an arid island. Estimates of precipitation range from 40 inches per year on the east coast to less than 20 inches in the south. Despite the low rainfall, Ni'ihau has the state's largest natural lake, 182-acre Halulu Lake, which, at an elevation of 2 feet below sea level, is also the lowest spot on Hawai'i. Close by is the playa, or intermittent lake, Halāli'i. Heavy rains can swell its area to 840 acres.

Eliza Sinclair, the family matriarch and widow of a sea captain, spearheaded the purchase of Ni'ihau. The captain and Eliza were born in Scotland, moving to New Zealand in 1840. Negotiations were conducted with G.H. Robertson, the Hawai'i Minister of the Interior. Kamehameha V approved the sale for $10,000 except for two small wedges of land that had already been sold. A condition of the sale was the right of the islanders to a little land to plant food, a place for a home and the right to fish the waters. Three months after the purchase, the Sinclairs engaged their friend Valdemar Knudsen to negotiate for the remaining land on the island. The landowner succumbed to Knudsen's tactic by accepting the offer of 1,000 shiny dollars laid before him.

Under Hawai'i law all beaches are held in trust by the state. Ni'ihau's owners believe they acquired the beaches as well as the rest of the land. Bruce and Keith Robinson have stated that their family has a separate deed unique in Hawai'i. They assert that they purchased the land from the Hawaiian monarchy when private property rights extended to submerged lands below the beach.

Limited access to Ni'ihau is granted to paying tour passengers of Ni'ihau Helicopters. The Robinsons purchased a helicopter to transport family members and employees between Kaua'i and Ni'ihau and to evacuate Ni'ihau residents to Kaua'i in medical emergencies. The tour service was instituted to help defray the costs of operating the helicopter. The helicopter flies over the island, being careful not to disrupt the quietness of Pu'uwai, and touches down on the north coast.

Lehua is the rocky, crescent-shaped islet about one-half mile north of Ni'ihau. Its highest point is 704 feet. A lighthouse is perched atop the islet. When it was built in the 1930s, it was the highest lighthouse in the U.S. Lighthouse Service. Lehua is uninhabited now but people have lived on it. Some residents of Ni'ihau chose to move to Lehua after their home island was sold to haoles in 1864. From there, they eventually moved to Kaua'i.

Nineteen miles southwest of Ni'ihau, the islet of **Ka'ula** stands on a submerged shield volcano that once was a substantial island. It is a vertical rock, 550 feet high and covering 136 acres. Ka'ula is uninhabited except for many birds. It has always been considered a special place by the people of Ni'ihau and appears in their *mele* (chants). The natives of Ni'ihau would travel to Ka'ula in the summer months to catch birds. Ka'ula is visible from the southwest shore of Kaua'i on a very clear day. Its profile can be seen to the left of Ni'ihau.

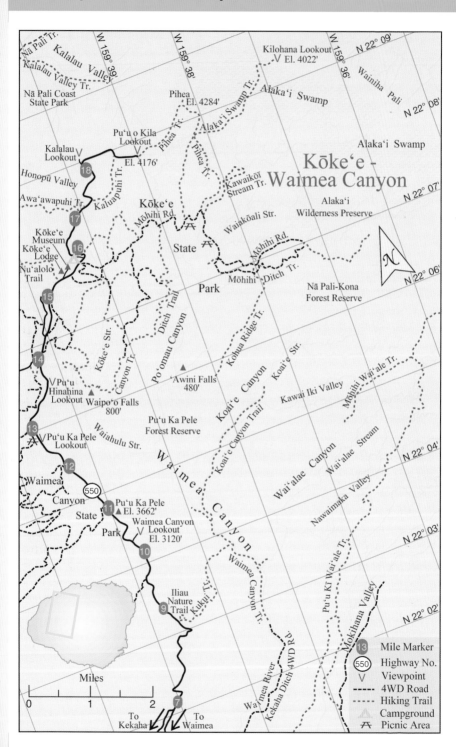

WAIMEA CANYON-KŌKE'E SIGHTS

Kaua'i's only accessible upcountry region is simply referred to locally as Kōke'e, although it is comprised of several areas: Waimea Canyon State Park, Kōke'e State Park and lands within Ku'ia Natural Area Reserve, Pu'u Ka Pele and Nā Pali Kona forest reserves, and Alaka'i Wilderness Preserve. All of these jurisdictions are on state land and protect important watershed and habitat critical to rare plants and animals. Balanced with the ecological considerations of the Waimea watershed are the extensive recreational opportunities Kōke'e provides. Hiking, mountain biking, birding, hunting, camping, and fishing are all pursued vigorously in the upcountry region.

Waimea Canyon is also a great place for sightseeing. Even on an island rife with scenic views, Waimea Canyon offers astonishing panoramas. Vistas along the paved road rimming the western wall of the canyon present streams shimmering on valley floors bounded by precipitous walls, arid cliffs built of rock and soil in a rainbow of hues that rivals the Grand Canyon, and sweeping views clear to the ocean. Mark Twain noticed the similarities when he visited Kaua'i and coined Waimea Canyon the "Grand Canyon of the Pacific."

The Waimea River and its tributaries have cut a gorge nearly 3,000 feet deep, a mile and a half wide, and 10 miles long. Feeding the waters is the Alaka'i Swamp, which acts as a giant sponge, soaking up the copious amounts of rainfall on Wai'ale'ale and releasing it in uniform flows. Smaller canyons branch to the east of Waimea Canyon, while its western flank is a singular, steep cliff. It seems incredible that such an immense natural feature could be tucked into a corner of a small island.

Waimea Canyon and Kōke'e State Park deserve a full day to visit, especially if you tackle one of the hiking trails. The return drive from Waimea is 38 miles. The gas stations at Waimea are the last ones on the west side. Bringing food and drink is a good idea, although there is a lunch wagon at the Waimea Canyon Lookout and a small restaurant at Kōke'e Lodge. Morning is often the best time to view the canyon—before the clouds roll down from Wai'ale'ale. Highway 550, Waimea Canyon Drive and then Kōke'e Road, is the steep route that takes 19 miles to wind from sea level to the Pu'u o Kila lookout, 4,176 feet above the Nā Pali's Kalalau Valley. Waimea Canyon Drive originates in the town of Waimea. Another route begins in Kekaha as Kōke'e Road and is joined by Waimea Canyon Drive seven miles uphill. Waimea Canyon Drive offers views of the lower canyon, while Kōke'e Road presents views of the Mānā Plain and the island of Ni'ihau in the downhill direction.

The first viewpoint on Waimea Canyon Drive is at the one-mile marker.

Here the view is to the southwest, looking over Waimea to the agricultural crops of the Mānā Plain and the island of Ni'ihau. Ni'ihau is the west flank remnant of a shield volcano older than Kaua'i. Secondary volcanic activity created Kawaihoa Hill on the southern tip and the islet of Lehua in the water to the north of Ni'ihau when blocks of older basalt and reef limestone blasted out during eruptions. On a clear day the islet of Ka'ula is visible, 19 miles southwest of Ni'ihau.

Kaua'i's trademark red soil

Waimea Canyon Drive is very steep in places. Roadside turnouts allow for views of the lower canyon on the right side and glimpses of sugar cane planted on the steep hillside to the left. The older Kōke'e Road joins with Waimea Canyon Drive just before mile marker seven. If you choose Kōke'e Road for your descent, watch for a growth of wiliwili trees at the hairpin curve, 3 miles above Kekaha. Wiliwili is a native tree that flourishes on hot, dry slopes below 1,500 feet. From March to May its flattened canopy and trios of round leaves blossom into clusters of yellow and peach-colored flowers.

Below mile marker nine is the sign marking the Kukui Trail. A paved apron across from the sign is the parking area. At the head of the Kukui Trail, which leads down into the canyon and eventually to the ocean, is the **Iliau Nature Loop Trail.** The loop leads a quarter of mile through flat land cleared by the Division of Forestry and Wildlife to allow native plants to grow naturally. Nametags identify plants and trees. Here grows the world's largest community of the rare and striking relative of the silversword plant of Maui, the iliau. Birds may have carried the barbed fruit of this descendant of the sunflower family on their feathers as they migrated from California. The iliau grows on slender stems that reach up to 12 feet high. In June and July it blooms spectacularly. After several years, a towering head emerges from the iliau's top, extending in great drooping tiers. Starting at the bottom, each tier opens to expose wheels of golden blossoms. Each plant blooms

The iliau blooms once and then it dies.

Hawai'i State Archives

Visitors enjoying Waimea Canyon in the 1930s

once in its lifetime, then dies. Along the trail you can also enjoy the deep red blossoms of the 'ōhia lehua tree, the orange blossoms of the 'ilima, yellow blossoms of the koa, and the red, white or pink berries of the pūkiawe shrub. A picnic shelter looks over the trail and the canyon.

Australian silky oak, paperbark and eucalyptus trees grow along the road above the Iliau Nature Loop as a result of reforestation efforts in the 1930s to control erosion. An irrigation ditch flows next to the road through unbelievably red soil. To satisfy the need for water in the sugar fields, water destined to cascade the 800 feet of Waipo'o Falls on the east side of the canyon is now diverted through 13 miles of ditches and 11 miles of tunnels to fill several reservoirs on the canyon's west side.

After mile marker 10 a large sign points the way to the **Waimea Canyon Lookout**. The lookout has a parking area, restrooms, a lunch wagon, and pathways leading to terraces overlooking the canyon. This lookout has the widest and grandest view of Waimea Canyon. As the sun moves over the gorge, its light changes

the hues of the red, ochre and gray earth, softened by green and gold vegetation. Clouds drift by, changing patterns that crawl across canyon walls. Your viewpoint stands beyond the western edge of a great caldera that spewed out much of the lava that built Kaua'i's original shield volcano. The peak to the left is **Pu'u Ka Pele**, a vent of the original shield. Its height gives an indication of the elevation of the shield before it succumbed to erosion. From this vantage point you can see three side canyons that drain Alaka'i Swamp and helped carve away the layer upon layer of lava flows that built the original volcano. Directly in front is Koai'e; Po'omau is to the left and Wai'alae is behind the ridge to your right. At one time these valleys emptied their waters straight out to the sea behind you. A huge part of Kaua'i's west side collapsed along a fault line, forming a wedge-shaped depression fanning out to the south. The streams from these side canyons diverted to the 'south and formed the Waimea River. Called the Makaweli Depression, it is clearly visible as you drive down Waimea Canyon Drive.

A few sandalwood trees grow in the parking lot of the lookout, next to the bus parking area. They are scarce vestiges of a large sandalwood forest decimated in the early 1800s. Hawaiian chiefs ordered sandalwood trees cut down so they could trade them for ships and luxuries and to pay off debts. The fragrant wood of the trees was prized in China for ornamental carving and cabinetry, incense, and as an insect repellent.

Waimea Canyon view from Pu'u Hinahina Lookout

Waimea Canyon from Pu'u Ka Pele Lookout

Only a few trees of Kaua'i's decimated sandalwood forests remain

Waimea Canyon

The peak that dominates the canyon's west side, Pu'u Ka Pele, means "Pele's Hill." Coinciding with geological evidence, Pele, the goddess that legend says created each of the Hawaiian Islands lived first on Kaua'i, then journeyed down the chain, creating a birth by fire on each stop. Pu'u Ka Pele is said to be the point where the fire goddess left Kaua'i for O'ahu. The pit at the top of the hill was supposedly made as she stamped her foot for the leap across the channel. Pele is said to now live in Kīlauea, the erupting volcano on Hawai'i, the chain's newest island.

As the road curves around Pu'u Ka Pele, several roadside viewpoints appear, followed by another lookout just shy of mile marker 13. This lookout is simply a railing at the roadside with parking on the opposite side of the road at the Kā'ana picnic area. From **Pu'u Ka Pele Lookout** you will have your closest opportunity to view **Waipo'o Falls**—if it is flowing. So much of its flow has been diverted for irrigation that it runs dry much of the time. After a heavy rain above the falls the flow is too much for the Kōke'e Ditch and a cascade returns to the falls. **Kā'ana Picnic Area** is a shaded clearing with picnic shelters, barbeque pits, bathrooms, and a pay telephone.

A large sign identifies **Pu'u Hinahina Lookout**, the last view of the canyon from this road. The view from Pu'u Hinahina looks south over the upper canyon. Watch for white-tailed tropic birds catching air currents rising from the canyon. The fish-eating seabirds with long, twin-pointed tails nest in the steep cliffs.

At mile marker 14, a paved road, called **Mākaha Ridge Road** heads to the sea cliffs. You can follow the road for 4 miles, where it ends at the restricted Pacific Missile Range Facility's tracking station. The only view near the road is over the red dirt mound to the north of the road just before the tracking station. Climb over the mound for a view of Mākaha Valley. Two picnic areas are situated along Mākaha Ridge Road.

The cluster of buildings that make up **Kōke'e State Park's headquarters** sits in a beautiful meadow rimmed by California redwood trees and centered by a giant Monterey cypress. At an elevation of

Waimea Canyon Lookout

Distance from lookout to:	
Waipoʻo Falls	2.2 mi.
Kāhililoa	1.7 mi.
Waiʻaleʻale	10.5 mi.
Kawaikini	10.6 mi.

Lookout Elevation	3120′
Waimea River Elevation Below Lookout	750′

Waipoʻo Falls

Kumuwela Ridge

Poʻomau Canyon

Kāhililoa El. 2760′

N   NNE   NE

Koai'e
Canyon

Kawai Iki
Valley

Kaluahā'ula
Ridge

Wai'ale'ale

Wai'alae
Canyon

Kawaikini

ENE

E

ESE

Koai'e
Stream

Waimea River

3,750 feet, the air at the meadow can be brisk. The **Kōke'e Lodge** has a dining room and gift shop. Next to the lodge is the **Kōke'e Natural History Museum**. There are interactive displays on Kaua'i's weather and geology and an excellent selection of natural history books for sale. An attendant is on duty daily to offer trail and wildlife information. The museum's exhibits include mounted taxidermy displays, botanical illustrations, and cultural artifacts. Sure to catch your eye is the mounted head of a truly ugly wild boar. The museum is open daily from 10:00 a.m. to 4:00 p.m. There is no admission fee but donations are accepted. Bathrooms are in the picnic pavilion and picnic tables sit in the meadow. Wild chickens cluck and scratch throughout the parking lot and meadow. They keep a close eye on every visitor who chooses to dine outdoors. The bright red birds are moa or descendants of the jungle fowl that Polynesians settlers brought with them. They and the escaped domestic chickens that roam Kaua'i flourish because the island luckily escaped the introduction of mongooses, which feed on bird eggs.

Monterey cypress tree at Kōke'e meadow

From the park headquarters Highway 550 winds through 'ōhia forest and around the Kōke'e Air Force Station with its dome that looks like a giant golf ball. At mile marker 18 a turnout to the left will take you to the **Kalalau Lookout**, the penultimate roadside vista along Highway 550. The view down the Kalalau Valley is breathtaking, but it gets even better at the last lookout. This is the last lookout where bathrooms are available.

The road ends in one mile at the **Pu'u o Kila Lookout.** In the bracing air of the lookout all but the sky is below you: the Kalalau Valley, birds in flight, vertical cliff walls, tour helicopters, even the clouds. Your vantage point is at the head of the valley's amphitheater. Knife-edged lava walls plummet to the sea, 4,176 feet below. The blue ocean, speckled in the shade of clouds, extends to an indistinguishable horizon. Warm air rising from the lower valley cools and often condenses into clouds at your feet. Be patient as winds eventually push the clouds away to again reveal the vista. The official viewpoint is paved and protected with a guardrail. Past the viewpoint is the start of the Pihea Trail, which follows the rim of the valley for a mile before traversing the Alaka'i Swamp. Follow the trail for a short distance and different views of the valley unfold before you. Stay away from the edge. The dirt is usually slippery from rain and the drop is sheer. Plants and stunted trees growing at the rim take root on the cliff wall many feet below. The trail to Pihea follows a badly eroded scar

Kalalau Valley

left by an ill-advised 1954 attempt to continue the road from Kōke'e, skirt Nā Pali and plunge to Hā'ena on the north shore. After eight months of labor, much of it done by prisoners, the Territorial Government abandoned the project. Determined hikers can reach the base of Kalalau Valley only by following the Kalalau Trail for 11 miles from its start at Kē'ē Beach. The trail ends at Kalalau Beach, hidden from view by a cliff at the left side of the valley floor.

Behind the viewpoint is the **Alaka'i Swamp**—the highest altitude swamp in the world. The crater atop the volcano that once belched fire and spewed lava is now a soggy marsh. Lava flowed into this natural reservoir in thick layers that resisted erosion. Trees grow slowly in the swamp's 30

square miles, stunted by rain that falls 350 days per year. It is a place of clouds and mist, mud, ferns, moss and birds. Listen and you will hear calls of endangered birds that survive only here. From Kaua'i's rooftop streams radiate like spokes of a wheel. These streams burdened with crumbling lava and silt join to form rivers that score valleys and gouge canyons. From the swamp's southwest edges the Po'omau, Koai'e, and Wai'alae streams cut through strata of lava to join with the Waimea River. Flowing south from Alaka'i, the Makaweli and Olokele streams also form confluences with the Waimea River near its mouth. The Hanapēpē River to the south, the Wailua River to the east, and the Wainiha to the north all originate at Alaka'i and the ridge of Wai'ale'ale.

HIKING

East Side Trails

Nounou Ridge (Sleeping Giant)

	KUAMO'O-NOUNOU	WEST NOUNOU	EAST NOUNOU
Distance (one way)	2.1 mi.	1.0 mi.	1.4 mi.
Duration (one way)	2.25 hr.	1.75 hr.	2 hr.
Difficulty	Moderate	Moderate	Moderate/Strenuous
Beginning Altitude	289'	304'	127'
Ending Altitude	1046'	1046'	1046'
Climbing Elevation	1127'	788'	1206'
Descending Elevation	370'	46'	288'
Average Grade	14	16	22
Map	Kapa'a/Wailua	Kapa'a	Kapa'a

There are three hiking trails on Nounou Ridge, culminating at the Sleeping Giant's chest. Approaches are from the east, west, and south. The south trail, called the Kuamo'o-Nounou trail, connects with the west Nounou trail, which in turn meets with the east Nounou trail at the crest of the ridge. The reward at the top is a wonderful view of Kapa'a, Wailua, and the Pacific Ocean to the east, Wai'ale'ale to the west and the formation called the Līhu'e Depression to the south.

The trailhead for **Kuamo'o-Nounou trail** is a mile past the 'Ōpaeka'a Falls viewpoint on Kuamo'o Road (Highway 580). If you are carrying a GPS receiver, the coordinates here are: N22° 3.09', W159° 22.05'. A sign across from Malia Road indicates the starting point. The trail contours along the base of the west side of Nounou Ridge, passing thickets of hau, scattered hala trees, and rows of planted Norfolk Island pine for nearly 2 miles before joining the west Nounou trail at coordinates: N22° 3.98', W159° 21.39'.

Starting the ascent on the **west Nounou trail** will take you to the junction of the Kuamo'o-Nounou trail in just under half a mile. To find the west trail's start, head up Kuamo'o Road for 2.8 miles and turn right onto Kamalu Road (Highway 581). This is about half a mile past the Kuamo'o-Nounou trailhead. Continue on Kamalu for 1.2 miles. The trailhead is a grassy right-of-way on the right, between two houses, at telephone pole # 11. Coordinates for the west trailhead are: N22° 4.11', W159° 21.77'. The trail leads up through a thick stand of guava and meets with the Kuamo'o trail at the rows of planted Norfolk Island pine. Head uphill, between the parallel rows of pine trees. As the trail steepens, it switchbacks to the ridge, where you'll get glimpses of the east shore. At 1.4 miles from the start, the trail joins the east Nounou trail, at coordinates N22° 3.83', W159° 21.23', and continues up the ridgeline to a picnic shelter. The joined trail forks on the way to the shelter. The right fork is the easier route. Coordinates for the shelter are N22° 3.80', W159° 21.26'. The covered shelter will provide protection from the rain or shade from the sun while you rest and enjoy the views. The peak of Nounou to the south interrupts a 360-degree view. An unofficial trail rises to the peak; however, it is covered with loose, crumbling rocks and has steep dropoffs.

The **east Nounou trail** is longer than the west trail, but not as steep. It is also more open and affords more views during the hike than the west trail. If you can arrange for a pickup, you can go up the mountain on one trail and down on the other. To find the east Nounou trailhead, turn *mauka* on Haleilio Road, which is the next road north of Kuamo'o Road on the Kūhiō Highway. Drive for one mile and park at the lot just past telephone pole # 38. Its coordinates are: N22° 3.68', W159° 20.77'. The trail soon leaves the cover of trees as it switchbacks up the brush and grass-covered mountainside. As the trail becomes steeper, it skirts around the side of the cliff exposed to the south, and leads west until it joins with the west trail. As one trail, the route continues south along the ridge to the shelter.

Kuilau Ridge Trail

Distance (one way)	1.5 mi.
Duration (one way)	1 hr.
Difficulty	Moderate
Starting Altitude	525'
Ending Altitude	999'
Maximum Altitude	1023'
Climbing Elevation	669'
Descending Elevation	195'
Average Grade	10
Coordinates	
Start:	N22° 4.296', W159° 24.992'
Picnic Shelter:	N22° 5.157', W159° 24.780'
End:	N22° 5.613', W159° 24.741'
Map	North East Trails

Kuilau Ridge Trail is popular because of its wonderful views along the lower levels of the ridge that extends down from east Kaua'i's Makaleha Mountains. The trailhead is on Kuamo'o Road, 6.6 miles from where it joins the Kūhiō Highway at Wailua. A few parking spots are available at the marked trailhead. If they are taken, there is more parking available 100 yards farther along the road at the Keahua Arboretum.

Footing is good along the trail as it starts out with side-by-side paths. Views are blocked in the early part of the trail by the ridge on the right and by trees. There is a remarkable diversity of trees and plants along Kuilau Ridge. Towering eucalyptus and monkey pods are the most common trees, with guava, hala, lantana, thimbleberry and 'ōhia lehua represented, as well. After a half mile of moderate rise, views to the west open from the trail. The almost vertical rise of Wai'ale'ale can be seen to the southwest—likely cresting in clouds. Kawi Stream's valley slopes below you, its forest cover highlighted by light-green splotches of kukui trees.

View of Sleeping Giant mountain from Kuilau Ridge

One mile into the hike, eastern views open to the Sleeping Giant Ridge, 4 miles to the east, and the ocean. A short while after that the trail crosses an open grassy knoll, where a picnic shelter and two tables are located. This is a great place to rest and eat lunch with green views of Kualapa Ridge and the Powerline Trail to the west and, to the northwest, the sharp peak of Kapehua'ala, high point of the Makaleha Mountains.

Kuilau Ridge Trail continues for a quarter mile past the picnic shelter. It descends slightly as it switchbacks. Ti plants grow 8 to 10 feet high along the side of the trail. As the trail follows the crest of the narrowing ridge, you will be able to see views from the ocean on the east coast inland to the heart of the island. A wooden bridge at 'Ōpaeka'a Stream marks the official end of Kukui Ridge Trail. The bridge also marks the end of the Moalepe Trail, which began 1.5 miles to the east.

North East Trails

Powerline Trail

Distance (one way)	10.5 mi.
Duration (one way)	4.5 hours
Difficulty	Strenuous
Starting Altitude	555'
Ending Altitude	521'
Maximum Altitude	2118'
Climbing Elevation	2195'
Descending Elevation	2229'
Average Grade	6
Coordinates Start:	N22° 11.060', W159° 27.419'
End:	N22° 4.293', W159° 25.099'
Map	Kīlauea/North East Trails

The Powerline Trail follows the right-of-way of the hydroelectric powerlines that run south from the power plant in the Wainiha Valley. The trail's northern trailhead is at the end of Po'oku Road, across the highway from Princeville. At the south end of the trail, the other trailhead is situated close to the Keahua Arboretum, 6 miles west of Wailua. Hikers can walk the length of the trail by arranging a car-shuttle, or they can walk in and out from either end. The trail's rate of incline is gentler from a northern start. Because the pathway is wider than regular trails, this is a good trail for mountain bikers, as well.

To find the northern trailhead, turn *mauka* shortly after the Kūhiō Highway's 27-mile marker onto Po'oku Road. After a mile and three-quarters

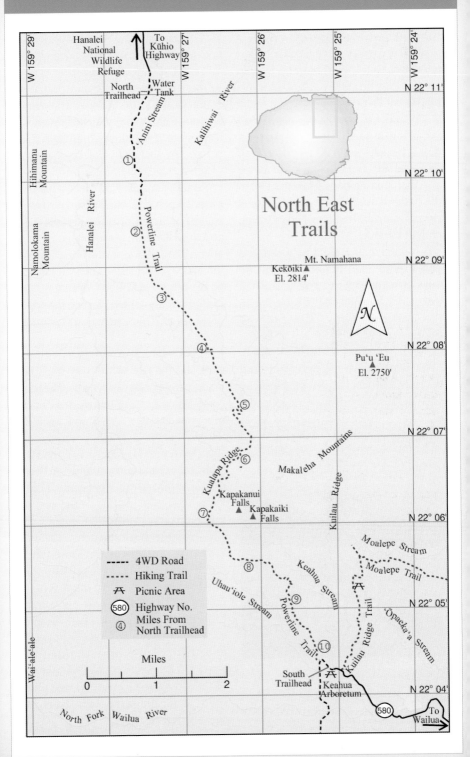

the paved surface degrades to a 4WD road. There is a parking area there, but passenger cars should have no trouble traveling the first 300 yards of the 4WD road to another parking area next to the water tank. If you have an off-road vehicle, you could drive another 1.5 miles. Hunters use the Powerline Trail on weekends and Mondays. Be aware also that hunting dogs often get lost in the brush here and that some hunters are replacing the traditional hounds with pit bull terriers.

After half a mile of walking a gentle grade and being enclosed by thick growths of ferns, guava, and hau trees, a view opens on the west side to the Hanalei Valley. The flatland bordering the Hanalei River is the Hanalei National Wildlife Refuge. Look north above the taro fields and the river and you can see the highway slice across the hill as it rises to the plateau of Princeville. At the Hanalei Valley viewpoint next to the highway, there will assuredly be many sightseers gazing back in your direction.

Hanalei Valley and Hihimanu from Powerline Trail

Another view opens to the west one mile from the trailhead. From there you can look across the Hanalei Valley to the steep green face and peaks of Hihimanu. From the highway, Hihimanu appears to have twin peaks that resemble the fins of a manta ray, but from this perspective the peaks bracket the ends of an extended ridge. South of Hihimanu is Namolokama. At 4,421 feet, it has the highest peak in Kaua'i's northern watershed. Intermittent waterfalls will appear on the steep face of Namolokama after a rainfall. Look down and to the left and you will see a waterfall farther up the ridge that you are ascending. Be careful not to step too close to the edge of the ridge. Thick vegetation covers a steep drop.

In another half mile the 4WD road ends and the rest of the way must be made on foot or on two wheels. The trail continues to rise and follows the center of a broader ridge. Views now open to the east and the highlands covered with 'ōhia lehua trees. The greenery is marked with the twisted gray stumps of dead trees victimized by Hurricane 'Iniki. Dominating the skyline to the east is the sharp peak of Mt. Namahana.

As the trail steepens, eastern views of the Makaleha Mountains come closer. Six miles from the northern trailhead, Kualapa Ridge marks the trail's highest elevation. More great mountain views are in store as the trail descends. To the southwest you will see the highest ridge on Kaua'i. The peaks of Wai'ale'ale on the north end and Kawaikini, one mile south along the ridge, will likely be shrouded in clouds.

At 7.4 miles from the north trailhead or 3 miles from the south trailhead, look through a clearing in the brush on the west side of the trail. To the north are two waterfalls. Kapakaiki Falls is the lower falls to the right. Kapakanui Falls, higher and to the left, drops 280 feet.

Frequent rain and hikers have combined to erode the trail badly. Large puddles and deep gullies will have to be negotiated. The trail ends at a hunter's check station next to a 4WD road. Turn left at the road to find the parking area next to the Keahua Arboretum. After fording Keahua Stream, the road heads east past small farms to become Kuamoʻo Road, ending at the Kūhiō Highway, next to the Wailua River.

Kalalau Trail

Nā Pali Trails

Kalalau Trail

Distance (one way)	11.1 mi.
Duration (one way)	Two days
Difficulty	Very strenuous
Starting Altitude	77'
Ending Altitude	77'
Maximum Altitude	866'
Climbing Elevation	6612'
Descending Elevation	6612'
Average Grade	28

Coordinates
Start: N22° 13.213', W159° 34.967'
Hanakāpīʻai campground:
          N22° 12.470', W159° 35.845'
Hanakoa Valley:
          N22° 11.439', W159° 37.182'
End: N22° 10.302', W159° 39.644'

Map   Nā Pali Coastline

Hiking the Kalalau Trail is Kauaʻi's ultimate outdoor adventure and its most grueling. It's by walking at the feet and sometimes the shoulders of the chiseled cliffs that their grandeur and captivating allure can be best appreciated. Hiking the length of Kalalau Trail should be attempted only by experienced backpackers. Hiking boots are essential equipment because footing along the trail includes soft cinders, dirt, mud, rocks, tree roots, and streams. A strong, waterproof tent is needed to stand up to gusty winds and frequent showers. A light sleeping bag or bedroll is adequate as the nighttime temperatures are mild. Firewood is difficult to find and tree cutting is not permitted, so a backpacking stove is recommended. A walking stick is a welcome aid when navigating the rocky terrain.

Elevation Profile of

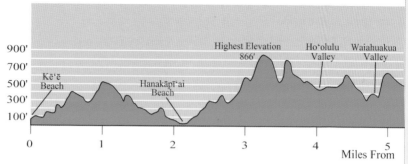

Running water is abundant along the trail but is not fit for drinking unless it is treated or boiled. The State Department of Health has issued a warning that, although portable water filters may protect against giardia, salmonella, and other bacteria and parasites, they do not protect from the bacterium that causes leptospirosis, a dangerous disease spread by animal urine and producing flu-like symptoms. Leptospirosis bacteria can enter the body through breaks in the skin or through mucous membranes. The long spiral-shaped bacteria, called spirochetes, are too skinny to be trapped by filters.

It isn't necessary to hike the length of Kalalau Trail to enjoy the beautiful sights of the Nā Pali coastline. A moderately strenuous day hike leads to Hanakāpī'ai Beach, 2 miles in from the trailhead at Kē'ē Beach. As many as 500 people use this trail daily in the summer and about 350 people walk its muddy path in the winter. The large majority of these hikers turn back at Hanakāpī'ai.

If possible, arrange to be dropped off and picked up at the trailhead if you are going to be on the trail for several days. The parking lot is small and cars left overnight are susceptible to break-ins. The Kalalau Trail begins at an information kiosk under tropical almond and kukui trees smothered with pothos plants. Footing is uneven, as the trail is covered with rocks and roots. After a half mile of steep ascent, you reach a lookout of Kē'ē Beach. Two hundred feet above the golden sand and turquoise water, you'll see the extent of the reef that forms the excellent swimming and snorkeling lagoon. To the southwest, cliffs serrate the coastline, becoming less distinct in the distance. The variability of rainfall is apparent as the green cliffs of Hanakāpī'ai Valley yield to the red ridges of the Honopū and Nu'alolo valleys and finally to the brown rock of Miloli'i Valley, 10 miles from your vantage point. Miloli'i Valley receives but a quarter of the rainfall than Nā Pali's northern extreme.

The trail rises steadily to the one-mile mark and then begins its descent into the **Hanakāpī'ai Valley**. As the trail switchbacks to the Hanakāpī'ai Stream, you'll notice a

the Kalalau Trail

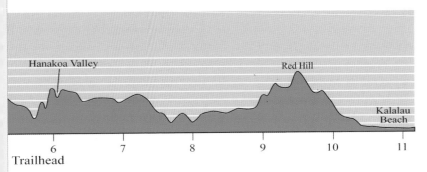

black-and-yellow-striped concrete pole imbedded in the ground. This is a marker for a safe elevation in the event of a tsunami. It seems to be incredibly high, but the V shape of the steep-sided valley would act as a funnel, pushing seawater higher as it surges inland. Hikers will have to hop slippery rocks in order to ford the stream. If the water level is too high, wait a while and it should recede. Flash floods can occur here when heavy rain falls on higher ground. Keep that in mind once you are on the other side.

Inland of the beach, where Kalalau Trail intersects with the trail to Hanakāpī'ai Falls, is a campground. Some people heading to Kalalau Beach will camp here, while others may choose to carry on to Hanakoa Campground, four miles farther along.

When Hawaiians lived in the Hanakāpī'ai Valley, they grew taro as well as banana, sweet potato and arrowroot in flooded rock terraces. In the 1800s, a Hanalei plantation farmer planted 20,000 coffee trees in the valley. A few coffee trees are still growing there.

Arrive in the summer and you will find gold sand covering Hanakāpī'ai Beach. Powerful winter surf scours the sand from the beach to leave boulder rubble. The sand is stored offshore until gentle summer surf pushes it back into place. Hanakāpī'ai Beach is a very dangerous place to swim. Many drownings have occurred here (see Beaches chapter).

Hanakāpī'ai Falls Trail leads from the camping area into the valley for 1.8 miles. It is a difficult hike to make, with a 1,800-foot elevation gain and several stream crossings. The difficult conditions are made worse by a trail that is poorly maintained by the state. Parts of the trail are heavily eroded, and in places the trail disappears under heavy growth. Persistent hikers will find **Hanakāpī'ai Falls** dropping 100 feet into a pool.

Day hikers return after they reach the Hanakāpī'ai Valley. Those who trek further must have a state camping permit (see Camping information). Kalalau Trail leaves Hanakāpī'ai Valley with a very steep ascent along 14 switchbacks, reaching its highest elevation of 866 feet in one mile. The trail does not return to sea level until it ends at Kalalau Beach. Sisal plants grow along the elevated portion of the trail. Its medium green leaves are armed with thorns. Sisal fibers were once prized for making ropes. The plants were introduced to the Islands in the hope of starting a rope industry.

Next, the trail traverses two small valleys. The first is **Ho'olulu Valley**, a hanging valley where the floor sits about 200 feet above the sea. Ho'olulu is thickly foliated with ti, guava, morning glory, mountain orchids, and ferns, along with kukui, koa and hala trees. Notice how goats have nibbled at the leaves of the ti plants.

Kalalau Trail cuts across steep Nā Pali cliffs

Waiahuakua Valley, another hanging valley, comes into sight 4-1/2 miles into the hike. From June to August, 'ōhia ai (mountain apple) abounds along the trail. Mountain apple trees have smooth, dark-green leaves and reach up to 50 feet high. Their fruit is a small, red or pinkish apple with a thin, waxen skin. The meat is delicious and juicy. Waves have cut sea caves into the cliffs below Ho'olulu and Waiahuakua valleys, but they are only visible to boaters.

The trail turns inland and follows the 500-foot contour into the **Hanakoa Valley**. The view along the green cliffs

of the valley is marked with waterfalls. Broad and terraced, Hanakoa Valley was once cultivated by Hawaiians. An 1835 census counted 50 individuals living in the valley. When they abandoned taro cultivation, the Hawaiians of Hanakoa modified the terraces for growing coffee bean trees. Campsites are found on both sides of Hanakoa stream, near mango and coffee bean trees. Campers are allowed to stay only one night at Hanakoa Valley.

Hanakoa Falls Trail is a half-mile diversion (one way) from the main trail taking hearty hikers 1,600 feet up Hanakoa Valley. The trail to Hanakoa Falls starts on the first terrace on the west side of the stream, exiting at its southeast corner. The distance to the falls is actually farther than the one-third mile that the sign indicates. Hanakoa Stream forks in two above the trail. You need to cross the west fork of the stream and then continue uphill along the west side of the east fork. Solitude and a pool will greet you at the base of the falls.

Hanakoa Falls

Many hikers save their energy for the Kalalau Trail and bypass this side trail. Your solitude will be broken frequently, however, by tour helicopters.

The last 4.8 miles of the trail lie ahead and will test the endurance of even the fittest hiker. The trail switchbacks alternately up and down along precipitous Manono Ridge. Underfoot, a loose conglomerate lacks the sure footing you might desire when navigating across a cliff with a 200-foot drop to the sea. The unobstructed view of the ocean is breathtaking, though. Vegetation becomes sparse on this section of the trail. After you pass a low point, the trail turns inland to cross two small gullies, the second has a running brook. As you approach the second gully, watch for the appearance of onion-skin boulders on the slope. They are so-named because the process of spheroidal weathering has gradually peeled away layers of lava rock from these boulders, much like peeling an onion. The boulders consist of a rounded core surrounded by concentric shells of fragile stone. Water penetrates imperfections in the outer surface of the rock and reacts with the underlying rock to form clay. The clay swells and forces the outer surface to separate from the inner surface.

Pōhakuao is the last small valley before Kalalau. A final steep incline brings you to the top of a steep red slope, appropriately named Red Hill. The welcome sight of the Kalalau Valley lies below. Kalalau is the largest valley along the Nā Pali coast—2 miles wide and 3 miles long. From Red Hill the trail snakes down to the cool rushing water of Kalalau Stream.

Camping is allowed on the beach, near the trees fronting the beach and in the caves at the far end of the beach. The westernmost cave collapsed in 1987, and a rock slide in 1980 sealed off the entrance to the next cave east. These are two good reasons to not choose the remaining caves as campsites. There are a pit toilet and a composting toilet near the east end of the camping area and a pit toilet near the west end. Ho'ole'a Falls, at the far end of the beach, is where most campers shower and replenish their water supply. Goats living in the hills above the stream require that its water is treated or boiled before drinking. Beyond the caves the steep walls of crumbling lava make any further progress on land impossible. Some people try swimming the four-tenths of a mile to neighboring Honopū Beach. This is risky even for strong swimmers, as an ocean current flowing from the north works against them on the return trip.

The state allows a maximum of five days to camp at Kalalau. While there, many campers hike up-valley on the **Kalalau Valley Trail** to Big Pool. The trail is 2 miles long one way and has an elevation gain of 900 feet. The trail into the valley begins on the west side of Kalalau Stream. From there, hikers follow the stream initially and then have to scramble up an eroded rise. Bare land transforms to areas wooded with orange, mango, guava and rose apple trees. A tributary stream and then Kalalau Stream have to be crossed. Big Pool is a pair of room-sized pools joined by a natural water slide. It is a delightful place to enjoy the sights of the Kalalau Valley.

TAKE A WALK ON THE SAFE SIDE

Kaua'i's natural beauty has long beckoned people to climb its ridges and peaks, to traverse its luxuriant tropical rain forests and to forge its rivers. The island's beauty can be as beguiling as it is enticing, for the unique beauty can be partnered with the unique dangers of Kaua'i's geography and weather. For instance, the millions of years of erosion that sculpted the magnificent pinnacles of the Nā Pali coast can also be a recipe for disaster for careless hikers on Kaua'i's many ridges and peaks. And the heavy rains necessary to feed the lush growth of the island's rain forests also spawn flash floods that can trap people in a narrow valley.

Kaua'i's backcountry trails are no walk in the park. Over the years a good number of people, many of them experienced hikers, have gotten themselves lost or injured. Some of them didn't return alive; some haven't returned at all.

Most official trails on the island are well marked, but there are hunter's trails and pig trails branching off the main routes that could lead to confusion. Another danger, besides getting lost, is falling off steep ridge trails from unsure footing. Volcanic rock often has a layer of crumbly gravel on top, which is like stepping on marbles.

An unlikely peril, but real nevertheless, is the uluhe, or false staghorn fern. It's a weed-like quicksand, which grows in places like Kōke'e. The uluhe reaches heights of 8 feet and is so dense it covers slopes and voids in the terrain. It grows in sunny, exposed areas and gives the false impression that there is dry, passable ground underneath. People leaving the trail to shortcut through the ferns can slip into mire and disappear.

Flash floods are possible hazards in the steep valleys of fast-moving streams. You can have a clear sky above but heavy rain can be falling higher up the mountain. A stream's level can rise very quickly, trapping hikers on one side or the other.

A hike of 2 or 3 miles in the Waimea Canyon may have an elevation loss and gain of 2,000 feet. The sun's heat re-radiates off the bare rock walls of the canyon and leaves unsuspecting hikers susceptible to heat exhaustion and dehydration.

Hikers need to be prepared for tropical conditions. Pack clothing and sturdy footwear that will protect you in hot, dry weather, as well as cool rainy conditions. Bring food and first aid supplies and twice as much fresh water as you think you'll need. Stay on marked trails and keep back from high ridges. Let someone know where you will be hiking and when you will be back. Know your physical condition and don't overtax your abilities.

Stay on the boardwalk when hiking in Alaka'i Swamp

View from the end of Awa'awapuhi Trail

Kōke'e Trails

Awa'awapuhi Trail

Distance (one way)	2.6 mi.
Duration (one way)	1.5 hr. going, 2 hr. returning
Difficulty	Strenuous
Starting Altitude	4060'
Ending Altitude	2754'
Maximum Altitude	4060'
Climbing Elevation	201'
Descending Elevation	1507'
Average Grade	12
Coordinates Start:	N22° 8.449', W159° 38.990'
End:	N22° 9.111', W159° 40.572'
Map	Kōke'e Trails

The Awa'awapuhi Trail begins at a marked trailhead, 1.5 miles past the turnoff to the Kōke'e Museum. After a short uphill start, the trail descends faithfully to the end, balanced on the spine of a ridge. Dry forest encloses the trail for most of its length. Some of the plants along the trail are identified with signboards. Shortly before the end of the trail, a connecting trail, called Nu'alolo Cliff Trail, branches to the left. It connects hikers with the Nu'alolo Trail, which leads back to the road on another ridge. The lack of views along Awa'awapuhi Trail is more than compensated for at the end. You are treated to a spectacular view down into Awa'awapuhi Valley on the right and Nu'alolo Valley to your left. The sight down to the floors of these rarely visited valleys is truly memorable. Green, fluted canyon walls contrast against the deep blue of the ocean. This is a great place to eat your packed lunch before heading back. Be sure to stay behind the metal railings. The cliff edges crumble easily and, as wonderful as this view is, you don't want it to be your last.

Nu'alolo Trail

Distance (one way)	3.6 mi.
Duration (one way)	1.75 hrs. going, 2.25 hrs. returning
Difficulty	Strenuous
Starting Altitude	3627'
Ending Altitude	2124'
Maximum Altitude	3737'
Climbing Elevation	397'
Descending Elevation	1,900'
Average Grade	12
Coordinates Start:	N22° 7.744', W159° 39.587'
End:	N22° 9.043', W159° 41.829'
Map	Kōke'e Trails

Nu'alolo Trail takes hikers through mostly endemic Hawaiian forest to broad views of the Nu'alolo Valley and the cliffs along the Nā Pali coast. The challenging trek begins at Kōke'e Road, several yards before the turnoff to Kōke'e State Park headquarters. From the trailhead you will ascend sharply for the first quarter of a mile as you enter the **Kuia Natural Area Reserve**. The rest of the trip is a steady descent. Between 1 and 2 miles in you will notice the forest change from wet to dry. The trail bends to the left and back to the right as you descend a broad ridge top. This part of the route is called the **Nu'alolo Bench Trail.**

Three miles from its start and after a very steep section, the trail meets with **Nu'alolo Cliff Trail** on the right. The cliff trail connects with Awa'awapuhi Trail, creating a lengthy loop trail back to the road. If you don't plan on making the loop, you can still walk a short distance on the cliff trail to see a view down into Nu'alolo Valley. Shortly after the junction with the cliff trail, another spur trail branches to the left. Keep to the right to follow Nu'alolo Bench Trail to the end viewpoint, called **Lolo Vista Point**. The last half mile to the viewpoint means walking on a narrow, steep-sided ridge that is exposed to wind and rain. An awesome view of the Nu'ololo Valley awaits. Below the almost vertical cliff you will see the silver sliver that is Nu'ololo Stream flowing to a rugged beach. The only access to Nu'ololo Beach and the valley is by boat. The edge of the ridge is covered with slippery, gravel-sized rocks. Be sure to admire the view at Lolo Vista Point from behind the metal railing.

Nu'alolo Cliff Trail

Distance (one way)	2.0 mi.
Duration (one way)	1 hr.
Difficulty	Strenuous
Starting Altitude	2889'
Ending Altitude	2505'
Maximum Altitude	2889'
Climbing Elevation	751'
Descending Elevation	1135'
Average Grade	18

Coordinates
  Start (from Awa'awapuhi Trail):
    N22° 9.114', W159° 40.492'
  End (at Nu'alolo Trail):
    N22° 8.696', W159° 41.450'

Map	Kōke'e Trails

Pihea Trail

Distance (one way)	1.1 mi.
Duration (one way)	0.5 hrs.
Difficulty	Moderate
Starting Altitude	4118'
Ending Altitude	4178'
Maximum Altitude	4178'
Climbing Elevation	351'
Descending Elevation	291'
Average Grade	10

Coordinates
  Start: N22° 8.839', W159° 37.917'
  Junction to swamp:
    N22° 9.244', W159° 37.109'
  End (at Nu'alolo Trail):
    N22° 9.305', W159° 37.046'

Map	Kōke'e Trails

High endurance hikers can use Nu'alolo Cliff Trail to connect Nu'alolo Trail with Awa'awapuhi Trail to make a loop trail that connects with Kōke'e Road. You can also walk partway onto the cliff trail for a view into Nu'alolo Valley and return by the same trail you came in on. The views from the cliff trail are intermittent as the trail passes through sections of forest. To make a loop out of the three trails will result in a total hike of 10.5 miles, including 1.6 miles along Kōke'e Road to return to your starting point. If possible, arrange for a car shuttle between the trailheads to shave some time and distance off the totals. Kōke'e Road is not good for walking at this section where it is narrow, winding and devoid of shoulders. Check with the attendant at the Kōke'e Museum on the latest condition of Nu'alolo Cliff Trail. It is eroded in places and is poorly maintained.

Mist from the Alaka'i Swamp rolls across Pihea Trail

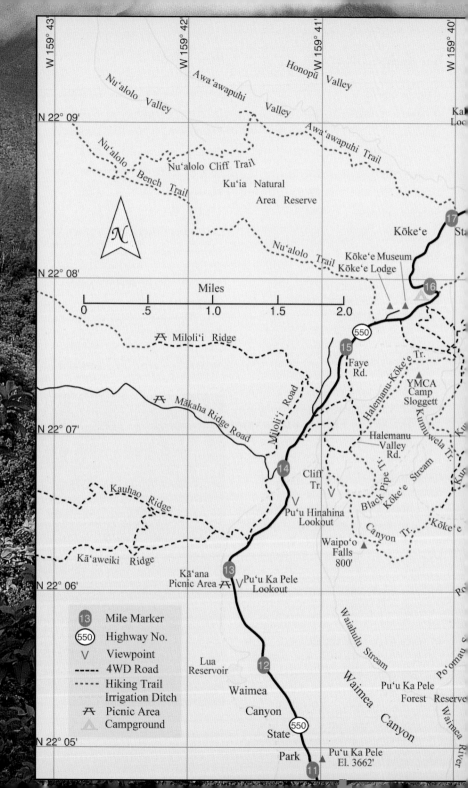

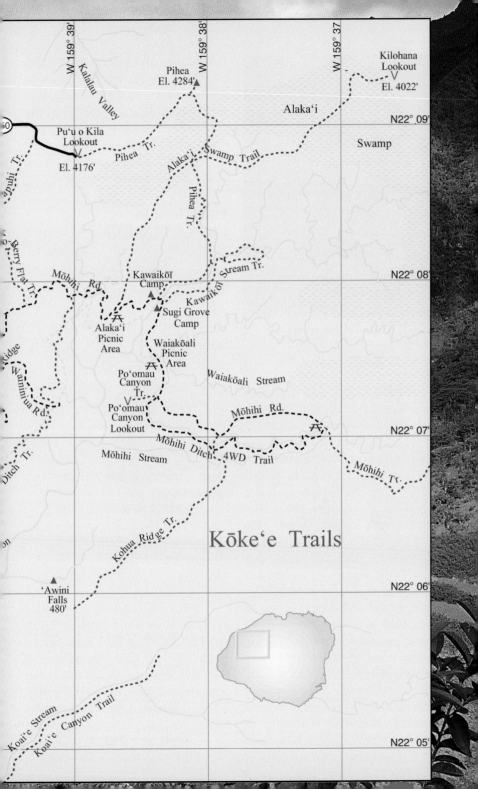

Hikers have to negotiate a muddy trench to reach Pihea Lookout

Pihea Lookout, the destination of this hike. Expect even steeper and muddier trail conditions on the final ascent to the lookout. Weather permitting, the view from Pihea Lookout will be from the highest point along the rim of the Kalalau Valley and treetop views of the Alaka'i Swamp to the north.

Pihea Trail to Kilohana Lookout

Distance (one way)	3.7 mi.
Duration (one way)	1.75 hrs.
Difficulty	Moderate to Strenuous
Starting Altitude	4118'
Ending Altitude	3931'
Maximum Altitude	4138'
Climbing Elevation	812'
Descending Elevation	999'
Average Grade	9
Coordinates Start:	N22° 8.839', W159° 37.917'
Fork to Alaka'i Swamp:	N22° 9.244', W159° 37.109'
Alaka'i Swamp Junction:	N22° 8.803', W159° 37.063'
End:	N22° 9.343', W159° 35.624'
Map	Kōke'e Trails

Pihea Trail starts at Pu'u o Kila Lookout, at the end of Kōke'e Road. The trail leaves the lookout of Kalalau Valley as a deeply eroded clay surface that was a road cut for an ill-conceived plan to build a road through the Alaka'i Swamp. On your left side are views of the Kalalau Valley even better than from the official lookout. Stunted 'ōhia trees grow on the edge of the Alaka'i Swamp on the other side of the trail. Pihea Trail degrades to a muddy pathway with deep cuts made by running water and hikers' boots. At some points it is necessary to grasp branches and tree roots while climbing through knee-deep cuts in the slippery clay. Wear old clothes, as they are sure to be stained dirt red. A hiking pole is a definite asset. A fork splits the trail one mile from its start. The trail to the right is described in the following hike. The short spur trail to the left leads to

This hike starts at Pu'u o Kila Lookout, at the end of Kōke'e Road, and follows Pihea Trail as described in the previous hike. One mile from the start, take the right fork at the junction and begin the section of the hike through the Alaka'i Swamp on a boardwalk.

Incessant rainfall has created about 20 bogs within the Alaka'i.

Moss grows easily in a swamp

Together, they make a series of unique biological communities that scientists say are the most fragile ecosystems in the state. Low-growing plants and shrubs dominate the bogs. 'Ōhia trees that grow to 50 feet in the forest stand a foot high in the swamp—fully mature, but stunted by excessive moisture. Bog plants such as native primrose and geranium are extremely imperiled. Some species are down to just a few remaining individuals or clusters. The Alaka'i oozes a primordial and mystical presence. Ghostly clouds float among moss-laden plants; shafts of sunlight highlight twisted trees; breezes blow mist across the faces of hikers.

Pihea Trail tracks through the swamp covered by a boardwalk. Concerned about the growing damage to the native forest by hikers, state foresters started building a system of wooden boardwalks on Alaka'i trails in 1990. Hurricane 'Iniki sidelined the project for a few years in 1992.

Volunteers joined the effort in 1995, helping to complete the boardwalk in 1998. You climb and descend many stairs on the boardwalk for seven-tenths of a mile until you reach a junction. A signpost at the junction points to destinations in four directions. A sharp left, onto the Alaka'i Swamp Trail, will lead to the destination of this hike, Kilohana Lookout. Continuing on the Pihea Trail will lead to Kawaikōi Camp and connect with 4WD Mōhihi Road. Turning right at the junction will follow the Alaka'i Swamp Trail south to Mōhihi Road, the destination in the following hike.

After the sharp left turn, Alaka'i Swamp Trail descends sharply. The boardwalk ends at a stream crossing and is picked up again after the trail rises from the stream's valley. Two miles from the trail junction, the trail ends on a wooden platform at the **Kilohana Lookout**. Here, on the edge of Wainiha Pali, you look down cliffs cloaked in rain forest to the valley of the Wainiha River. The Wainiha River, one of seven rivers to drain the Alaka'i, empties into the ocean on Kaua'i's north shore. Above the songs of rare birds you can hear the river rushing, thousands of feet below.

Trees stunted by excessive rainfall in Alaka'i Swamp

Pihea Trail - Alaka'i Swamp Trail

Distance (one way)	3.2 mi.
Duration (one way)	1.5 hrs.
Difficulty	Moderate to Strenuous
Starting Altitude	4118'
Ending Altitude	3679'
Maximum Altitude	4138'
Climbing Elevation	453'
Descending Elevation	892'
Average Grade	8
Coordinates Start:	N22° 8.839', W159° 37.917'
Fork to swamp:	N22° 9.244', W159° 37.109'
Alaka'i Swamp Junction:	N22° 8.803', W159° 37.063'
End:	N22° 7.802', W159° 37.670'
Map	Kōke'e Trails

In this hike follow the directions given in the preceding hike to the junction of the Pihea and Alaka'i Swamp trails, 1.7 miles from the Pu'u o Kila Lookout. At the junction, turn right to head south. The destination from here is 1.5 miles away at the Alaka'i picnic area on Mōhihi Road. As the boardwalk transits the south edge of the swamp, you will come across fallen telephone poles, abandoned vestiges of a WWII communications project. The trail widens into a lane bordered by evergreens and ends at a grassy field about 300 yards from Mōhihi Road. Across the road is a shelter and picnic area overlooking Po'omau Canyon.

The hike can also begin at this trailhead, or a shuttle from the Pu'u o Kila Lookout can be arranged. Mōhihi Road is a 4WD road that begins at Kōke'e Road. Take the first right after the Kōke'e Museum turnoff, across from the campground, onto a dirt road and follow it for 3.1 miles to the Alaka'i picnic area.

Po'omau Canyon Lookout Trail

Distance (one way)	0.2 mi.
Duration (one way)	10 minutes
Difficulty	Easy
Starting Altitude	3476'
Ending Altitude	3301'
Maximum Altitude	3476'
Climbing Elevation	12'
Descending Elevation	187'
Average Grade	18
Coordinates Start:	N22° 7.255', W159° 37.334'
End:	N22° 7.217', W159° 37.515'
Map	Kōke'e Trails

Mōhihi Road has only two canyon vistas, one is at the Alaka'i picnic area and the other is at the end of the Po'omau Canyon Lookout Trail. Follow the directions in the preceding hike to locate Mōhihi Road and follow it for 4.6 miles. Look for the trail sign two-tenths of a mile after the Wai'akoali picnic area. The Po'omau Canyon Lookout Trail starts on the right side of Mōhihi Road. A short walk over a footbridge and through groves of Norfolk and sugi pines and

A short walk leads to vista of Po'omau Canyon

koa trees will take you to a viewpoint at the head of Po'omau Canyon. From your viewpoint you can see Po'omau Stream flowing to meet the Waimea River. Together, the Waimea River and Po'omau Stream form the second longest waterway on Kaua'i after the Wailua River.

Kukui - Waimea Canyon Trails

Distance (one way)	2.3 miles
Duration (one way)	1.75 hrs. down, 3 hrs. up
Difficulty	Strenuous
Starting Altitude	2927'
Ending Altitude	686'
Maximum Altitude	2927'
Average Grade	24
Coordinates Start:	N22° 3.102', W159° 39.595'
End:	N22° 3.778', W159° 38.523'
Map	Kōke'e-Waimea Canyon

Steep Kukui Trail is the only access to the floor of Waimea Canyon from Kōke'e. Prepare for a difficult and hot hike. The temperature rises noticeably from the cooler conditions of the upcountry to the canyon floor, where the sun's heat is re-radiated off the canyon walls. The trailhead for Kukui Trail is marked with a sign shortly before mile marker nine on Highway 550. Hikers can take a short diversion through the Iliau Nature Loop situated at the start of Kukui Trail (see Waimea Canyon-Kōke'e Sights chapter).

After passing a picnic pavilion, the trail starts switchbacking down the grade. As well as the ever-closing view of the Waimea Canyon, hikers can look to the northeast into Wai'alae Canyon, a view mostly obscured from Waimea Canyon Lookout back at the highway. Standing out from the red and earth-toned canyon walls are the light-green canopies of kukui trees. About one-half mile and one mile along the trail, benches give you a chance to rest and take in the views. As the trail descends into the depths of the canyon, it takes you under a dense cover of kukui, silk oak and swamp mahogany trees. The trail emerges from the forest at Wiliwili Camp, where a dark-red cliff on the other side of Waimea River looms above. Wiliwili Camp provides a pavilion, picnic table, and a pit toilet.

CAMPING ON KAUA'I

Camping is permitted at designated campgrounds at many of Kaua'i's state parks, county parks, and forest reserves. Permits are required for an overnight visit to any campground and must be obtained in advance.

State Park Campgrounds

State park campgrounds are open seven days per week, all year. Permit applications must be received at least seven days before the camping event and are issued up to one year in advance. The maximum length of stay at any one park is five consecutive nights. Tent camping is $5 per campsite per night, except for Nā Pali Coast State Park, which is $10 per person per night. Permit applications are available by contacting:

Hawai'i State Parks
Island of Kaua'i District Office
Department of Land & Natural Resources
3060 Eiwa Street, Room 306
Līhu'e, HI 96766-1875
Tel. (808) 274-3444
Hours: 8 a.m. to 4 p.m., Monday to Friday
A permit application is available in PDF format at the state's website at:
<www.state.hi.us/dlnr/dsp/dsp.html>.

Nā Pali Coast State Park

You need to apply early for a permit to camp at the Kalalau campground. Two-thirds of all permits during the summer are issued one year in advance. Campsites are situated at the Hanakāpī'ai, Hanakoa, Kalalau and Miloli'i valleys. These campsites are considered primitive, and drinking water is unavailable. Miloli'i campsite, which can be reached only by boat, is closed indefinitely.

Kōke'e State Park

The campsite is in a lovely meadow close to the Kōke'e Museum. Drinking water, bathrooms, a restaurant, and a picnic shelter are available at the park headquarters.

Polihale State Park

The Polihale campsite is located on Kaua'i's largest beach on the hot and arid west coast. Facilities include bathrooms, showers, barbeque pits, picnic tables, and a pavilion.

County Park Campgrounds

Camping permit fees are $3 per adult per night for nonresidents and free for state residents. Stays at the campsite are limited to seven nights. Applications are available by contacting:

County of Kaua'i
Department of Public Works
Division of Parks and Recreation
4444 Rice Street
Mo'ikeha Building, Suite 150
Līhu'e, HI 96766
Tel. (808) 241-6660
A permit application is also available at the county's website at:
<www.kauaigov.org/parks.htm>.

The county park campsites are:
Hā'ena Park (closed Mondays); Black Pot Beach on Hanalei Bay (weekends and holidays only); 'Anini Beach Park (closed Tuesdays); Anahola Beach Park (closed Thursdays); Hanamā'ulu Beach Park (Wednesdays); Salt Pond Beach Park (closed Tuesdays); and Lucy Wright Park in Waimea (closed Mondays).

BEACHES

Making sand sculptures at Kalāpaki Beach

K Kaua'i's glorious beaches contribute greatly to its appellation of a tropical paradise. Fifty-eight beaches circle this small island, bestowing nearly 45 percent of its coastline with a gold-colored buffer between the sea and the land. Ocean temperatures average 75° F in the winter and 81° F in the summer months. Some beaches are perfect for lying on motionless and others invite beachgoers to swim, snorkel, SCUBA dive, surf, sail, or windsurf. You may find that your favorite beach is right in front of your resort, a few steps from a roadside parking lot, or secluded at the end of an unmarked trail. All beaches are for everyone's use. Hawai'i law prevents private ownership of any beach below the upper reaches of the waves as evidenced by the vegetation line. Even the most exclusive resorts provide public access to the beaches they front.

Wind direction and surf levels are the two important factors directing the day-to-day character of Kaua'i's beaches. For most of the year, the trade winds prevail from the northeast. At any time of the year, but more often in the summer, humid *Kona* winds blow from the south (in Hawaiian, *Kona* means leeward wind). The trade winds blowing over vast areas of open water create dangerous ocean currents.

Storms that may be thousands of miles away can determine surf conditions. In the winter months, North Pacific storms drive waves to Kaua'i's north shore, with the opposite occurring to the south in the summer. The geographic isolation of the Hawaiian Islands means there is no landmass to intervene and diffuse the ocean swells and no continental shelf to cushion their impact. Fair weather on Kaua'i is not an indication that ocean conditions locally will be calm and safe, nor should the presence of local surfers be taken as an indication of safe water. Fortunately for recreational beach users, coral reefs and rocky points offer a degree of protection. Call (808) 245-3564 for high surf advisory.

Beach Safety

Only a handful of beaches on Kaua'i provide lifeguard service. More drownings occur on Kaua'i beaches than on any other Hawaiian island. During the last decade, Kaua'i has averaged 11 drowning deaths per year. Visitors comprise three-quarters of the drowning fatalities. Understanding the behavior of the ocean, heeding posted hazards, and the use of common sense are needed to safely enjoy the beach and the ocean.

Shorebreaks

Places where waves break directly on or near the shore with downward force are known as shorebreaks. They occur where a deep ocean bottom changes abruptly to a shallow bottom and the incoming wave is forced upwards. Swimmers could be injured if they try to jump through or over a large shorebreak; instead, they should take a breath and swim under the wave. Be aware of the potential danger even if you are not in the ocean. Typical waves are interrupted by an occasional aberrantly large wave that could knock down someone on the shore. Each year in Hawai'i, unsuspecting people drown by being swept away by such waves. Never turn your back on the ocean.

Backwash

When a wave washes up on shore, the water must return to the sea. Backwash is the spent wave rushing back down the beach. On a steep beach the backwash may be powerful enough to sweep you off your feet and out into deeper water.

Rip Current

Because waves generally come in sets, with short lulls between sets, the backwash is partially prevented from returning by the next wave coming in. As a larger volume of water builds up, it moves along the shore looking for a point of release, usually a trough in the sand or a channel in the reef. This river-like movement of water out to sea is a rip current. A swimmer who gets caught in a rip current should try to flow along with it or swim sideways to it until it diminishes. Trying to swim against a rip current will cause exhaustion.

Undertow

Sometimes the returning water has no channel of escape and must back out under the incoming wave. This creates the condition known as an undertow. A swimmer caught in an undertow will be pulled under an incoming wave and released as the wave passes. It lasts only a few seconds; granted it will seem longer.

Tsunami

A tsunami is a series of waves set into motion by great disturbances such as earthquakes or landslides and are capable of traveling across the ocean at high speed. When the possibility exists of a tsunami reaching Hawai'i, the public is warned by the sounding of sirens located along the coastlines. If the sirens sound, immediately evacuate coastal areas. An elevation of 50 feet has been arbitrarily set as safe ground. Turn on a radio and listen for information and instructions from civil defense agencies. The sirens are tested at 11:45 a.m. on the first working day of each month.

Marine Life

Jellyfish, and in particular the Portuguese man-of-war, live in Hawai'i waters. The man-of-war has a translucent, bubble-shaped body, usually less than 6 inches long. As it generally drifts with winds and currents, the man-of-war is more of a problem on beaches where there is a strong onshore wind. For an unknown reason, jellyfish become more numerous in offshore waters 9 to 10 days after a full moon. Their tentacles are capable of delivering a severe sting and cause a red welt on the skin. If stung, the affected area should be cleaned immediately with fresh water and a solution of household ammonia or baking soda. Some people may develop allergic reactions and should seek immediate medical treatment.

Eels are found in nearly every reef in Hawai'i, hiding in holes and crevices. They are not aggressive unless threatened. Armed with powerful jaws lined with sharp teeth, eels are best left alone.

Sharks are more likely to be met in open water than close to beaches. If a swimmer or diver encounters a shark, he or she should remain calm until the curious shark moves on. The most dangerous shark found in Hawai'i waters is the tiger shark. They love to eat turtles and, from below, surfers with their hands and feet dangling over a board look like turtles. Of the 15 deaths attributed to shark attacks on Kaua'i since 1970, 13 were surfers.

If a sea urchin is stepped on or brushed against, the needle-like spines break off and embed in the skin. The spines are difficult to remove but will dissolve after about a week. A common folk remedy is to apply urine to the afflicted area. The uric acid is said to hasten the dissolution of the spines. Coral is very abrasive and can cause cuts that are susceptible to infections and slow to heal.

The Sun

Spending too much time in the sun can spoil your entire vacation. The tropical sun is higher in the sky than most visitors are used to and, therefore, the atmosphere filters less of the burning ultraviolet rays. As well, water intensifies the effect by reflecting UV rays. Sunblocks of every factor are readily available everywhere on Kaua'i. Remember that sunblock takes 20 to 30 minutes to take effect, so it should be applied before going outside.

East Side Beaches

Kalapakī Beach

Location: In front of Marriott Hotel in Līhu'e

Coordinates: N21° 57.63', W159° 20.97'

Length: 0.2 miles

Facilities: Boat rentals, showers and telephone at Marriott, bathrooms, showers, and picnic tables at Nāwiliwili Park.

Being the beach closest to Līhu'e and fronting the Marriott Hotel causes Kalapakī to be one of Kaua'i's most popular and heavily used beaches. Its gently sloping, sandy bottom and its partial protection from the open ocean make for favorable swimming conditions. Beginner surfers and bodyboarders try out the gentle waves that break across a shallow sandbar. Hule'ia Stream empties into nearby Nāwiliwili Bay, causing the water at Kalapakī to be a bit murky. To the west of the beach is Nāwiliwili Park, which is a popular picnic spot for Līhu'e residents. Luxury houses balance precariously, perched like aeries, 100 feet above Kalapakī on the cliff to the east.

The Marriott Hotel, formerly the Westin Kaua'i, which suffered severe damage from Hurricane 'Iniki, is the latest building to occupy this site. The first structure built on Kalapakī was a beach house owned by the Rice family. The son of missionaries William and Mary Rice purchased the land in 1870 from Princess Ruth Ke'elikolani. Ancient Hawaiians also surfed the waves at Kalapakī. The name, Kalapakī, means "double-yolked egg." How the beach was connected with eggs has been lost over time.

Public access is available from Nāwiliwili Park or from a public parking lot east of the Marriott.

Ninini Beach

Location: Below Kiele Golf Course on Nāwiliwili Bay

Coordinates: N21° 57.52', W159° 20.51'

Length: 100 yards

Facilities: None

This small pocket of sand, protected from prevailing winds and currents on the north entrance to Nāwiliwili Bay, normally has appealing swimming conditions. When Kona storms kick up the surf, the beach is sometimes used for bodyboarding. To find this out-of-the-way beach, follow the road across the Kiele Golf Course to the beach access sign just before Whalers Brew Pub. A short path leads to the beach from the parking lot.

Hanamā'ulu Beach Park

Location: On Hanamā'ulu Bay, north of Līhu'e Airport

Coordinates: N21° 59.59', W159° 20.49'

Length: 0.2 miles

Facilities: Picnic shelters, bathrooms, camping

Hanamā'ulu was given its name, which means "tired bay," because it was off the main island trails and a traveler had to walk extra miles to get there. The beach park at Hanamā'ulu Bay is popular with local residents, particularly on weekends. That means the noise from picnics and parties is competing with the din from jets and helicopters taking off and landing at nearby Līhuʻe airport. The narrow sand beach has fine-textured sand and the bay is protected from the open ocean, but the murky water is not inviting to swimmers. Ocean currents don't make their way into the bay to flush away the silt deposited from Hanamāʻulu Stream.

To find the beach park, turn off Highway 56 at the town of Hanamāʻulu, between the school and the Shell station. After three-tenths of a mile, turn right onto Hehi Road and follow it to the end.

Nukoliʻi Beach Park

Location: In front of Outrigger, Aston Beach Villas and Wailua Golf Course
Coordinates: N22° 00.41', W159° 20.17' (south entrance)
Length: 2 miles
Facilities: Bathrooms, shower, picnic tables

This long stretch of sand is rarely visited even though it lies between the populated areas of Līhuʻe and Kapaʻa. The beach is narrow at spots, with rock ledges exposed on the southern section. Ocean currents and surf make swimming conditions marginal. Debris from fishing boats washes up here, making it a good place for beachcombing.

The south access is from the entrance road to the Outrigger and Aston Beach Villas, between mile markers three and four on the Kūhiō Highway. Just south of mile marker four is another road that connects the highway to the section of the beach in front of the Wailua Golf Course.

Lydgate State Park

Location: In front of Holiday Inn Sunspree Resort
Coordinates: N22° 02.48', W159° 20.08'
Length: 0.5 miles
Facilities: Bathrooms, showers, picnic shelters, telephone, lifeguard, barbeques, playground

The park and beach at Lydgate were named after the Reverend John Lydgate, a former pastor and prominent Kauaʻi civic leader who died in 1922. It's a wonderful destination for family outings. The park features a large pavilion, a new playground, shade trees, and a grassy field. The beach starts on the south bank of the Wailua River and is backed with a lawn and a few shade trees. A large seawater pond enclosed by walls of boulders centers the beach. Built in 1970 to provide a safe swimming area protected from the waves and currents of Kauaʻi's east coast, it has a partition wall that divides the pool into an area for small children and one for adults and older children. The shallow and calm water inside the rock wall is an excellent place for young or inexperienced snorkelers. Fish swim through gaps between the boulders looking for handouts. The water outside the rock wall and along the beach south of the wall is treacherous. Even with lifeguard protection, Lydgate has experienced 21 drownings since 1970.

To find the park when traveling from the south, turn *makai* from the Kūhiō Highway at mile marker five onto Leho Road and then right at Nalu Road. The entrance road is marked with a sign. If you are traveling from the north, turn left at the Holiday Inn Sunspree Resort and then left again at Nalu Road. A left turn is not allowed further south on the highway at Leho Road.

Wailua Beach

Location: Next to Kūhiō Highway, north of Wailua River

Coordinates: N22° 02.93', W159° 20.08'

Length: 0.5 miles

Facilities: None

You won't have any trouble finding Wailua Beach; it's right next to the highway, north of the Wailua River. A sandbar close to shore causes waves to break into the curls the surfers and bodyboarders look for. Powerful rip currents develop when the surf is high, so swimmers should be cautious here. From the beach you can walk under the bridge that crosses the Wailua River at its mouth. Sand accumulates at the river's mouth when the river flow is low. When the river flow increases, the sand is quickly pushed back into the sea. It's not a good idea to swim at the river's mouth, as the bottom drops off quickly and the currents can be treacherous.

Waipouli Beach

Location: In front of Kaua'i Coconut Beach Resort

Coordinates: N22° 04.20', W159° 19.00'

Length: 1.5 miles

Facilities: None

Possibly, observers of an eclipse there gave Waipouli its name, which means "dark water." Waipouli Beach is long and narrow, reaching from the resorts at the Coconut Plantation to the Waika'ea Canal in Kapa'a. A pedestrian walkway runs along the length of the beach and continues on a former train bridge over the canal into Kapa'a Beach. The canal was built to drain the inland marshes to make the land suitable for growing sugar cane and rice. It has the only boat ramp on the windward shore of Kaua'i. Markers guide boaters through a channel in the reef to the open ocean.

Beach rock is exposed along much of Waipouli Beach. Ocean currents are usually strong here and the surf reaches the shore at several places. It is not considered a safe beach for swimming.

The beach and walkway can be reached from any of the resorts along the Royal Coconut coast. To reach the north end of the beach at the canal, turn onto Akia Street, across from the Burger King.

Kapa'a Beach Park

Location: Next to Kapa'a's town center

Coordinates: N22° 04.51', W159° 18.99'

Length: 0.8 miles

Facilities: Picnic shelter, bathrooms

A reef protects much of the beach in front of the town of Kapa'a. Pockets of sand on the offshore bottom make for some reasonable swimming spots. In the winter the high surf can crash past the reef and create strong currents. Located at the center of the beach is a park featuring a large concrete statue of a Japanese lantern. North of the park, the beach is split by the Mo'ikeha Canal, which does not have a pedestrian crossing. Take Niu Road *makai*, one block north of the ABC store.

Keālia Beach

Location: One-half mile north of Kapa'a, at mile marker 10

Coordinates: N22° 05.90', W159° 18.30'

Length: 0.7 miles
Facilities: None

Driving north from Kapa'a, right after the scenic overlook, you will see the long and wide curve of golden sand that is Keālia Beach. Kapa'a Stream crosses the beach at the south end, and a rocky point and the remains of a jetty define its north end. Powerful waves rolling down the island's northeast coast break onto an offshore sandbar at Keālia. This feature attracts many surfers and bodyboarders. Most of them will congregate at the north end of the beach where the best waves are usually found. During periods of high surf, rip currents are powerful along this beach. Many drownings and near-drownings have occurred here.

Keālia means "salt land," because of the shallow ponds formed behind the beach from high surf and high tides. Salt was an important commodity to the Hawaiians, who harvested the accumulated salt deposits to use for flavoring of poi and preserving fish. Every Hawaiian island has an area named Keālia.

Donkey Beach

Location: Two miles north of Kapa'a
Coordinates: N22° 06.89', W159° 17.81'
Length: 0.3 miles
Facilities: None

Sugar plantations once utilized donkeys and mules to haul seed cane and fertilizer into the fields where plantation workers would plant the cane and spread the fertilizer by hand. The Līhu'e Plantation Company kept a herd of donkeys and mules in the pasture behind the beach north of Palikū Point, thus giving the beach its name. To reach this isolated beach, you must follow a trail for a quarter mile across a cane field. The trail begins at the Kūhiō Highway, at the emergency call box seven-tenths of a mile north of mile marker 11. As the trail approaches the ocean, follow it to the right to find Donkey Beach. You may be sharing the trail with dirt bikers.

Ocean conditions there are too treacherous for safe swimming. The foreshore is steep, causing a strong backwash. You may see experienced surfers challenging the powerful rip currents and pounding shorebreak. The beach's soft sand, sunny conditions, and isolated location make it popular for nude sunbathing.

The Līhu'e Plantation Company has sold its land behind the beach and it's not clear yet if the new owners of the residential subdivision will continue to allow public access to Donkey Beach. Also, some island residents object to public nudity, which is illegal in Hawai'i. On rare occasions, police have issued citations to nude sunbathers here. Kaua'i's mayor has even ventured to Donkey Beach to personally chastise the naked beachgoers.

Anahola Beach Park

Location: In the town of Anahola
Coordinates: N22° 08.78', W159° 18.07'
Length: 0.6 miles
Facilities: Bathrooms, showers, lifeguard, picnic tables, camping

The east-coast town of Anahola is populated mainly with people of Hawaiian descent. Anahola Beach Park can be busy on weekends, with local residents enjoying picnics and swimming. On weekdays it may be nearly deserted. The beach covers the south half of Anahola Bay, extending more than half a mile west of Kahala Point to the mouth of Anahola Stream. A small reef protects the beach in the lee of Kahala Point. The reef ends at the ruins of a century-old landing. This is the only area of the beach safe for swimming. A shorebreak on the sandbar west of the old landing attracts bodyboarders and surfers.

To find the park, turn *makai* at Anahola Road, between mile markers 13 and 14 on the Kūhiō Highway. Turn left at Poha Road for an entrance to the beach or continue on Anahola Road to the park, seven-tenths of a mile from the highway.

'Aliomanu Beach

Location: North of Anahola Bay
Coordinates: N22° 09.05', W159° 18.38' (south end)
Length: 1.5 miles
Facilities: None

This narrow beach begins at Anahola Stream and ends at the sea cliffs forming Pāpa'a Bay. Swimming conditions are not good here and snorkeling is safe only when the ocean is very calm. The wide fringing reef along the beach brings out the locals for pole and throw-net fishing and for seaweed harvesting.

The beach may be approached from 'Aliomanu Road, just north of mile marker 14. A parking area is six-tenths of a mile from the highway. 'Aliomanu Road continues north behind the beach but ends at a bridge washout. The other part of 'Aliomanu Road connects again with the Kūhiō Highway north of mile marker 15.

Pāpa'a Bay

Location: Below newly developed 'Aliomanu Estates
Coordinates: N22° 10.37', W159° 18.84'
Length: 250 yards
Facilities: None

Pāpa'a Bay is a small, secluded bay backed by a 120-foot-high sea cliff. A shallow reef runs across the bay with a channel cutting through the center. When the surf is low, the near-shore waters offer good swimming and the reef offers good snorkeling opportunities. Hawaiians use the bay for spearfishing and throw-net fishing. When the surf is up, waves roll over the reef and create a dangerous rip current in the channel.

To find this picturesque little beach, turn *makai* on Pāpa'a Road, six-tenths of a mile north of mile marker 15. Pāpa'a Road turns to the right in three-tenths of a mile. A blue and white beach access sign points to the left, past the new housing sites of 'Aliomanu Estates. At the end of the road the beach is partially visible on the shoreline to the north. A steep trail leads down to the beach. A tenth of a mile to the south is a parking area and another beach trail. This trail leads down to the north end of 'Aliomanu Beach.

North Shore Beaches

Moloa'a Bay

Location: Kaua'i's northeast corner
Coordinates: N22° 11.64', W159° 19.99'
Length: 0.6 miles
Facilities: None

When sea conditions are calm and the sky is sunny, the beach at Moloaʻa Bay presents a beautiful sight. The golden-sand beach curves around the half-moon-shaped bay filled with turquoise water. Moloaʻa Stream flows through the center of the bay. Bluffs, 200 feet high, terminate at both entrances to the bay. Beachrock protrudes at the north end of the beach, which is exposed to the surf rolling in from the ocean. Windblown debris accumulates in this part of the bay, making it a good place for beachcombing. The south side of the bay is calmer and partially protected by a reef. When the surf is high, a rip current runs from the south side, along the shorebreak, and then out the center of the bay. This rip current has been responsible for many drowning and near-drownings.

This lovely beach is not well known to visitors. A few homes line the back of the beach south of the stream. To find Moloaʻa Bay, turn *makai* onto Koʻolau Road between mile markers 16 and 17 of the Kūhiō Highway. After 1.2 miles, follow Moloaʻa Road to the right. At the end of the road is a beach access sign pointing left.

Larsen's Beach

Location: *Makai* of Koʻolau Road
Coordinates: N22° 12.25', W159° 20.17'
Length: 0.9 miles
Facilities: None

Larsen's Beach is named in honor of L. David Larsen, the former manager of Kīlauea Sugar Plantation, who had a beach house there. The beach is a straight, narrow ribbon of coarse sand, with several outcroppings of beach rock. Cattle pasture covers the hill behind Larsen's Beach. Shells and glass balls litter the beach, making it a good beachcombing spot. Seaweed of the *limu kohu* variety is harvested from the shallow reef offshore.

Swimming conditions at Larsen's are poor and dangerous. The offshore bottom is shallow and rocky. A channel through the reef, situated in front of Pākalā Point, allows a very fast rip current to flow back to the sea. The channel is visible from the top of the trail as you approach the beach.

West of Pākalā Point are two pockets of sand, the last being on the east side of Kepuhi Point. A colony of wedge-tailed shearwaters lives at the point. Also watch for the frigate bird or man-of-war bird. In Hawaiian, this seagoing bird with a wingspan that can reach 7 feet, is called ʻiwa. The ʻiwa feeds by forcing smaller fishing birds to regurgitate their catch, which it then scoops up in midair. Hawaiians would use the word ʻiwa figuratively to mean a thief.

To find Larsen's Beach from the south, turn off the Kūhiō Highway between mile markers 16 and 17 onto Koʻolau Road. The road immediately turns left and in 1.2 miles you'll reach an intersection with Moloaʻa Road. Keep to the left until you have traveled 2.3 miles from the highway. Take a hard right onto a dirt road. If you see a small cemetery, you have driven too far and missed the turnoff. The correct road has a white "Beach Access" signpost. Follow this road of deep-red dirt nine-tenths of mile to its end. A trail leads down to the beach from there. If you are approaching from the north, turn onto Koʻolau Road where it meets the Kūhiō Highway at mile marker 20. From there, it is 1.2 miles to the red dirt road to the beach.

Pīlaʻa Beach

Location: Three-quarters of a mile west of Kepuhi Point

Coordinates: N22° 12.68', W159° 21.53' and N22° 12.69', W159° 21.84'

Length: 250 yards each

Facilities: None

Pīla'a Beach is actually two sections of sand divided by a rocky point. The eastern section is protected somewhat by Kepuhi Point. A stream crosses the western section of sand. A wide reef extends from Kepuhi Point to Kīlauea Bay, 2 miles to the west. During calm conditions, the western section has a couple of sandy bottom areas that are good for swimming. The outer section of the reef has a channel that is a major drainage point for the reef. A powerful rip current runs through this channel during periods of high surf. It is visible from the access trail on the hill to the west. The reef in front of Pīla'a and the rocky shoreline west of the beach are popular with experienced snorkelers and spearfishers.

The property behind Pīla'a is privately owned and there is no direct right-of-way to the beach. Both pockets of sand can be seen from the hill to the west. A trail from the base of the hill leads over the rocky shoreline to the west section of the beach. The trail drops 180 feet in elevation and is about a half mile long. See the description of Waiakalua Iki beach for directions to the trail.

Waiakalua Iki Beach

Location: One-half mile east of Kīlauea Bay

Coordinates: N22° 12.92', W159° 22.29'

Length: 0.2 miles

Facilities: None

Waiakalua Iki Beach is the eastern part of two isolated beaches. The western and smaller part is Waiakalua Nui Beach. The beach is narrow on the east end and widens on the west, where the Waiakalua Stream flows from the valley behind. The near-shore bottom has some sandy spots but generally isn't good for swimming. The Kapinao *heiau* is visible above the beach, but it is on private land and not accessible.

Chances are good that you will be the only visitor on the beach. Its isolated location and fresh-water stream sometimes attract people who unofficially call the area home. To find this beautiful stretch of shoreline, turn onto North Waiakalua Road, eight-tenths of a mile past the Kūhiō Highway's mile marker 20. Follow the paved road for seven-tenths of a mile to the end, then turn left onto a dirt road that leads three-tenths of a mile to the trail. From the trailhead you can see Pīla'a Beach to the right. It takes 5 minutes to descend the steep dirt trail. Make sure you haven't left valuables in your car. At the bottom of the trail, the approach to Pīla'a Beach is over the boulders to the right. The Waiakalua beaches are to the left.

Waiakalua Nui Beach

Location: One-quarter mile east of Kīlauea Bay

Coordinates: N22° 12.98', W159° 22.49'

Length: 200 yards

Facilities: None

Waiakalua Nui Beach is on the other side of the rocky point that marks the western end of Waiakalua Iki Beach. The beach is wide and sandy, with beachrock cropping up in the offshore water. Swimming conditions are poor here. A deep and narrow valley behind the beach isolates it from the rest of the island. After rainy periods, a stream will flow across the beach.

Kāhili Beach

Location: On Kīlauea Bay

Coordinates: N22° 13.05', W159° 23.08'

Length: 0.2 miles

Facilities: None

Kāhili Beach lines the back of Kīlauea Bay to the east of the mouth of Kīlauea Stream. The west end of the beach has patches of coral reef offshore. The waves breaking over the reef here attract surfers. A wide, shallow reef protects the east end of the beach, which is popular for throw-net and pole fishing. Swimming is not suggested here unless the surf is calm. Rip currents run back through the gaps in the west reef. False kamani and ironwood trees grow in the sand dunes behind the beach.

The easiest approach to Kāhili Beach will bring you to the east end. From the Kūhiō Highway, turn onto North Wailapa Road, which is six-tenths of a mile past mile marker 21, but doesn't have a sign. Follow the paved road for half a mile and then take the left fork onto a dirt road. After another half mile this road ends at the beach. The west end of the beach can be reached by turning right, off Kīlauea Road, three-quarters of a mile from the highway. A badly rutted dirt road will end 1.4 miles later on the banks of Kīlauea Stream, next to an abandoned quarry. The stream must be crossed to reach the beach.

Kauapea (Secret) Beach

Location: West of Kīlauea Point National Wildlife Refuge

Coordinates: N22° 13.39', W159° 24.97'

Length: 0.8 miles

Facilities: None

Kauapea Beach is commonly called Secret Beach locally. Its informal name came from its seclusion and its difficulty to find. An improved access road makes it a little easier to find now and it's certainly worth the effort. The large beach is great for taking long walks while taking in the sights of the pounding surf, small springs trickling down the cliffs behind the beach, and Kīlauea Point to the east. Winter surf will prevent swimming, but it is possible during especially calm days in the summer. You will likely come across unofficial campers and nude sunbathers at Secret Beach. Both activities are illegal but not enforced enough to become a serious deterrent.

Turn off the Kūhiō Highway 100 yards before mile marker 24 onto the first Kalihiwai Road. The road immediately bends to the left. Take the dirt road cut into the hill on the right and follow it three-tenths of a mile to a parking area. The beach trail follows the barbed wire fence before turning down the hill. It takes 7 minutes to walk down to the beach.

Kalihiwai Beach

Location: On the eastern half of Kalihiwai Bay

Coordinates: N22° 13.02', W159° 25.59'

Length: 0.2 miles

Facilities: Picnic tables

The beach at Kalihiwai Bay is widest at its western end, where the Kalihiwai River meets the ocean, and narrows to a point where it becomes a boulder beach at the base of a sea cliff.

Surfers ride the steep and fast waves that break close to the cliff. A grove of tall ironwood trees lines the backshore, providing for shaded places to park your car. Swimming conditions are dangerous during periods of high surf, with a pounding shorebreak and strong rip currents. During calm, summer conditions the swimming is pleasant.

Take the first Kalihiwai Road from the Kūhiō Highway and follow it past the "Dead End" sign for one mile. The road ends at Kalihiwai River. The remnants of a bridge wiped out by a tsunami in 1957 remain on the river. On the other side of the river, Kalihiwai Road picks up again and returns to the highway.

'Anini Beach Park

Location: Between Kalihiwai Bay and Princeville
Coordinates: N22° 13.43', W159° 26.75'
Length: 2.2 miles
Facilities: Picnic shelters, bathrooms, showers, camping

The near-shore waters of 'Anini Beach are as calm as you'll find anywhere on Kaua'i. This is due to the protection of a fringing reef that follows the shoreline for 2 miles and broadens to 1,600 feet offshore at its widest point. The reef extends from Kalihiwai Bay to the cliffs of Princeville. A sandy bottom covers the shallow near-shore area, making it a good place for children to swim. The shallow water and wide reef offers excellent snorkeling. A channel in the reef is visible from shore at the west end. During periods of high surf, the rip current that flows through the channel out to the ocean can be dangerous.

'Anini Beach Park is situated midway along the beach. It's a popular place for picnics, camping and fishing. Across the road from the beach is the playing field for the Kaua'i Polo Club, which holds polo matches on Sunday afternoons in the summer.

The first road sign here read Wanini. Irate because of a misspelling, born and raised Hanalei resident Walter Sanborn shot the *W* off the sign with his shotgun. After that incident, people starting calling the beach 'Anini, even though the sign misspelled its true name, Wainini, which means "spilled water."

To reach 'Anini Beach, take the second Kalihiwai Road, between mile markers 25 and 26 on the Kūhiō Highway. Drive left at the fork in the road towards the "No Outlet" sign. The road follows the back of the beach, taking you past several large homes, some of which are getaways for celebrities.

Sealodge Beach

Location: Princeville
Coordinates: N22° 13.74', W159° 28.65'
Length: 100 yards
Facilities: None

This lovely pocket of coarse sand is located in a cove at the base of a sea cliff, near the Sealodge condominiums. The beach is protected by the same reef that extends from 'Anini Beach. Swimming conditions here are fair because the ocean bottom is shallow and rocky. False kamani trees line the backshores and the exposed roots of hala trees can be seen clinging to the cliff overhead.

There are two points of entry from Princeville to the beach. The trails from both these points converge into one steep trail, which winds through thickets of Java plum, guava and Christmasberry trees. One path begins behind Building A of the Sealodge condominiums. The other is to the west at the end of Keoniana Road. It starts at the paved driveway to the left of house no. 3583. The walk down will take about 15 minutes and will be slippery if it has been raining. You also will have to scramble over large boulders at the trail's end.

Pali Ke Kua Beach

Location: Princeville
Coordinates: N22° 13.39', W159° 29.71'
Length: 100 yards and 250 yards
Facilities: None

Pali Ke Kua Beach is two pockets of sand divided by a rocky point and is sometimes called Hideaways. The eastern pocket is below the Pali Ke Kua condominiums. A trail leads down to the beach from the condominiums but there is no public right-of-way. The western beach is below the Puʻu Pōā condominiums. A trail begins between Puʻu Pōā and a public parking lot that can accommodate only nine cars. The trail is very steep and can be treacherous when it is wet and muddy. Steps and handrails help your descent for the first half of the trail.

Once reached, the beach is lovely, with a view of Makana peak (Bali Hai) to the west. Patches of reef protect the beach but high surf will still make its way to the shore. The surf break is good enough here to entice surfers to lug their boards down the precipitous trail. Hawaiian monk seals come ashore here to rest. Remember, federal law prevents anyone from getting closer than 100 feet to them or bothering this endangered species in any way.

Puʻu Pōā Beach

Location: Princeville
Coordinates: N22° 13.16', W159° 29.89'
Length: 150 yards
Facilities: Showers and bathrooms for guests of Princeville Hotel

Primarily guests of the luxurious Princeville Hotel use this beach. Guests may use the hotel's elevator to descend the hill to the beach; others will have to follow the steps that start near the hotel's gatehouse.

The beach is on the east shore of Hanalei Bay, extending from the north bank of the Hanalei River to the hotel. Kayakers, outrigger canoe paddlers, surfers, snorkelers, and boaters fill a beautiful scene; backdropped by the peaks of Puʻu Ka Manu across the bay, and Makana, three and a half miles behind that. Swimming is difficult at Puʻu Pōā because of an irregular ocean bottom strewn with rocks and coral.

Hanalei Bay

Location: Town of Hanalei
Length: 2 miles

Hanalei Bay is an almost perfectly shaped crescent incised from the heart of Kauaʻi's north shore. In Hawaiian, Hanalei means "crescent bay." A beautiful sandy beach lines the bay for 2 miles. In a recent poll, readers of *Hawaiʻi* magazine picked Hanalei Bay as Hawaiʻi's best beach. Although the bay is a continuous stretch of sand, it is traditionally segmented into four areas: Black Pot, Pavilion, Waiʻoli, and Waikoko.

Black Pot Beach Park

Coordinates: N22° 12.82', W159° 29.83'
Facilities: Picnic tables, bathrooms, telephone, camping

Black Pot Beach is situated on the east side of Hanalei Bay, between the Hanalei River and the pier. It was given its name because Hanalei residents used to keep a large, black, iron cooking pot there for use during large community social gatherings. That tradition continues today; the pot is gone, but many residents gather at the beach for picnics and parties. Recreational boaters use the small boat ramp at the mouth of the Hanalei River. The pier is used regularly for fishing and is a fine place for a scenic stroll and photographic opportunities, especially at sunset. Diving is not allowed off the pier. To reach Black Pot Beach and the pier, turn *makai* off the highway at Hanalei and then right onto Weke Road, following it to its end.

Hanalei Pavilion Beach Park

Coordinates: N22° 12.42', W159° 29.90'

Facilities: Picnic shelter, bathrooms, telephone, lifeguard

South of the Hanalei pier, a concrete picnic shelter and bathrooms occupy a beachfront lot neighbored by large homes. In the summer months, the water in front of the pavilion is calm and safe for swimming. The beach has a sandy bottom and a very gentle slope. Winter brings high surf, which attracts experienced surfers but can create unsafe swimming conditions onshore. The pavilion can be reached from Weke Road.

Wai'oli Beach Park

Coordinates: N22° 12.18', W159° 30.21'

Facilities: Bathrooms, showers, lifeguard, volleyball nets

Wai'oli Beach Park anchors the south end of Hanalei Bay, near the mouth of Wai'oli Stream.

The beach is lined with tall ironwood trees, which lend it the botanically incorrect nickname of "Pinetrees." Being half-moon shaped, the bay directs the advancing surf towards its center and Wai'oli Beach. Swimming is safer here during the calmer summer months while the surfers are out enjoying the surf breaks of Wai'oli (which means joyful water) in the winter. Wai'oli Beach Park can be found by turning *makai* from Weke Road onto either He'e or 'Ama'ama Roads.

Waikoko Beach

Coordinates: N22° 12.28', W159° 30.86'

Facilities: None

Waikoko Beach includes the westernmost section of Hanalei Bay. The reef extending from Makahoa Point, marking the bay's western entrance, provides swimmers with some protection. The sandy beach narrows as it traces the shoreline west from Waipā Stream. Waikoko Beach can be entered from a roadside turnout next to the four-mile marker.

Lumaha'i Beach

Location: One-half mile west of Hanalei Bay

Coordinates: N22° 12.86', W159° 31.23' (east end); N22° 12.98', W159° 31.91' (west end)

Length: 0.8 miles

Facilities: **None**

Lumahaʻi is a wild and beautiful beach where powerful surf crashes unimpeded on its steeply sloped foreshore. Vegetation-covered cliffs and Highway 560, 150 feet above, back the wide beach. No tourist brochure will pass up the opportunity to point out that Lumahaʻi Beach was the locale for the scene in *South Pacific* where Mitzi Gaynor "wash(ed) that man right out of my hair." There is an east entrance and a west entrance to Lumahaʻi. The east entrance is via a trail that descends from a roadside pullout, just before the five-mile marker. Lava-rock outcroppings at this end of the beach provide some protection for swimmers when the surf is relatively calm. When the surf is high, which is most of the year, Lumahaʻi becomes literally a killer beach. Every year, drownings occur here. The ocean waves hit the beach hard and the bottom drops off quickly. The steep foreshore creates a powerful backwash that pushes strong swimmers away from land. Drowning victims have included not only swimmers, but sightseers who have been knocked down by surging surf sweeping across the beach or by being swept off the lava point.

The west end of the beach is marked by the Lumahaʻi River and can be easily reached from a parking area under a grove of ironwood trees, just before the highway crosses the river. Flash floods from heavy rains higher in the valley can cause the river's depth to rise dangerously in a matter of minutes. But, in spite of its dangers, the beauty of Lumahaʻi Beach contributed to its being voted "Hawaiʻi's Most Romantic Beach" by readers of *Hawaiʻi* magazine.

Wainiha Beach

Location: **On Wainiha Bay**
Coordinates: N22° 12.90', W159° 32.52'

Length: 0.2 miles
Facilities: **None**

At Highway 560's seven-mile marker you will drive by the beach at Wainiha Bay. No fringing reef protects the bay, so the beach is subjected to a powerful shorebreak. Swimming is dangerous here at any time of the year.

Kepuhi Beach

Location: **In front of Hanalei Colony Resort**
Coordinates: N22° 13.27', W159° 32.67'
Length: **1 mile**
Facilities: **None**

A shallow reef fronts much of Kepuhi Beach with deep channels running through it. High surf rolling over the reef creates strong rip currents of water flowing back to the ocean through the channels. These rip currents make for dangerous swimming along Kepuhi Point. The Hanalei Colony Resort is situated at Kepuhi Beach and many of their guests enjoy beachcombing the long stretch of sand. The easiest point of entry to the beach is at the Hanalei Colony Resort, halfway between mile markers seven and eight of Highway 560.

Tunnels Beach

Location: **Behind the half-moon-shaped reef of Hāʻena Point**

Coordinates: N22° 13.54', W159° 33.56'

Length: 0.7 miles

Facilities: None

Tunnels Beach tied with O'ahu's Hanauma Bay as Hawai'i's best snorkeling beach in a reader's poll by *Hawai'i* magazine. Surfers, windsurfers, and divers also favor this site. The large, horseshoe-shaped reef has an outer and an inner section with a channel between them running east to west. Snorkelers can float above abundant sea life and coral formations in the inner reef that extends right up to the shore. Divers head out to the deeper channel where underwater arches and tunnels await—hence, the beach's name. Also contributing to its name is the tunnel-shaped surfing break created over the outer reef. High winter surf can break through to the inner reef, keeping snorkelers out of the water.

The setting for Tunnels Beach is especially beautiful. Fluted, green mountains descend to the white sand of Hā'ena Beach to the west. Behind them, Makana Peak, the famed "Bali Hai," rises above jagged spires.

Tunnels is a popular area with few parking spots. The closest right-of-way from the Highway 560 is four-tenths of a mile past the eight-mile marker. Another access is two-tenths of a mile to the west. If both of these options are full, you can park at Hā'ena State Park and walk back along the beach.

Hā'ena Beach Park

Location: In front of Hā'ena Dry Cave

Coordinates: N22° 13.23', W159° 33.97'

Length: 0.7 miles

Facilities: Bathrooms, showers, picnic tables, camping

Tunnels Beach continues uninterrupted to the west to become Hā'ena Beach. Behind the beach are Hā'ena Beach Park, a large parking lot, and the Maniniholo Dry Cave (see North Shore Sights chapter). The large reef that protects Tunnels Beach stops at Hā'ena Beach, leaving the shore exposed to the hard-hitting surf. During periods of high surf, a pounding shorebreak, a strong backwash, and powerful rip currents make for hazardous water conditions. A shallow reef on the west end of the beach creates a surfing break locally called Cannons. The breaking of the hollow waves can shoot out a blast of compressed air and spray, which early surfers in the area likened to the firing of a cannon. Behind the nearly white sand of the wide beach is a county campground. A concession truck is usually set up in the parking lot.

Kē'ē Beach

Location: At the north end of Highway 560 and the beginning of the Nā Pali Trail

Coordinates: N22° 13.27', W159° 34.98'

Length: 0.4 miles

Facilities: Bathrooms, showers, telephone

When you can't drive any further on Highway 560, you've arrived at Kē'ē Beach. This small beach, with its lagoon and reef, is a real gem. The large reef ends at the beginning of the Nā Pali coastline and creates a shallow lagoon with calm water and a sandy bottom. Abundant reef fish, such as wrasse, butterflyfish, damselfish, goatfish, convictfish and surgeonfish populate the reef and clear water. A sandy beach with outcroppings of shelf rock continues around Ka'ilio Point to the north. Take a walk north along the beach to the point and you are treated to a view of the Nā Pali coastline. Here, channels in the reef create dangerous rip currents. Swimmers and snorkelers should stay in the protected area in front of the parking lot.

Next to the cliffs, at the western end of the reef, a channel allows a rip current to flow out to sea. This rip current has claimed the lives of snorkelers who have ventured too far past the reef. In the winter, high surf may roll over the reef, spoiling the calm conditions for swimmers and snorkelers. At low tide, especially in the summer when the ocean is calm, the reef is exposed enough to allow people to walk over it. The far side of the reef is a dangerous place to swim even when the ocean is calm. A strong current flows past the reef towards the Nā Pali coast.

The question of liability has kept lifeguards off Kē'ē for years. Kē'ē is a state-operated beach. The state historically has not placed lifeguards at its beach parks. The county of Kaua'i is allowed to place lifeguards at a state beach but it becomes vulnerable to lawsuits if it does so. Unlike the state, however, the county is not immune to lawsuits and county officials feel they cannot expose their taxpayers to this risk. Strangely enough, by virtue of state Act 90, the county and state are relieved of liability as long as they post strong current and dangerous shore break signs at their beaches.

This is a very popular beach and in recent years parking has become a problem. The dirt parking lot, which also is used by hikers starting on the Kalalau Trail, fills quickly. You need to arrive early to find a spot in the lot or be lucky enough to find someone leaving. Additional parking is available in Hā'ena State Park, just before the wet caves, about a half mile from the beach.

Nā Pali Beaches

Hanakāpī'ai Beach

Location: Two miles from the start of the Nā Pali Trail

Coordinates: N22° 12.51', W159° 35.89'

Length: 200 yards

Facilities: Camping

Hanakāpī'ai Beach is the first of two beaches accessible by foot on the Kalalau Trail. The hike, which begins at Kē'ē Beach will take most people one-and-a-half hours to reach Hanakāpī'ai. This is a popular area for many day hikers to enjoy and rest before heading back to the start of the Kalalau Trail. The trail continues for a grueling 9 miles, not returning to the ocean until it ends at Kalalau Beach.

In summer months, the large boulders of Hanakāpī'ai Beach are covered with sand. During the winter months, high surf storms the beach, completely eroding the sand covering the boulders.

While it looks inviting, especially after a strenuous hike in hot weather, the beach and water at Hanakāpī'ai are very hazardous places. Do not go into the ocean here. More drownings occur here than at any other beach on Kaua'i. Over the last three decades this beach has averaged a drowning every year. This is in spite of it receiving far fewer visitors than more accessible beaches and its sand disappearing in the winter. A strong current flows across the beach, sweeping swimmers and even waders away from shore and to their deaths. In 1996, a man from Arizona tried to pick up an empty bottle in waist-deep water and was swept out to sea. In 1997, a native of Texas got caught in the current while swimming in shallow water and drowned in the struggle to reach shore. There are no lifeguards or telephones in this remote area. By the time a message for help reaches the fire department rescuers in Hanalei, it will likely be too late.

Kalalau Beach

Location: At the end of the Kalalau Trail, 11 miles from its start

Coordinates: N22° 10.36', W159° 39.56'

Length: 0.5 miles

Facilities: Camping

The long and wide beach at Kalalau Valley is backed by low, vegetated sand dunes. At the west end of the beach, seasonal depositing of sand makes sea caves accessible by foot. Even with its remote location, Kalalau Beach is frequently visited. During the summer, when the trail to the valley carries most of its hikers, the beach attracts many swimmers. Although the ocean may appear calm, caution is still needed. A shallow sandbar runs parallel to the beach but drops off quickly to overhead depths. Currents generated by trade winds run along the length of the beach.

In the winter, high surf assaults the beach, erodes the shoreline, and carries the sand away from the sea caves. The surf creates backwashes and rip currents and the sandbar endures a pounding shorebreak. Remember, this is a wilderness park without lifeguards or rangers to look out for swimmers who don't heed the dangerous conditions.

Honopū Beach

Location: One-half mile west of Kalalau Beach

Coordinates: N22° 10.04', W159° 40.06'

Length: 0.4 miles

Facilities: None

Honopū Beach sits picturesquely at the base of a high sea cliff just half a mile down the coast from Kalalau Beach. A thick wall of lava divides the beach into two pockets. Wave action on the wall has carved an arch in the lava rock, 65 feet high and 200 feet wide, joining the two pockets of sand. Helicopter tour companies invariably point out the beach and its landmark arch. Helicopters are not allowed to land at Honopū and there is no trail to the beach. The only access is from the sea. Kayakers often stop at Honopū as they paddle along the Nā Pali coast.

Nu'alolo Kai Beach

Location: Between Alapi'i Pt. and Makuaiki Pt. on the Nā Pali coastline

Coordinates: N22° 09.54', W159° 42.04'

Length: 0.5 miles

Facilities: None

Nu'alolo Kai is a long, narrow beach lined with beachrock at the water's edge. It occupies a narrow coastal flat bounded by steep sea cliffs.

A reef extends 600 feet from the beach. A deep channel penetrates the reef, allowing boats to bring in snorkelers and divers. At the turn of the twentieth century a small Hawaiian fishing village was located here. Its residents deserted the remote valley and beach for other parts of the island, leaving only a few ruins and a *heiau*. There is no land route to Nu'alolo Kai Beach.

Miloli'i Beach

Location: Last westward beach on the Nā Pali coastline
Coordinates: N22° 09.07', W159° 43.09'
Length: 0.5 miles
Facilities: Portable toilets, picnic shelter, camping

Miloli'i Beach is the last of the remote beaches in Nā Pali Coast State Park. The Nā Pali coast ends at Polihale beach, 4 miles to the southwest. As is the case with the two beaches up the coast, Miloli'i is accessible only by boat. This beach once hosted a fishing village, but the residents vacated the coastal flat and the valley behind a century ago. During periods of calm seas, the fringing coral reef of Miloli'i affords excellent snorkeling opportunities. Boat access to the beach is via a narrow channel blasted out of the reef. Beach sand generally erodes from winter's high surf and accretes during the summer.

South Side Beaches

Kīpū Kai Beach

Location: South of Hoary Head Ridge
Coordinates: N21° 54.69', W159° 23.36'
Length: 0.7 miles
Facilities: None

The Hā'upu Range, or Hoary Head Ridge, isolates Kīpū Kai from Hule'ia Stream and Līhu'e to the north. The land in the valley behind the Hā'upu Range has been operated as a cattle ranch for many years. The last owner of the land was John T. Waterhouse, who died in 1984. He bequeathed the land to the state of Hawai'i with the hope that it would be used as a nature and wildlife preserve. The bequest doesn't take effect however, until the end of the lifetimes of his nieces and nephew. For now, all the land behind Kīpū Kai Beach is private, and the dirt road over the ridge is gated.

Boat tour companies occasionally institute tours departing from Nāwiliwili Harbor, taking passengers around Kawai Point to Kīpū Kai Beach. Kīpū Kai has four pockets of sand. The longest pocket curves around at its eastern end to form a protected cove for swimming, snorkeling, and anchoring boats. Prevailing currents and the trade winds sweep debris around this corner, making the beach an excellent place for beachcombing.

Māhā'ulepū Beach

Location: Two miles northeast of Po'ipū

Length: 1.5 miles

East of Po'ipū, at the end of a cane haul road, is a mile-and-a-half reach of beautiful and interesting shoreline called Māhā'ulepū Beach. The coastline consists of three areas, Gillin's Beach, Kawailoa Bay and Ha'ula Beach, which are described individually. The area is noted for hosting a catalog of interesting geological features: lithified sand dunes, caves, wave-cut terraces, coral formations, sea cliffs, and a small sea stack.

Archaeological evidence indicates that the area was once well populated in the pre-contact era. The fertile land of the inland valley, in conjunction with the bountiful fishing grounds near shore, would have made Māhā'ulepū an ideal area for habitation. Grove Farm planted the land behind the sand dunes in sugar cane until they closed their Kaua'i sugar operations. Attempts have been made at growing other agricultural products on the land. The fate of undeveloped Māhā'ulepū now lies in the hands of its new owner, Steve Case, founder of AOL.

To find the beaches at Māhā'ulepū, drive past the Hyatt Regency and Po'ipū Bay Golf Course on a dirt road for 1.8 miles. Turn right at the stop sign and follow the bumpy road to a gate. The gate has a sign indicating it is open 7:30 a.m. to 7:00 p.m. Likely, no one will be attending the gate and you may continue to the parking area for Gillin's Beach, seven-tenths of a mile from the stop sign. The road turns to the left at the parking area and leads to Kawailoa Bay and Ha'ula Beach.

Gillin's Beach

Coordinates: N21° 53.33', W 159° 24.90'

Length: 0.4 miles

Facilities: None

From the parking area at Gillin's Beach, follow the path through a dense thicket of trees for a few yards to reach the shore.

Gillin's Beach was named for the long-time engineering supervisor of the Grove Farm Company, the owners of the sugar plantation behind the beach. Gillin was best known for supervising the construction of the Hā'upu Tunnel. The half-mile-long, dirt-lined tunnel cuts through the ridge to provide direct access between the sugar cane fields north of the ridge and the Kōloa Mill to the south.

Broken patches of beachrock protrude through the sand covering the crescent of Gillin's Beach. Vegetated sand dunes back the beach as well as the original house built by Elbert Gillin in the 1920s. Boogie boarding and windsurfing are popular recreational activities on this beach.

Kawailoa Bay

Coordinates: N21° 52.53', W159° 24.66'

Length: 200 yards

Facilities: None

Follow the dirt road east from Gillin's Beach for three-tenths of a mile to find Kawailoa Bay. Often there are local families here for picnics and fishing. The shoreline is covered with active and lithified sand dunes. Waves have deeply undercut the sea cliffs below the dunes. A small mushroom-shaped sea stack projects above a shallow reef next to the outer point.

Ha'ula Beach

Coordinates: N21° 53.93', W159° 24.23'

Length: 200 yards

Facilities: None

Follow the dirt road four-tenths of a mile from Kawailoa Bay to the entrance to Ha'ula Beach. The trail to the beach takes about 5 minutes to walk and is marked by two metal posts that stop vehicle traffic.

The small pocket beach sits at the center of a large cove, with a low, flat, rock shelf fronting the rest of the beach. Behind the beach are the highest sand dunes on the south shore. Adding to the rugged beauty of the area, waves have cut jagged edges, spires, and caves into the lithified dunes and sea cliffs.

The rocky offshore bottom and surf preclude swimming in the cove. This shoreline is prized for its beauty and solitude. The beach is occasionally visited by fishermen, trail riders from CJM Stables, and Hawaiian monk seals looking for a quiet place to rest.

Shipwreck Beach

Location: In front of Hyatt Regency Kaua'i Resort

Coordinates: N21° 52.48', W159° 26.24'

Length: 0.4 miles

Facilities: Lifeguard, showers, bathrooms

The wide sandy beach in front of the Hyatt Regency sees some of the island's best boogie boarding and bodysurfing conditions. The best surf breaks are at the east end of the beach. High surf and a pounding shorebreak make conditions difficult for novice oceangoers.

The shipwreck that gave the beach its name is long gone. An unidentified wooden boat lay at the water's edge for many years, scavenged by people for firewood. In 1982, Hurricane Iwa ravaged the south coast of Kaua'i and destroyed the remains of the shipwreck. The Hawaiian name of the beach is Keoneloa, which means "the long sands."

The much-photographed Makawehi Point, a high bluff of lithified sand dunes, marks the eastern end of the beach. Pole fishermen use the bluff, as do some reckless cliff divers. Public access to the beach is at the end of Ainako Road, between the Hyatt Regency and the Po'ipū Bay Golf Course. The road ends at a paved parking lot. Public bathrooms and showers are located next to the parking lot.

Brennecke Beach

Location: One-tenth of a mile east of Po'ipū Beach

Coordinates: N21° 52.38', W159° 27.09'

Length: 50 yards

Facilities: None

Brennecke Beach is just a small pocket of sand in a cove east of Po'ipū Beach. It is a popular boogie boarding and bodysurfing site. Long surfboards and boards with fins are not allowed here because of congestion from the large number of wave-riding enthusiasts trying to use the small area. The beach suffered severe damage from Hurricane 'Iniki. Kaua'i County hired an engineering firm to restore the beach and protect it from further erosion. They removed an old cement sea wall, creating more beach area for recreation and improving the wave patterns so that sand now moves to the beach instead of being swept away. A 250-foot-long revetment was constructed next to Ho'ōne Road, which was threatened by beach erosion. Several truckloads of sand were brought to the site to speed up the natural recovery.

The beach's namesake, Dr. Marvin Brennecke, owned a home across the road from the sea wall. Brennecke came to Kaua'i in 1931 and worked as a plantation doctor on Kaua'i for 40 years.

Po'ipū Beach Park

Location: End of Ho'owili Road, south of Po'ipū Road

Coordinates: N21° 52.40', W159° 27.27'

Length: 0.2 miles

Facilities: Bathrooms, showers, picnic shelters, lifeguard, telephone, playground

Po'ipū Beach is the south shore's most popular beach for visitors. A recent poll of readers of *Hawai'i* magazine picked Po'ipū Beach as Kaua'i's Best Beach and Hawai'i's Best Kid's Beach. When clouds and rain threaten elsewhere on Kaua'i, the most likely place for fair weather is the heart of the south shore, which has earned its moniker of "Sunny Po'ipū." This is likely to be the island's busiest beach, especially on weekends and holidays, when local families are enjoying their time off at the beach.

The beach is divided into two crescent-shaped coves by a spit of sand that carries out to a rocky islet called Nukumoi Point. Wave action sweeping around both sides of the point deposits sand behind it, creating the bridge to the main island. This phenomenon is called a tombolo and it occurs at only three places in Hawai'i, all on Kaua'i. The other two examples are at Kīpū Kai Beach and at Crater Hill, near Kīlauea. Po'ipū's tombolo is the only one readily accessible to the public. At high tide, waves manage to just sweep over the sand.

Rocky breakwaters shelter the cove to the west of the tombolo, creating a calm and safe swimming area. Here is where families can bring their children to swim and ride boogie boards on the gently rolling waves. The sandy offshore bottom deepens gradually to overhead depths. On a calm day look closely into the water from the shore. Someone has arranged large beach rocks in the shallow water to spell out the name of the beach.

The east side of the tombolo is less desirable for swimming, but has some of the south shore's best snorkeling. A small reef grows inside the breakwater, harboring many colorful fish waiting for handouts from visitors. During high surf conditions, waves can sweep over the breakwater. Don't swim past the breakwater, as a rip current flows out to rough water.

A large parking lot is directly behind the park and beach. Turn south from Po'ipū Road onto Ho'owili Road and drive another tenth of a mile.

Sheraton Beach

Location: In front of the Sheraton Kaua'i Resort

Coordinates: N21° 52.55', W159° 27.60'

Length: 0.3 miles

Facilities: Showers belonging to the resorts

Also referred to as Wai'ōhai Beach or Po'ipū Beach, this lovely curve of sand is 150 yards west of a rocky point separating it from Po'ipū Beach Park. Generally the water conditions here are favorable for swimming. When a south swell brings in high surf, the beach is a popular place for surfing. The beach is backed by the Sheraton resort on its west side and by the Outrigger and Castle Resorts to the east. Public parking lots are situated north and east of the Sheraton.

Beach House Beach

Location: Next to Beach House restaurant on the road to Spouting Horn
Coordinates: N21° 52.90', W159° 28.56'
Length: 100 feet
Facilities: None

Sunbathers should use this beach at low tide, because at high tide this tiny, roadside beach nearly disappears. During calm surf conditions, the offshore reef has good snorkeling and diving. The beach is named after the Beach House restaurant next door. Beach House Beach is next to Lāwaʻi Road on the route to Spouting Horn blowhole. A public parking lot is across the road.

Kukuiʻula Beach

Location: Off of Lāwaʻi Road, at Kukuiʻula Small Boat Harbor
Coordinates: N21° 53.08', W159° 29.23'
Length: 100 yards
Facilities: Bathrooms, shower, picnic shelters, telephone

Kukuiʻula Small Boat Harbor is popular with recreational and commercial boaters alike. At the back of the harbor is a sheltered, sandy beach. The sand, however, came from somewhere else. One of the conditions imposed by Kauaʻi County on the Kukuiʻula Development Co. before they could build a planned resort and residential development was to improve the beach at the harbor. The company removed loose rocks, shoreline debris, and scrub vegetation before nearly doubling the size of Kukuiʻula Beach by dumping 500 cubic yards of sand on it. Floats, indicating the swimming area, are planned. Ledge rocks are exposed at the shoreline and most of the swimming area has a rocky bottom.

The water here is sheltered by a breakwater and is calm in all but the strongest of south swells. Facilities are available in the adjacent harbor park. Beachgoers may use the harbor parking lot or park along Lāwaʻi Road.

Lāwaʻi Bay

Location: Six-tenths of a mile west of Spouting Horn Park
Coordinates: N21° 53.30', W159° 30.17'
Length: 200 yards
Facilities: None

Lāwaʻi Stream flows through the wide crescent-shaped beach that lines the head of Lāwaʻi Bay. All the land behind the beach at Lāwaʻi Bay is owned by the Allerton estate and is the site of the Pacific Tropical Botanical Garden. There is no public land access to the beach, but it can be seen when touring the garden. The high cliffs on either side of the bay add to its sense of seclusion.

Pālama Beach

Location: Three miles south of Kalāheo
Coordinates: N21° 53.16', W159° 31.35'
Length: 0.4 miles
Facilities: None

Pālama Beach borders Nōmilu Fishpond. Filling a volcanic cinder cone and covering 20 acres, Nōmilu is one of the largest fishponds in Hawaiʻi. It is actually a saltwater lake fed by natural springs, which turns the water brackish. The fishpond was famous throughout Hawaiʻi, and the mullet raised there was said to be especially delicate. The Pālama family has owned the fishpond for many years and has lent their name to the nearby beach.

The beach has a steep slope and a raised shelf of rock at the water's edge along most of its length. When the surf is high, the rocks create a good surfing break. A half mile offshore, Lanipu'ao Rock nearly breaks the surface of the ocean. It is marked by Pālama Buoy and is a popular diving destination. The only roads near Pālama Beach are private cane haul roads.

West Side Beaches

Wahiawa Bay

Location: One mile east of Port Allen
Coordinates: N21° 53.84', W159° 34.48'
Length: 150 yards
Facilities: None

Wahiawa Bay deeply indents the shoreline east of Hanapēpē Bay and is lined on both sides with low sea cliffs. With this excellent protection from prevailing winds and currents, it is a suitable anchorage for small boats. A straight beach with a level foreshore lines the head of the bay. Runoff from Wahiawa Stream mixes silt with the sand and water. There is no development around the bay. The land behind the beach is owned by the McBryde coffee plantation and is posted with "No Trespassing" signs.

Glass Beach

Location: Port Allen
Coordinates: N21° 53.90', W159° 35.06'
Length: 100 yards
Facilities: None

This beach has more value as a curiosity than for recreation. The land behind the beach was the site of a dump. Decades of wave action have ground thousands of broken glass bottles into millions of multicolored grains of glass. Mixed with the natural sand of the beach, the smooth glass beads glint and sparkle in the bright west side sunlight. Glass Beach is in front of the fuel storage tanks of the electric generating station at Port Allen. Take the last left before the Port Allen dock and follow it past the four exhaust stacks. A dirt road leads a few yards down to the beach.

Salt Pond Beach Park

Location: One-half mile west of Hanapēpē
Coordinates: N21° 53.99', W159° 36.47'
Length: 250 yards
Facilities: Picnic shelters, bathrooms, showers, lifeguard, telephone, camping

A ridge of rocks connects the two rocky points that mark the ends of Salt Pond Beach. Inside this barrier of basalt lies the best swimming beach on the south shore. The calm waters, sandy beach, and the large park behind it attract many families for water fun and picnics.

Next to the park are the only functioning salt ponds left in Hawai'i (see West Side Sights chapter). The Hawaiians were the only people of the Pacific Islands to make salt crystals from the sea and use it to preserve fish and meat. Whaling ships took on salt to preserve meat, and fur traders from Europe and America used the Islands' salt to preserve their animal skins.

Salt Pond Beach Park is one-half mile south of Highway 50 at Hanapēpē. The turnoff south onto Lele Road, at the western edge of Hanapēpē, is marked with a sign.

Pākalā Beach

Location: One and a half miles east of Waimea

Coordinates: N21° 56.29', W159° 38.96'

Length: 0.2 miles

Facilities: None

Pākalā Beach is home to a surfing break known as Infinities—one of the best summer surfing sites in Hawai'i. Infinities was given its name in 1962 by a young surfer who felt that riding the seemingly endless waves was akin to surfing into infinity. Discharge from a nearby stream muddies the water, which is an attraction to sharks.

The public is allowed to use the 150-yard path across private land to reach the beach from Highway 50. The right-of-way is located near a small bridge just west of mile marker 21. A string of vehicles parked along the road will mark the entrance.

Lucy Wright Beach Park

Location: At the mouth of the Waimea River

Coordinates: N21° 57.14', W159° 39.98'

Length: 1.5 miles

Facilities: Camping, bathrooms, showers, picnic table, pavilion, barbeques

Captain Cook made his first landing in what he soon named the Sandwich Islands at this beach near the mouth of the Waimea River on January 19, 1778. In spite of this important event happening here, the honor of being the namesake of the beach goes to Lucy Wright, a Native Hawaiian schoolteacher who taught for 35 years at Waimea.

The beach sand at the park is dark and the waters muddy from soil carried downstream by the river. While the beach and water are unappealing, the adjoining park is a good place for south side travelers to stop, rest, and have a picnic lunch under the large shade trees. A sign immediately west of the bridge spanning the Waimea River points the way to the park, one block south of Highway 50.

Kekaha Beach Park

Location: At the small town of Kekaha, three miles west of Waimea

Coordinates: N21° 58.09', W159° 43.13'

Length: 3.7 miles

Facilities: Bathrooms, shower, picnic tables

Hawai'i's longest beach starts here at Kekaha and stretches 15 miles to Polihale at the south end of the Nā Pali coast. From the arid and sunny southwest coast of Kaua'i you can see the island of Ni'ihau, 22 miles to the west. Breaking the water to the north of Ni'ihau is the tiny islet of Lehua.

Kekaha beach is wide, and the deep, small-grained sand is nearly white. The unprotected beach experiences pounding shorebreak, rip currents, and along-shore currents, particularly in the winter. These conditions are best left to the experienced surfers who ride the waves of Kaua'i's west side.

A beach park is situated across the highway from the beach between Alae Road and Amakihi Road in the town of Kekaha. Highway 50 runs next to Kekaha beach, with parking available at several roadside turnouts.

Pacific Missile Range Facility

Location: Skirting the Mānā Plain on Kaua'i's western shore

Coordinates: N22° 00.56', W159° 46.75' (Major's Beach)

Length: 8.2 miles

Facilities: Bathrooms, shower, telephone, four covered picnic tables with barbeques.

The U.S. Navy's Pacific Missile Range Facility is a large operation designed to detect and track aircraft and vessels over a huge area of the Pacific Ocean. Just past mile marker 32 of Highway 50 is the entrance road leading to the guarded main gate. Unless military operations are being conducted, the public is allowed access to the beach. A recorded message at 335-4229 informs callers when the beach is closed to the public. Visitors will be asked to present a driver's license and then will be issued a visitor's pass for their vehicle. Visitors are usually directed to Majors Beach at Recreation Area #3, one and a half miles south of the main gate. The beach in front of the range is exposed to the open ocean. During the winter, high surf may generate pounding shorebreaks, strong backwashes, and powerful rip currents. With calmer conditions, throw-net fishermen, surfers and windsurfers use the beach. Beachgoers are not allowed to cross behind the beach's vegetation line.

Polihale State Park

Location: The last beach before the southern limits of the Nā Pali coastline

Coordinates: N22° 05.51', W159° 45.07' (north campground)

Length: 2.6 miles

Facilities: Shelters, picnic tables, bathrooms, showers, camping

The last beach before the south end of the Nā Pali coastline is an impressively wide, long and deep stretch of sand. The readers of *Hawai'i* magazine voted Polihale as Hawai'i's best hidden beach in a recent poll. In places, Polihale obtains widths of 300 feet and the dunes may reach 100 feet high. The sand in this dry, sun-baked area is loose and deep. Just walking on the beach is vigorous exercise. Be sure to bring water and protection from the sun.

Swimming at Polihale is dangerous. The ocean bottom drops off sharply to overhead depths. A strong backwash can force swimmers into the rip current that runs along the length of the beach. An area called Queens Pond is located about midway up the length of Polihale. It is a shallow, sand-bottomed pool formed by a reef adjoining the beach. During calm surf conditions, the reef protects swimmers from waves

and currents. When waves from high surf sweep over the reef, however, a rip current flows through a channel in the reef's south limit.

At the south end of Polihale Beach is an area of 60-foot-high dunes called Barking Sands. Like other coastal dunes in Hawai'i, these grew rapidly during the ice age when the low sea level exposed reefs and offshore sediment to the wind. Supposedly, if conditions are right, stepping on the sand or sliding down a dune will cause it to emit a barking noise. Mr. W.R. Frink of Honolulu described the barking phenomenon as far back as 1875 in a letter to the California Academy of Sciences. Don't be surprised if you are unable to duplicate Mr. Frink's success.

The Hawaiians, of course, have a legend to explain the beach sand that barks. One variation of it tells of an old fisherman who lived near the beach with his nine dogs. When he went fishing, the man would stake his dogs in the sand, three to a stake. After returning from an exhausting fishing trip where he was caught in a bad storm, the fisherman forgot to untie the dogs. When he awoke the next morning, the dogs were gone. In their place were three mounds of sand. Walking over the mounds produced a low bark. Believing the dogs to be buried because of the storm, the fisherman began to dig. But the digging was futile, with each shovelful just producing more sand. Finally, the fisherman gave up, and every day after that, he could hear the low barking of dogs when he crossed the beach.

To reach Polihale, follow Highway 50 to its end and follow the signs. A wide and bumpy road cuts through sugar cane fields for 5 miles to the parking areas and campgrounds of the park. Queens Pond is located before the campgrounds. Two large monkeypod trees mark a fork in the access road to Queens Pond. Turn left at the trees and follow a smaller road to the dunes. Watch for drifting sand that can trap rental cars.

FLORA AND FAUNA

So dire has the plight of endemic species in the Hawaiian Islands become, that conservationists have bestowed the Islands with the unhappy distinction of being the endangered species capital of the country. Already, Hawai'i has lost hundreds of original life forms, while hundreds more teeter on the brink of extinction. The U.S. has 526 plant and 88 bird species on the endangered and threatened species list; more than a third are found in Hawai'i. Three-quarters of the United States' extinct plants and birds once lived only in Hawai'i, even though its islands represent just two-tenths of one percent of the nation's total land area.

Creatures and plants have been vanishing ever since Polynesian voyagers—and later European explorers—first set foot in the Islands about 1,500 years ago. Having evolved on the most remote group of islands on earth, native species were not equipped to survive the onslaught of predators and competitors that accompanied human arrival. Twenty species of flightless birds—easy prey for the hunter—were among the first decimated.

The original Hawaiians' presence was not as benign as was once thought. The settlers brought with them breadfruit, bananas, sugar cane and taro, clearing lowland forests to cultivate them. They brought small pigs that escaped to become feral. The first humans in Hawai'i caused the extinction of 35 species of birds. Later, in the several decades following the arrival of Captain James Cook in 1778, outsiders introduced cattle, goats, sheep, and large European pigs. Many of these animals escaped and flourished. Settlers introduced guavas, Java plum, lantana, bamboo, and ginger, which pushed aside and destroyed numerous indigenous species and native flora in the wild.

Most of the threatened and endangered species in Hawai'i find refuge among uplands too steep for development. More than a quarter of Hawai'i's land remains unspoiled, giving conservationists cause for hope. By restoring and maintaining healthy ecosystems, conservationists hope to give native species the respite and protection they need to survive. Work crews kill feral animals, erect fences to keep ungulates away from fragile plants, breed birds in captivity, pollinate flowers by hand, and destroy nonindigenous plants.

Plants and Trees

There are more than 2,500 species of plants that occur only in the Hawaiian Islands. Native plants are common today only in such remote places as the headwalls of deep valleys, on steep cliffs, and on mountain ridges and peaks. The coconuts, orchids, sugar cane and pineapples that visitors associate with Hawai'i are neither native nor unique. Native plants have evolved from about 275 species of successful natural immigrants, which arrived in Hawai'i on the average of once every 100,000 years since the time when the islands emerged from the sea.

Bird of Paradise

This African native has become a trademark of Hawai'i. Their orange and blue flowers nestle in green bracts, looking somewhat like birds in flight. Bird of Paradise are abundant in the gardens of vacation resorts and in cut-flower arrangements in hotel lobbies.

Ginger

Some of Hawai'i's most fragrant flowers are white and yellow ginger. They are usually found growing 4 to 7 feet high in areas blessed with frequent rain. Their flowers are 3 inches wide and composed of three dainty, petal-like stamen and three long, thin petals. White and yellow ginger were introduced in the nineteenth century from Malaysia. More exotic-looking is the torch ginger. The red flower stalks are about 6 inches long and resemble the fire of a lighted torch.

Hibiscus

The yellow hibiscus is Hawai'i's official state flower. Hibiscus grow on hedges up to 15 feet high. The 4 to 6-inch flowers, which resemble crepe paper, bloom in colors from white to deep red, with stamens and pistils protruding from the center. Because it shrivels quickly, it is unsuitable for use in a lei but it is a favored flower to tuck behind the ear. Tradition says that a flower behind the left ear means a lady's heart is committed and behind the right ear means that she is available.

Taro

Originally from Sri Lanka, taro is a food crop planted in flooded patches and found growing wild around pools and streams. Taro resembles the ornamental plant, elephant ears, with heart-shaped leaves arising from its base. The Polynesian staple, poi, is made from the starchy corm of the taro plant.

African Tulip Tree

The flaming red flowers on these large trees provide a welcome contrast to the multihued greens of the rain forests they live in. The trees produce globes of frilly, tulip-shaped flowers on branch tips.

Koa Tree

The beautifully grained wood of the koa is prized for the making of canoes, paddles, bowls, furniture, and even surfboards. Its beauty and diverse uses has resulted in the harvest of nearly all of the large trees. A native tree, the koa is frequently mentioned in Hawaiian legends and songs.

Kukui Tree

Early Polynesians imported the kukui because of its many uses. Kukui nuts are rich in oil and were used as candles or made into leis. When baked, the kernels are edible. The roots and shell of the fruit yield a black dye. Kukui oil was used to soften skin as part of pre-wedding rituals.

'Ōhia Lehua Tree

The 'ōhia is the most abundant of the native Hawaiian trees and is usually the first life to appear on new lava flows. 'Ōhia can grow as a miniature tree in wet bogs or as an 80-foot giant on cool slopes at high elevations. Its petal-less flowers, the lehua blossom, are composed of a large mass of brightly colored stamens, usually red but sometimes orange, yellow, or white. The flowers are an important source of nectar for rare endemic birds.

Birds

Because of Hawai'i's isolated location in the middle of the Pacific Ocean, the first birds to arrive were probably blown off course during migration or floated in clutching on to driftwood. Here, with abundant food and no predators, they were free to evolve into 67 species highly adapted to their environment. Human settlement of Hawai'i caused the demise of 40 percent of native bird species and endangered another 40 percent. Early Polynesians cleared lowland vegetation and replaced it with introduced plants that were used for food and fiber. As a result, when foreigners from many lands made Hawai'i their new home during the nineteenth century, there were no songbirds in the lowlands. It was natural for them to want to import familiar birds from their homelands. When sugar cane, pineapple, and cattle became economically important, settlers introduced foreign birds that would feed upon the insect pests of the crops and cattle. Since 1796, when the first pigeons or rock doves were released, 170 different species of exotic birds have gained their freedom in Hawai'i.

Just as the Hawaiian people had never developed resistance to measles, Hawaiian birds had no resistance to avian malaria. Common among mainland birds, avian malaria is caused by a microscopic parasite in the blood. Caged pet birds and foreign birds introduced by the early colonists likely carried this parasite. An incident that occurred in the port of Lahaina, Maui, in 1826 led to the spread of this disease to the native bird population. In that year the ship *Wellington* put in at Lahaina to fill its water casks, having last filled them on the west coast of Mexico. Released from those casks into a clear Maui stream were the larvae of a particular mosquito, *Culex pipiens fatigans*, which inhabits tropical and subtropical regions. It is now found on all the main Hawaiian Islands from sea level to an elevation of 3,000 feet. These mosquitoes were the vector that transmitted blood parasites and viruses from migratory birds and domestic poultry to Hawai'i's endemic birds. Birds that lived above the level of the mosquito infestation but migrated to lower levels during winter storms were also bitten and mortally infected. Today, it is only in the highlands that Hawai'i's rare endemic birds are found.

Cattle Egret

Cattle egrets are tall, white birds with slender bodies and long necks. They were introduced to Hawai'i in the mid-twentieth century to reduce pest insects near cattle. Egrets are commonly seen on Kaua'i following cattle as they graze, waiting for them to stir up insects and small vertebrates.

I'iwi

The 'i'iwi is one of over 50 species of honeycreepers that evolved from a single ancestral species that colonized the Islands millions of years ago. It is easily distinguished from other Hawaiian forest birds by its bright red feathers, pink curved bill, and black wings and tail. In the mountains where it lives, its presence can be detected by the sound its wings make as it flutters from tree to tree. The movements of the 'i'iwi are also unique, as it spends much of its time hanging upside down poking its long, curved bill into flowers. The lehua blossom is one if its favorites. Hawaiians prized the 'i'iwi's bright red feathers for adorning capes, helmets, and other ornaments for the *ali'i*. Some large cloaks required the sacrifice of 8,000 birds to make them.

'Io

The 'io, or Hawaiian hawk, lives in the forests of Hawai'i, where it preys on rats and spiders. Adults grow to 18 inches in length and have a light brown color. Regally circling the Hawaiian skies, the endangered bird is esteemed by some as an ancestor spirit. Its name honors 'Iolani Palace in Honolulu.

Java Sparrow

A member of the finch family, the Java sparrow was introduced to Kaua'i in 1865. A population did not take hold until it was reintroduced in the 1960s. Male and female Java sparrows have white bodies, gray wings, and black tail feathers. Their black-and-white heads sport large, round beaks that they use to strip seeds from stalks of grass. In their native Indonesia, Java sparrows have experienced a significant drop in population. The birds are trapped intensively for the pet trade.

Moa

Polynesians brought the moa or red junglefowl with them when they settled the Hawaiian Islands. Moa are found mostly in the upland forests and are not to be confused with the many domestic chickens that roam the lowlands, although interbreeding does occur. Chickens and moa prosper in the wild on Kaua'i because it doesn't have a resident population of mongooses to devour their eggs as they do on the other Hawaiian Islands. Visitors to the meadow and parking lot of the Kōke'e Museum will be visited by numerous moa looking for handouts of food.

Nēnē

The endangered nēnē is Hawai'i's state bird. It is believed to be a descendant of the Canada goose, which it still resembles. The large, colorful bird grows to weigh 5 pounds and measure 28 inches in length. Nēnē can be found only in and near the crater of Haleakalā on Maui; on the slopes of Mauna Kea and Mauna Loa on the Big Island; and in Kōke'e, Kīlauea Point, and near Līhu'e on Kaua'i. Predation of their nests by mongooses,

rats, and feral cats, coupled with overhunting, nearly drove the nēnē to extinction. By 1951 only 33 individuals were known, half of which were in captivity.

Survival of the nēnē can be primarily credited to the work of the late Sir Peter Scott, who founded the Wildfowl and Wetlands Trust in England. Shortly after the trust's formation in 1946, its officers suggested to the territorial government of Hawai'i that steps be taken to save the nēnē. At the time only 50 of the birds remained. The International Union for the Protection of Nature, a United Nations-sponsored organization, placed the nēnē on a list of 13 most threatened bird species in the world. In 1949, a rancher on the Big Island who was keeping many of the surviving nēnē, shipped a breeding pair to England. Nine goslings were hatched from them in the following year. That same year the Hawaiian government started its own breeding project on the Big Island with the help of the trust's curator. Slowly, the population of nēnē in England grew, and, in 1962, 30 were returned to the

Islands and released—five at Haleakalā crater. Over the years, breeding projects have returned more than 2,000 birds to the wild.

Pueo

The Hawaiian short-eared owl, or pueo, has brown and white markings and heavily feathered legs. It grows to 13 to 17 inches long. Unlike most owls, the pueo is often active at midday. As it soars at high altitudes, watchful for its prey of mice and rats, it is sometimes mistaken for the 'io or Hawaiian hawk by observers. Pueo build their nests on the ground, usually in grass, which leaves their eggs vulnerable to rapacious feral cats and mongooses. The pueo can be found from sea level to 8,000 feet in elevation on all the main Hawaiian islands, in areas dominated by both native and alien vegetation, and from pastures and grasslands to dry and wet forest. Many Hawaiians consider the pueo to be an ancestor spirit and spotting one to be a good omen.

Western Meadowlark

Kaua'i is the only Hawaiian island where the western meadowlark, which was introduced in 1931, has become permanently established. Both male and female meadowlarks are mid-sized birds with yellow, black, and brown markings and long, conical bills. Meadowlarks punctuate the evening air of the grasslands with their long, distinctive call.

Mammals

Because of its geographic isolation, only two land mammals arrived in the Hawaiian Islands through natural dispersal and became established. They are the hoary bat and the Hawaiian monk seal. Marine mammals such as whales and dolphins, widely distributed throughout the world and of ancient origin, likely have been in Hawai'i waters since very early times. Seafaring Polynesians brought with them dogs and pigs (both for eating) and stowaway rats. Most of the land mammals found in Hawai'i today were introduced after Captain Cook's landing in 1778. These aggressive, implanted species have profoundly affected Hawaiian wildlife.

Hawaiian Monk Seal

It may be their monk-like preference for solitude, or the loose skin around their necks that resembles the hood of a monk's robe, that gave these seals their name. Monk seals are sometimes referred to as "living fossils" because, as the oldest living members of the pinniped order, they have remained virtually unchanged for 15 million years.

There have been three known species of monk seals: Hawaiian, Caribbean, and Mediterranean. Last sighted in 1952, Caribbean monk seals are thought to be extinct. Mediterranean monk seals survive in small numbers in isolated caves and beaches rarely visited by humans in the Mediterranean. The Hawaiian monk

seal is considered an endangered species, with its population currently estimated to be between 1,200 and 1,500 individuals.

Hawaiian monks seals breed in the remote Northwestern Hawaiian Islands, which stretch 1,200 miles northwest from Kaua'i. A few seals live in the sea and on the beaches of the main islands. Kaua'i's monk seal population is between 15 and 20 individuals.

Adults measure about 7 feet in length and weigh between 400 and 600 pounds. Because Hawaiian monk seals have evolved free of terrestrial enemies, they did not develop the need or the instinct to flee from predators. Being easily approached by humans has proven to be one of the major factors leading to the population decline of the species. In the early nineteenth century, sealers took Hawaiian monk seals for their oil and pelts. Within a few years, the population had been drastically culled to a point where hunting the seals commercially was no longer worthwhile.

Hawaiian monk seals are extremely sensitive to human activity. Mothers will abandon preferred pupping areas, and even their pups, when disturbed by human visitors. It is illegal in Hawai'i to approach the seals.

Hoary Bat

Theirs is a remarkable example of wayward migration. The hoary bats of North and South America are strongly migratory and regularly reach the Farallon Islands off California, The Galápagos, and Bermuda. Flights that brought bats to Hawai'i may have been rare. The local bats have formed their own subspecies after likely being isolated from their progenitors for tens of thousands of years. Even now, the reddish-brown Hawaiian bat accumulates a reserve of body fat late in summer in preparation for a migration it no longer takes. Their principal breeding ground is on the island of Hawai'i, but bats can be spotted on all the islands. It is not known if they reside there or move regularly between the islands.

Humpback Whale

Warm Hawai'i waters provide the winter habitat for humpback whales migrating from Alaska and the Bering Sea. Fifth largest of the great whales, humpbacks feed all summer in the plankton-rich northern waters to develop the layer of blubber they will need to sustain them through the winter. Humpbacks screen small schooling fish such as herring, mackerel, pollock and haddock, and crustaceans such as krill through baleens in their mouths. From their summer feeding grounds, the whales migrate more than 3,500 miles to the warm tropical waters of Hawai'i to mate and give birth. They fast for the six months that they are migrating and living in Hawai'i waters. Humpbacks can be seen near all the Hawaiian Islands, but the favorite area for their winter habitat is the shallow water surrounded by Maui, Moloka'i, Lāna'i, and Kaho'olawe. Migrating humpback whales don't arrive at or depart Hawai'i en masse, but begin filtering in each year around November and start returning north around May. The North Pacific population of humpbacks is estimated at between 2,000 and 3,000, with approximately two-thirds of them migrating to Hawai'i and the rest traveling to Mexico.

Humpbacks display the white underside of their pectoral fin

On average, adults grow to 45 feet in length and 45 tons in weight. They have long flippers, reaching one-third of body length. A newborn calf weighs 1.5 tons and can range in size from 10 to 16 feet. In five to nine years the humpback will reach sexual maturity and can expect to live for 30 to 40 years. Their gestation period is 10 to 12 months. Females calve every second or third year, although some have been known to calve every year for several successive years. Births usually occur between January and April. A third whale called an escort whale often accompanies mothers and calves. The escort whale, assumed to be a sexually active male, only remains with the pair for less than a day.

Generally, humpback whales have dark-blue or gray backs with white marking on their fins, sides, and ventral surfaces. Individuals can be identified by the unique markings on the underside of their tails, or flukes. Researchers catalog photographs of humpback whale flukes to study the movements and social interactions of individuals.

There is little evidence indicating when the humpbacks first began wintering in waters around the Hawaiian Islands. The whale doesn't seem to figure prominently in Hawaiian folklore. Whales appear in Native Hawaiian chants but they have only one generic word for whale, koholā, which translates to mean hump dorsal. The koholā was *kapu* to common people. *Ali'i* valued the ivory teeth and bones. A whale carcass was called pala'oa. A pala'oa that drifted ashore became the property of a chief. Native Hawaiians believed that a whale breaching and blowing foreshadowed a storm.

Hawai'i was a major port of call for the Pacific whaling fleet during the early and mid-nineteenth century. Initially, whalers hunted the larger sperm, blue and right whales. Humpback whales were faster swimmers and had less whale oil than the other great whales, giving a smaller return for the greater effort it took to kill and process them. Whalers eventually depleted the other whale populations, subjecting the humpbacks

The whale shows its tail when it is about to dive

to intense whaling in the first half of the twentieth century. Between 1905 and 1965 whalers reduced the North Pacific humpback whale numbers from 15,000 to about 1,000. Since 1965, when commercial whale hunting was substantially curtailed globally, the humpback whale has slowly made a comeback; however, it remains on the Endangered Species list.

Humpback whales are noted for their long and highly complex vocalizations, called songs. Singers are usually lone males or males escorting cow-calf pairs. A song generally lasts between 6 and 18 minutes and may be repeated many times. Singing occurs only during the breeding/birthing season. Small changes in the song may occur as the season progresses. Humpbacks breeding off the coast of Mexico sing virtually the same songs as Hawai'i's humpbacks.

Pig

Without hesitation, conservation biologists would indict the feral pig as the most significant threat to native Hawaiian rain forest species today. Pigs uproot shrubs and till the soil with their snouts in search of grubs and worms. They sow the seeds of alien plants in their droppings. Those seeds grow into tangles of vines like the South American banana poka and small trees like the Brazilian strawberry guava, which form dense thickets that crowd out native trees. More than 100,000 pigs roam the Islands.

The pig that the Polynesians brought with them was much smaller than the tusked troublemakers roaming the forests now. When Captain Cook bartered with the Hawaiians for larder for his ships, he complained that the largest of their pigs weighed only 50 to 60 pounds. After many generations, the Polynesian pigs have bred with imported domestic breeds and the resulting feral pig is large, resembling the European wild boar.

Reptiles and Amphibians

None of Hawai'i's terrestrial reptiles and amphibians are thought to be native to the Islands. Reptiles such as geckos were introduced unintentionally, either as stowaways in cargo shipments or as escaped pets. Farmers and sugar growers released toads into agricultural and settled areas in efforts to control insects. The Hawaiian Islands are now home to five species of amphibians, 20 species of land reptiles, plus five types of sea turtles and one sea snake. Hawai'i is essentially snake-free and authorities are ever vigilant to keep it that way. On Guam, the brown tree snake is blamed for virtually wiping out the native bird population after it arrived. Snake-sniffing dogs aid inspectors in Hawai'i ports and airports in finding stowaway snakes in cargo.

Gecko

Of their own volition, geckos have become Hawai'i's "house lizards." Geckos invade houses and buildings and become ubiquitous wall ornaments. It is their ravenous appetite for insects, especially cockroaches, which make them welcome nighttime visitors. The small lizards, usually gray or brown with bulging eyes, scurry about walls, windows and ceilings, seemingly oblivious to gravity. They accomplish such feats with the aid of miniscule hair-like structures on the bottom of their toes that provide attachments to walls and ceilings by something akin to surface tension—the same property that allows some insects to walk on water. Adult geckos are about 2 inches long in the body with its tail doubling its length. Their tails are fragile and frequently break off, then regenerate.

Giant Toad

The giant toad reaches 7.5 inches long and weighs up to half a pound. Often shades of olive green or brown, they have a lumpy, wart-strewn appearance. They were introduced to the Islands in 1932, when sugar growers imported them from Puerto Rico to control insect pests. In the evenings they endanger their safety by hopping out of the cane fields onto nearby roads. Toads adapt to human behavior and can be found around settlements, sometimes eating dog or cat food that has been left out. Some people find them to be pests because they are noisy in the evening, occasionally poison curious pets, and hop into homes. Others appreciate their insect-eating ways, especially when it comes to cockroaches.

Sea Turtles

The two most commonly seen sea turtles in Hawai'i waters are the green sea turtle and the hawksbill. The green sea turtle is so named because of its greenish body fat. They can reach 4 feet in length and have a gray, green, or brown back. The hawksbill is about a foot shorter and can be easily identified by its narrow head and tapering hooked "beak." Green sea turtles and their eggs were probably important food sources for the early Hawaiians. The hawksbill was less palatable and was not eaten. All sea turtles are currently endangered due to illegal hunting and drowning in fishing nets. Sea turtles are always a delight to see when diving or snorkeling in Kaua'i's offshore waters, but it is illegal to pursue them. Green sea turtles are frequently spotted in the choppy surf of Queen's Bath in Princeville (see North Kaua'i Sights chapter).

DO NOT DISTURB

They may act friendly, or almost tame, but Hawai'i's endangered marine animals are protected by law from interference or harassment by people. Under the Marine Mammal Protection Act, the term harassment is defined by "any act of pursuit, torment, or annoyance" that "has the potential to disturb a marine mammal or marine mammal stock in the wild by causing the disruption of behavioral patterns, including but not limited to, migration, breathing, nursing, breeding, feeding, or sheltering." For example, when a pod of spinner dolphins comes into a secluded bay or cove, they may be in a rest mode; their movement is slow. If swimmers or boaters move close to the pod and cause them to change from the relaxed, slow mode to a fast, swimming or leaping mode, that would be a change of behavior, which constitutes harassment. Should dolphins approach a boat in open ocean there is no problem, but a boater chasing a group of dolphins is certainly considered harassment.

Special provisions in the federal Endangered Species Act protect humpback whales even further. The law states it is unlawful "to operate any aircraft within 1,000 feet of any humpback whale; or, approach by any means, within 100 yards of any humpback whale." Boats should maneuver out of the path of an approaching whale, should not cut across the path of a whale or pass between a mother and a calf, and should not purposefully "leap-frog" or go around a whale to get in its path. If a boat is floating with motors off, while bottom fishing for example, it's not a violation if a whale comes and approaches the boat.

Hawaiian monk seals face more human encounters than other marine mammals on Kaua'i due to their habit of basking on beaches. They are attracted to popular beaches for essentially the same reasons that people are there: to rest and relax in the warm sun. Monk seals can't sleep in the ocean, so they need the opportunity to rest unbothered. Also, they are slower moving after feeding, and beaches provide protection from sharks. A person moving closer than the allowed 100 feet may cause the seal to retreat to the ocean and waiting predators. Witnesses to a case of monk seal harassment may contact volunteers of the Hawaiian Monk Seal Watch Program by calling pager numbers. They are: north shore 644-1673; eastside 644-1775; south shore 644-1849; westside 644-1745.

The federal Endangered Species Act and related state legislation protect the green sea turtle. It is unlawful to capture any threatened or endangered wildlife or take any egg, offspring or dead body part. Owning the shell of a green sea turtle is outlawed, even if you didn't directly cause the death of the animal.

ACTIVITIES

Boat Cruises

The Nā Pali coast offers spectacular offshore scenery and several tour boat companies have taken advantage of this blessing. Along the rugged coast, multihued cliffs tower above the sea. Streams flow from hanging valleys to cascade into the ocean. Voyagers will see secluded beaches that are accessible only by boat and caves cut into the cliffs by relentless surf.

All the large tour companies depart for the Nā Pali from Port Allen on the south coast. Port Allen is not close to Nā Pali but it is the only commercial boat harbor available for their purposes. Some Nā Pali boat tours used to embark on their tours from Hanalei Bay on the north shore, until state legislation banned commercial boat tours from the area. A round-trip boat tour of Nā Pali from Port Allen covers about 70 miles—twice the distance traveled when they departed from Hanalei Bay. The greater distance also means that larger boats are needed. Power catamarans are the favored choice for most operators and passengers who are looking for a reasonably smooth voyage. Large oceangoing rafts take thrill seekers on a bumpy ride and are subject to greater limitations when the weather worsens.

A cruise leaving Port Allen sails west along the south coast and sugar cane country. Tilted cane land rises above the towns of Waimea and Kekaha. You will have a view of the longest continuous stretch of sand in the state as it reaches from Kekaha, around the Navy's Pacific Missile Range Facility to Polihale and the southern edge of the Nā Pali. There are good opportunities to spot sea life, as well. Spinner dolphins and the larger and less common bottlenose dolphins often visit the boats. Turtles and flying fish can be spotted and, in season, the humpback whale. It takes at least 90 minutes to reach the beginning of the Nā Pali cliffs from Port Allen. Keep that in mind when looking at the total time of the cruises.

Most operators offer a chance to snorkel on an offshore reef as part of their cruise. The area often chosen is Mākole reef, one and a half miles north of Polihale. Snorkel gear and a quick lesson are provided. Boats moor in about 20 feet of water and about 100 yards from shore. Fish populations at the reef can be sporadic. Better snorkeling can be found at Lehua rock from operators that include the side trip to Ni'ihau on their tour.

The tour will continue to Miloli'i Valley and its beach. The sandy beach is the site of a state park. Camping on the beach was suspended when funding cutbacks prevented the replacement of a composting toilet. Next to Miloli'i is the valley of Nu'alolo and Nu'alolo Kai Beach. The beach here is protected by a large fringing reef (see Beaches chapter). Only a few operators are licensed to take passengers ashore at Nu'alolo.

The most dramatic scenery begins at Awa'awapuhi Valley and continues through the Honopū and Kalalau Valleys. Waterfalls, towering pinnacles, and sea caves treat the eye. At Honopū Beach, waves have eroded an arch into the lava flow and deposit sand on either side. The tours generally end at Kalalau, but favorable weather conditions may allow for further progress along the coast.

A Nā Pali Eco Adventure

Phone: (808) 826-6804
Website: www.napali.com
Vessels: 34' and 40' power catamarans running on recycled vegetable oil
Cruises: Nā Pali Coast Tour, 6 hrs., $132; Nā Pali Coast Tour, 5 hrs., $105; Nā Pali Coast Sunset Tour, 3.5 hrs., $85; Whale watching Tour, 2 hrs., $49
Departure: Port Allen

Blue Dolphin Charters

Phone: (808) 335-5553, (877) 511-1311
Website: www.kauaiboats.com
Vessels: 63' power catamaran; 56' trimaran
Cruises: Ni'ihau/Nā Pali Coast Tour, 7 hrs., $159; Nā Pali Coast Tour, 5 hrs., $119; Nā Pali Coast Sunset 3.5 hrs., $85; Po'ipū Sunset 2 hrs., $60
Departure: Port Allen except for Po'ipū Sunset, which departs from Kukui'ula Small Boat Harbor

Bluewater Sailing

Phone: (808) 828-1142
Website: www.sail-kauai.com
Vessels: 42' Pearson ketch-rigged yacht; 42 single hull powerboat
Cruises: Half-Day Sail to Nā Pali, 4 hrs. $105; Sunset Sail, 2 hrs., $60; Nā Pali Coast on powerboat, 5 hrs., $110; Sunset/Nā Pali on powerboat, 4 hrs., $90
Departure: Port Allen

Capt. Andy's Ocean Adventures

Phone: (808) 335-6833
Website: www.capt-andys.com
Vessels: 65' power catamaran; 55' sailing catamaran
Cruises: Nā Pali Coast Tour, 5.5 hrs., $109; Nā Pali Coast Sunset Tour, 4 hrs., $99; Po'ipū Sunset Tour, 2 hrs., $59
Departure: Port Allen except for Po'ipū Sunset, which departs from Kukui'ula Small Boat Harbor

Captain Sundown

Phone: (808) 826-5585
Website: www.captainsundown.com
Vessel: sailing catamaran
Cruises: Nā Pali Coast, 6 hrs., $99; Sunset Sail, 3 hrs., $50
Departure: Hanalei Bay

Catamaran Kahanu

Phone: (808) 335-3577
Website: www.catamarankahanu.com
Vessel: 36' power catamaran
Cruises: Nā Pali Coast Morning Tour, 5 hrs., $105; Nā Pali Coast Sightseeing Tour, 4 hrs., $85
Departure: Port Allen

Holoholo Charters

Phone: (808) 335-0815, (800) 848-6130
Website: www.holoholocharters.com
Vessels: 61' power catamaran; 48' sailing
    catamaran
Cruises: Ni'ihau/Nā Pali Coast Tour,
        7 hrs., $156;
    Nā Pali Sailing Tour, 5 hrs., $109;
    Nā Pali Sunset Tour, 3.5 hrs., $85
Departure: Port Allen

Owners Kevin and Marcie Millett ensure that
all their passengers receive attentive and pro-
fessional service and the boat crews create a
fun atmosphere on the cruises. Kevin Millett is
an accomplished boat designer, having built
both of Holoholo's catamarans. The *Leila* sails
a good deal of the time during its tour. If conditions are favorable, the 48-foot catamaran will
attain 18 knots under sail.

Kaua'i Sea Tours

Phone: (808) 826-7254, (800) 733-7997
Website: www.seatours.net
Vessels: 60' catamaran motor-sailer; rigid
    hull ocean raft
Cruises: Nā Pali catamaran tour with beach
    landing at Nu'alolo Kai, 6 hrs., $135;
    Half-Day Nā Pali catamaran tour, 5 hrs.,
        $119;
    Nā Pali sunset catamaran tour, 4 hrs., $85;
    Nā Pali raft tour with beach landing at
        Nu'alolo Kai, 6 hrs., $132;
    Half Day raft tour, 5 hrs., $108;
    Nā Pali sunset raft tour, 4 hrs., $85

Nā Pali Explorer

Phone: (808) 338-9999, (877) 335-9909
Website: www.napali-explorer.com
Vessels: 26', 16-passenger Hurricane Zodiac;
    48', 35-passenger Explorer class
    adventure craft
Cruises: Nā Pali Snorkel Expedition,
        5 hrs., $118;
    Nā Pali Coast Expedition, 3.5 hrs., $79
Departure: Kīkīaola Small Boat Harbor

Golf

Kaua'i is a golfer's paradise.
Spectacular views surround challenging
holes at all nine of Kaua'i's resort and
public courses. Golf courses anchor
three major resort developments on
Kaua'i's north, east, and south coasts.
Visitors may tee off at very posh and
expensive clubs or enjoy a round under
the tropical sun on reasonably priced
public courses.

Kaua'i Lagoons Resort

The two courses of the Kaua'i Lagoons Resort,
the Kiele and the Mokihana, are laid out along
Līhu'e's Nāwiliwili Bay, next to the Marriott
Hotel. The fairways of the more challenging
Kiele Course skirt ocean cliffs and weave
through fresh-water lagoons. This championship layout designed by Jack Nicklaus rewards
players who can hit the ball high in order to
carry the assorted drainage creeks, ravines and
lagoons, as well as reach the couple of island
greens that finish the course. The signature hole
is called "The Turtle." It offers a spectacular
view of Nāwiliwili Harbor and the harbor lighthouse. All the holes are named for animals and
the par-3, 13th hole, which requires a steep shot
over open ocean, is fittingly titled "The Frog."

Kaua'i Lagoon's Kiele Course

The Mokihana Course is laid out with Scottish-
style rolling links. Designed for players of all
skill levels, Mokihana is marked by its open
fairways and its relative lack of forced carries.
The real challenges of the course are its undulating greens.

Reservations for both courses: 241-6000,
    (800) 634-6400

Golf facilities include: lessons, driving range, chipping range, rental clubs, rental shoes, restaurant, bar, health club/spa.

Kiele Course

Par: 72

Yardage: Gold 7070, Blue 6674, White 6164, Red 5417

Designer: Jack Nicklaus

Green Fees: $170, Kaua'i Marriott guest $120, Junior $65

Cart included in green fees. Rated by *Golf Digest* as 6th best course in the state from 1995 to 1996 and 7th best in 1997. In addition, *Golf Magazine* nominated Kiele 64th among the Top 100 Courses You Can Play in The U.S. in 1998.

Mokihana Course

Par: 72

Yardage: Gold 6960, Blue 6578, White 6136, Red 5607

Designer: Jack Nicklaus

Green Fees: $120, Kaua'i Marriott guest $75, Junior $42

Cart included in green fees. *Golf Magazine* rated Mokihana as one of the ten most playable courses in America.

Kiahuna Golf Club

Kiahuna's main boast is not its play but the ancient remains around which the course is built. Historical and natural landmarks include a *heiau*, irrigation aqueducts, two lava tubes, and the remains of a Portuguese house and crypt built in the 1800s. Robert Trent Jones, Jr. designed the links-style course with large undulating greens, rock gardens, and 70 deep bunkers. Located in Po'ipū, the course has mountain and ocean views but does not border the ocean. Access is on Kiahuna Plantation Road, next to Po'ipū Shopping Village. Lately golfers have complained that the course is not as well maintained as it once was.

Reservations: 742-9595

Par: 70

Yardage: Back 6363, Middle 5631, Front 4871

Designer: Robert Trent Jones, Jr.

Green Fees: $75, Twilight $45, Junior $45

Cart included in green fees. Golf facilities include: lessons, driving range, rental clubs, rental shoes, restaurant, bar.

Kukuiolono Golf Course

This picturesque and historically rich golf course is one of the best golf bargains on the island. It is situated in Kukuiolono Park, on a bluff above the town of Kalāheo. Walter McBryde, who co-founded the McBryde Sugar Company, acquired the land for the park in 1907 for use by the locals. He added the golf course to the park in 1928 for the enjoyment of the mill workers, many of whom were Scots like himself. At the time it was only the second golf course built on Kaua'i and the eighth in the Hawaiian Territory.

In its nine holes Kukuiolono has almost everything except a water hazard. One fairway is laid around a park monument. There also are Japanese Gardens and Hawaiian artifacts near the 8th tee (see South Kaua'i Sights chapter). The driving range opens to a vista of the south shore and ocean. At Kalāheo, turn *makai* at the lights onto Papalina Road and follow it up the hill for seven-tenths of a mile.

Reservations: 332-9151

Par: 36

Yardage: Back 3173, Front 2981

Green Fees: $7, Juniors $3

A golf cart may be rented for $6. Golf facilities include: driving range, putting green, rental clubs snack bar, bar.

Po'ipū Bay Resort Golf Course

The Po'ipū Bay course weaves through gentle contours that feature ancient stone walls and the remains of *heiaus*. Golfers rate this as a tough course with windy conditions. Holes 16 to 19 follow 80-foot sea cliffs downwind to the clubhouse. Since 1994, this course has hosted what some call the most exclusive golf tournament in the world—the PGA of America's Grand Slam of Golf. To be invited, participants must have won the Masters, the U.S. Open, the British Open, or the PGA Championship. The entrance to the clubhouse is off Po'ipū Road, just past the Hyatt Regency.

Reservations: 742-8711

Website: www.kauai-hyatt.com/golf.html

Par: 72

Yardage: Gold 6959, Blue 6499, White 6023, Red 5241

Designer: Robert Trent Jones, Jr.

Green Fees: Hyatt guests $120, Nonresident

$170, Twilight $95 after noon, $65 after 3:00 p.m., Junior $45

Cart and range balls included in green fees. Golf facilities include: lessons, driving range, practice green, practice sand and chipping area, rental clubs, rental shoes, restaurant, bar.

Princeville Resort

To quote the words of world-famous golf course architect Robert Trent Jones, Jr., "In all the world, I never expected to find a more spectacularly beautiful place to build a golf course." The natural beauty of mountains, sea and luxuriant tropical foliage frame the Princeville courses from every angle. From the beginning, developers planned for the two courses to be the focal point of the north shore community. With 45 holes of play, Princeville offers more golf opportunities than any other resort in the state.

Reservations: 826-5070, (800) 826-1105
Website: www.princeville.com/play/
 pvgolf.html

Prince Course

Golf Digest has named the Prince Course the number one golf course in the state of Hawai'i. It is also included in their prestigious list of "America's 100 Greatest Golf Courses." The Prince Course is designed to accommodate golfers who are serious about their game and not beginners or recreational golfers. It is a very difficult course with up-and-down terrain, small greens, deep bunkers, and rolling fairways marked by rolls, mounds, and hollows. Even with five different tee positions, there is little relief. Only players with a handicap of 9 or below are permitted to play the back tees. Guests are asked to take many extra balls and to not waste time looking for errant shots.

Par: 72
Yardage: Prince 7309, Championship 6960,
 Ali'i 6521, Resort 6025, Princess 5338
Designer: Robert Trent Jones, Jr.
Green Fees: $175, Resort guest $145, Hotel
 guest $125

Cart and spa pass included in green fees. Golf facilities include: lessons, driving range, putting green, rental clubs, rental shoes, restaurant, bar, health club/spa.

Makai Course

The Makai Course is comprised of three distinct nine-hole courses, named for their most dominant features—the Ocean, Lakes, and Woods courses. Each nine is a course unto itself and has its own distinctive flavor, but all are similar in distance and demands on the player. They flow into each other, making any combination of the three a well-integrated round of golf.

Par: Ocean 36, Lakes 36, Woods 36
Yardage: Ocean Nine-Blue 3430, White
 3157, Red 2802; Lakes Nine-Blue 3456,
 White 3149, Red 2714; Woods Nine-Blue
 3445, White 3208, Red 2829
Designer: Robert Trent Jones, Jr.
Green Fees: $120, Resort guest $105, Hotel
 guest $100

Cart and range balls included in green fees. Golf facilities include: lessons, driving range, chipping range, putting green, rental clubs, rental shoes, snack bar, free pass to Prince Course Health Club.

Puakea Golf Course

Formerly known as Grove Farm Golf Course, Puakea was voted one of the Top Ten 9-Hole Golf Courses In The U.S. by *Sports Illustrated*. Actually it has ten holes, but *SI* probably doesn't have that category. The course plays around ravines and streams, and as is the case with most Kaua'i golf courses, it has mountain backdrops. Puakea is located in a new subdivision of Līhu'e, west of the Kukui Grove Shopping Center. Turn onto Pīkake St. at Border's Bookstore and then right onto Kalepa St.

Reservations: 245-8756
Website: www.puakeagolf.com
Par: 40 (10 holes)
Yardage: Green 3803, Blue 3520, White
 3279, Red 2778
Designer: Robin Nelson
Green Fees: 10 holes $45; 20 holes $65,
 Twilight 20 holes $50

Cart included in green fees. Golf facilities include: lessons, driving range, rental clubs.

Wailua Municipal Golf Course

The Wailua course is located just off the Kūhiō Highway, between Līhu'e and Kapa'a. The U.S. Public Links Amateur Golf Championships were twice held here—back in the days when it was regularly rated as one of the top public or municipal courses in the United States. It now exists on past reputation rather than current reality. The course was badly damaged by Hurricane 'Iniki in 1992 and never was restored to its former glory. Despite the installation of a new irrigation system, four holes remain marginally playable. Wailua is the oldest course on Kaua'i and the first built on any of O'ahu's neighboring islands. Like most seaside courses in Hawai'i, Wailua gets more than its share of wind and sand. The fairways are narrowed by the abundance of mature trees and tropical foliage. This is a popular golf course for the locals and the early tee times fill quickly. Reservations are not taken more than seven days in advance.

Reservations: 241-6666
Par: 72
Yardage: Back 6981, Middle 6585,
    Front 5974
Designer: Toyo Shira
Green Fees: $35 weekends and holidays,
    $25 weekdays, Twilight half-price

A golf cart may be rented for $14 but is not mandatory. Golf facilities include: driving range, putting green, lockers, pro shop, club rentals, lunch wagon.

Helicopter Tours

The best way to take in Kaua'i's legendary scenery in a short time is on a helicopter tour. If you can afford to spend $150 or more for an hour's flight and accept some of the limitations of helicopter flight, you'll be in for a thrilling time. Flight times range from 30 minutes to an hour and a half. Flying for less than an hour will just whet your appetite and leave you wanting more. Most tour operators are based at the heliport at Līhu'e airport. One operator flies out of Port Allen airport and another is based at the Princeville airport. These operators tend to have shorter flights because they start and end their tours closer to the popular sights of Waimea Canyon and the Nā Pali coast.

More than 90 percent of helicopter tour passengers in Hawai'i are taking their first ride on a helicopter. Window seats, of course, are the best vantage points in a helicopter, but you can't be guaranteed to sit in one unless you're the pilot. The windows on tour helicopters are large and the view from an inboard seat is still excellent. The tour companies assign the seats to even the weight distribution on board. People weighing more than 250 pounds are assigned two seats and charged 50 percent extra. Whether assigned a window or inside seat, expect cramped quarters. The trips are of short duration and the sights so splendid that you probably won't notice anyway.

Most tour operators sell a video of your flight. This is a fun souvenir to have but don't expect the production quality to rival that of a pre-produced video. Nearly everyone brings a camera on his or her helicopter tour. A zoom telephoto lens, in the 28mm to 80 mm range, works best. Use fast film to help counteract the vibration from the engines. Wearing dark clothing and using a circular polarizing filter will help eliminate glare and reflection on the inside of the windows. Some of the Bell Jet Ranger helicopters are equipped with portholes that open for photographers; the ASTARs don't have opening windows. And, finally, don't

Left: Waiānuenue Falls

Right: Many of Kaua'i's waterfalls can be seen only by helicopter

Bottom: Bird's-eye view of Nā Pali coast

spend your whole trip looking through the camera's viewfinder—put the camera down occasionally and marvel at the scenery below you.

Bali Hai Helicopter Tours

Phone: (808) 335-3166, (800) 325-8687

Website: www.balihai-helitour.com

Fleet: Four-passenger Bell Jet Ranger with opening windows for glare-free photography.

Video: Not offered

Tours: Bali Hai Splendor, 45 minutes, $110; Bali Hai Grandeur, 55-60 minutes, $139 Both tours depart from Port Allen Airport, on the south coast next to Salt Pond Beach.

Heli USA Airways

Phone: (808) 826-6591

Website: www.heliusa.com

Fleet: Six-passenger, Executive AS-350 ASTAR

Tours: Menehune, 35 minutes, $99; Kama'aina, 45 minutes, $135; Ali'i Nui, 60 minutes, $179. Tours depart from Princeville Airport.

Island Helicopters

Phone: (808) 245-8588, (800) 829-5999

Website: www.islandhelicopters.com

Fleet: Four-passenger Bell Jet Ranger, six-passenger ASTAR

Video: One, pre-made tour video per couple included in price.

Tours: Kaua'i Grand Deluxe, 55-60 minutes, departs from Līhu'e Airport, $197.50.

Jack Harter Helicopters

Phone: (808) 245-3774, (888) 245-2001

Website: www.helicopters-kauai.com

Fleet: Two 4-passenger Bell Jet Rangers with portholes that open for photographers.

Video: No video is offered. The pilot narrates all tours.

Tours: 60-Minute Tour, $165; 90-Minute Tour, $235. Both tours depart from Līhu'e Airport. The 90-Minute Tour is the longest and most detailed helicopter tour offered on Kaua'i.

Ohana Helicopter Tours

Phone: (808) 245-3996, (800) 222-6989

Website: www.ohana-helicopters.com

Fleet: Three 6-passenger ASTARs

Video: Not offered

Tours: Mokihana Tour, 50-55 minutes, $146; Maile Tour, 65-70 minutes, $186. Both tours depart from Līhu'e Airport.

Safari Helicopters

Phone: (808) 246-0136, (800) 326-3356

Website: www.safariair.com

Fleet: Six-passenger, super ASTAR 350B27s featuring more legroom

Video: Customized video of your flight accompanied by music and pilot narration available at extra cost.

Tours: Deluxe Waterfall Safari, $149, 55 minutes, $159. Pilot narration of tour with two-way communication. Tours depart from Līhu'e Airport.

Safari is the only helicopter tour company to actually weigh their passengers on a scale. They have found that passengers tend to underestimate their weight by 20 percent. The scale discretely displays the weight to the counter worker only. Passengers wear new, X-generation Bose noise-canceling headsets. A multiple camera video system gets the best views for the video purchaser, plus the pilot is taped and monitored by company personnel for the safety of passengers.

South Sea Helicopters

Phone: (808) 245-2222, (800) 367-2914
Website: www.southseahelicopters.com
Fleet: Four-passenger Bell Jet Ranger, six-passenger Bell Long Ranger
Tours: Kaua'i Special Flight, 45-50 minutes, $135; Golden Eagle Flight, 55-60 minutes, $159. All tours depart from Līhu'e Airport.

Will Squyres Helicopter Tours

Phone: (808) 245-8881, (888) 245-4354
Website: www.activities-kauai.com
Fleet: Six-passenger ASTAR 350 BA with air conditioning and bubble windows.
Video: A pre-made video that can be personalized is available for $30. The pilot narrates tours.
Tours: 60 minutes, $159. Private charter, $950/hr. (1-6 guests). Tours depart from Līhu'e Airport.

Horseback Riding

Private ranches and stables are located throughout Kaua'i and welcome riders with every level of riding experience. Most of the horseback tours take place on private property, making this an excellent opportunity for many visitors to get to places that they would otherwise miss. All riding tour companies require reservations. During busy times, they fill up quickly, so book early. Bring your long pants and closed shoes but you can leave your chaps and spurs at home.

CJM Country Stables

Phone: 742-6096
Website: www.cjmstables.com
Area: Po'ipū and Māhā'ulepū areas on the south shore.
Tours: Secret Beach Breakfast Ride, 2 hours on horseback, 3 hours total, $80. Includes a packed-in continental breakfast. Hidden Beach Ride, 2 hours on horseback, $70. Beach Swim, Picnic Ride, 1-1/2 hours on horseback, 3-1/2 hours total, $90. Includes time for a swim in the ocean at Māhā'ulepū Beach and a deli-style lunch.
Restrictions: 7 years or older, under 250 pounds, no riding on the beach.

These rides are through the Grove Farm property under the Hoary Head ridge. Likely, the weather will be hot, sunny and breezy. The rides cut through and around sugar cane fields and pasture land on the way to Māhā'ulepū Beach. Although it is private land, access to the beach is granted to the public (see Beaches chapter). CJM Country Stables is on Po'ipū Road, just past the Hyatt Regency.

Esprit de Corps Riding Academy

Phone: 822-4688
Website: www.kauaihorses.com
Area: East Kaua'i, in the high country above Kapa'a
Tours: Fast Half, 3 hours, maximum five riders, $99. There are ocean and mountain views on this active ride with trotting and cantering. Picture Perfect, 2 to 3 hours, minimum two riders, $250. For the less-experienced rider, this package includes a riding lesson in the arena before venturing on the trail. The Wow Ride, 5 hours, maximum five riders, $250. This is a fast-paced ride into the mountains with a break for lunch and a stretch. All Day Adventure, 8 hours, $350 for a minimum of two riders and $300 for a minimum of four riders. It's an all-day ride into the interior of Kaua'i with timeout for lunch and a cool swim in a stream.
Restrictions: Ages 10 and up

A state trail maintenance fee of $7 is added to the cost of trail rides. Rides begin with stretching exercises and an orientation lesson with your horse. Raincoats are provided, if needed. Esprit de Corps is about 15 minutes from

Kapaʻa. From the Kūhiō Highway, turn mauka at Kuamoʻo Road (Highway 580) and head uphill for 2.7 miles. Turn right on Kamalu Road (Highway 581) and drive 1.6 miles to the end and turn left onto Olohena Road. Go 1.5 miles and turn right onto Kualapa Pl. At the end of Kualapa Pl., drive down the gravel road.

Keapana Horsemanship

Phone: 823-9303

Website: www.keapana.com

Area: East Kauaʻi

Tours: Keapana Valley, 1-1/2 hours, $89; Kalalea View Ride, 2 hours, $119; Kalalea Exploration Ride, 3 hours, $195. Specially requested rides on the Moalepe trail to the arboretum, to Sleeping Giant and on Contour road in Waimea Canyon are available.

Princeville Ranch Stables

Phone: 826-6777, 826-7473

Website: www.princevilleranch.com

Area: North shore, next to the community of Princeville.

Tours: Hawaiian Country Ride, 1-1/2 hours, $55. This ride takes you across rangeland with close-up views of the Hanalei Mountains. Waterfall Picnic Ride, 4 hours, $110. The highlight of this ride involves a short, steep, 10-minute hike (without horses) down to the base of an 80-foot waterfall. They recommend that you be in good physical condition for this. ʻAnini Bluff To Beach Ride, 3 hours, $100. Riders cross lush green pastures and meander along the bluff. Horses are ridden down the trail and are tied off near ʻAnini Beach. Riders can stop at the beach for a snack and swim. Cattle Drive Ride, 1-1/2 hours, $125. Riders can pretend to be *paniolo* (cowboys) and help to round up a herd of cattle at sunrise and drive them across the ranch to their grazing area.

Restrictions: 8 years and up, under 220 pounds for men and 180 pounds for women. A sign on the Kūhiō Highway, across from the Prince Golf Course, indicates the access road to the Princeville Ranch.

Silver Falls Ranch

Phone: 828-6718

Website: www.sfrkauai.com

Area: Kalihiwai Ridge, near Kīlauea.

Tours: The Greenhorn Ride, 1-1/2 hours including instruction, $69. Beginner riders receive individualized instruction within an enclosed area before setting out. The Hawaiian Discovery Ride, 2 hours, $78. This is a leisurely trail ride along winding streams, through paperbark and wild guava forests near the base of Mount Namahana. The Silver Falls Ride, 2 hours on horseback and one-hour stop, $105. Ride to a natural mountain pool and waterfall for a swim and a picnic.

The rides on Silver Falls Ranch are on private property. Turn *mauka* just west of Kīlauea, at Kalihiwai Ridge, onto Kahiliholo Road. Drive 2.3 miles to Kamoʻokoa Road and turn left to Silver Falls Ranch.

Kayaking

Without a doubt, Kauaʻi offers the best combination of river and sea kayaking in Hawaiʻi. Most popular among the river trips is Wailua. The **Wailua River** is considered Hawaiʻi's only navigable river. Because of that, many motorized craft ferry sightseers to the Fern Grotto, 2 miles upstream of the marina on the island's east shore. The motorboats stay on the south side of the river and the kayaks keep to the north. Kayak outfitters provide foam boat racks and straps so that the lightweight boats can be carried to the launch site by rental car. A state-owned small boat launch is available on the north side of the Wailua River. From the Kūhiō Highway, turn onto Highway 580 (Kuamoʻo Road) and take the second left turn.

The Wailua River flows between two mountain ridges, Kālepa Ridge on the south and Nounou Ridge to the north. Forty minutes upriver, as green and black cliffs tower above you, the river branches into north and south forks. Explore the north fork first for an opportunity to hike to a beautiful waterfall. After turning right into the north fork, take the left choice when reaching the next fork. Deep water soon ends and you have to pull the kayak ashore. Follow the trail upstream for 20 minutes where you cross a shallow stream that flows from your left. Five minutes further on the trail will take you to the foot of **Ho'olalaea Falls**. You can swim in the pool at the base of the 100-foot-high falls and enjoy a picnic lunch on the boulders surrounding the pool.

After paddling back to the fork in the river, turn right and head upstream on the south fork to the fabled **Fern Grotto**. The large motorized barges have the rights to exclusive use of the pier at the grotto, but kayakers may tie-up on the bank next to the pier. Anyone may enjoy the grotto, which is part of Wailua River State Park (see East Kaua'i Sights chapter). With good timing you can walk up to the grotto between boatloads. A short distance upstream from the Fern Grotto is a rope swing on an overhanging tree branch and a cliff dive about 15 feet above the river. Beyond this swimming area the south fork becomes too shallow for even kayaks to negotiate. The trip back to your launching point is usually against a wind. Total time for the tour, including the hike, is about 5 hours.

Hulei'a Stream flows along the north slope of Hā'upu Ridge, or Hoary Head Ridge, into the Kīpū area, emptying into Nāwiliwili Bay. The views of Hā'upu Ridge from the stream are majestic. Kayakers can paddle past the Menehune Fish Pond, but are not allowed to go inside its rock-walled enclosure. In fact, boaters can't legally land on any shore along Hulei'a Stream, as it is all private property. The land in Kīpū is owned by the Rice family, which zealously guards their property rights. Only guided kayak tours that have negotiated landing rights can take you on private property. Hulei'a Stream is closed to recreational boating on Sundays.

The third major waterway popular for kayaking is the north shore's **Hanalei River**. Unfortunately, the views of taro fields and mountains that you see from the Princeville viewpoint are mainly obscured to kayakers by tall grass growing along the riverbank. After paddling more than a mile from Hanalei and passing under the one-lane bridge, mountain views begin to open. As is the case with Hule'ia Stream, the property along the Hanalei is either privately owned or a National Wildlife Refuge. In the summer when the ocean surf is calm, kayakers can turn downstream and paddle out of the river's mouth into Hanalei Bay. You have spectacular views from the bay and you can land your boat and enjoy the beach.

Another north shore kayaking opportunity is the **Kalihiwai River**. The

Kayaking the Wailua River

These secluded waterfalls can be reached only by kayaking the north fork of the Wailua River

river flows through the lush and beautiful Kalihiwai Valley, between Kīlauea and Princeville. You certainly would have noticed its beauty if you drove over the gracefully curving concrete bridge on the Kūhiō Highway. The Kalihiwai River is navigable by kayak for only 1.2 miles. You will see a waterfall to the left of the bridge as you paddle upstream. After passing under the bridge, your attention will be drawn to a four-tier waterfall on the right side. It's just a 10-minute hike to the waterfall. A steep trail follows the stream up the hillside to the other levels of the waterfall. Guided stable rides create some congestion at the falls between 11:00 a.m. and 2:00 p.m. when they arrive for a picnic lunch.

Knife-edged cliffs, waterfalls, sea caves and hanging valleys make the **Nā Pali coast sea voyage** a stunning kayaking experience. Paddlers put in at Hā'ena on the lush north shore and pull out 16 miles later at Polihale Beach on the arid west coast. Sights on the coast include sea caves, beaches, and reefs. The trip is made arduous by never-ceasing ocean swells and exposure to the sun and wind. Aiding the paddlers are favorable winds and

ocean currents. Guides say that sea sickness is the most common malady among their charges. Tours of Nā Pali take place only from mid-May to mid-September. The trip requires 5 to 6 hours of intermittent paddling. Be sure to bring sun protection, water, a bathing suit, footwear that can get wet, such as sandals or tabis, and a change of clothes.

Aloha Canoes and Kayaks

Phone: (808) 246-6804
Rental: Single $25, Double $50
Guided Hule'ia River Tour,
    Nāwiliwili $70-$82
Location: Kalapakī Market Place,
    3366 Wa'apa Rd., Nāwiliwili

Aloha Canoes and Kayaks launches their guided tours of Hule'ia Stream from the Nāwiliwili Small Boat Harbor. Kayakers paddle upstream for 2.5 miles and start a hike on the private property of the Kīpū Ranch, owned by the Rice family. The hike leads to a swimming pond with a waterfall and a rope swing. Only kayakers/hikers that are part of the guided tour have permission to travel there.

For the return trip downriver, the kayaks are tied to a double-hulled launch and towed back to Nāwiliwili. The hike lasts about 30 minutes and the total tour is 3 hours for the morning and afternoon tours and 3.5 hours for the mid-day tour where a picnic lunch is provided.

Chris The Fun Lady

Phone: (808) 822-7759
Rental: Single $25-$45, Double $50-$85
Location: Kūhiō Highway, Waipouli, across from Foodland

Island Adventures

Phone: (808) 245-9662
Rental: Single $10/hour or $30/day, Double $15/hour or $45/day
Guided Huleʻia River Tour $49
Location: Kalapakī Market Place, 3366 Waʻapā Rd., Nāwiliwili

The guided tour of Huleʻia Stream launches from Nāwiliwili Small Boat Harbor and lasts for 2 hours. You are taken ashore at the National Wildlife Refuge. Kayak rentals are launched at Kalapakī Bay.

Kayak Kauaʻi

Phone: Kapaʻa (808) 822-9179
(800) 437-3507; Hanalei (808) 826-9844
Website: www.kayakkauai.com
Rental: Single $26, Double $50
Guided Nā Pali Coast Tour $160/person
Guided South Shore Tour $115/person
Location: Kapaʻa, south end of Coconut Marketplace; Hanalei, on main highway at east end of town

In Hanalei, Kayak Kauaʻi has its own launch site on a canal that connects to the Hanalei River. In Kapaʻa, they include a foam roof rack for your vehicle. The guided Nā Pali Coast Tour runs mid-May to mid-September. All kayaks are reinforced double sea kayaks with rudders. They put in at Hāʻena Beach and try to determine if you are up to the task by the time they paddle to Kēʻē Beach. Occasionally someone is overcome with sea sickness and has to end the trip early. The guide will lead you through sea caves and pull in at Miloliʻi Beach for lunch and a rest. The last leg is to Polihale Beach where a waiting van will take you on the long drive back to Hanalei.

When winter seas are too rough for kayaking the Nā Pali coast, Kayak Kauaʻi offers a south shore guided kayak journey. Paddling west from Poʻipū, they pass Spouting Horn, Lāwaʻi Beach, Nōmilo Pond, and Wahiʻawa Bay. Some of the sights along the coast are on private land and not accessible except by sea. The tour involves 3 to 4 hours of intermittent paddling. Windy conditions and sun exposure require participants to be in good physical condition. The south shore tour operates from October to April.

Kayak Wailua

Phone: (808) 822-3388, 822-4274
Website: www.kayakwailua.com
Rental: Single $20-$35, Double $35-$55
Location: Kinipopo Shopping Center, Wailua

Outfitters Kauaʻi

Phone: (808) 742-9667
Rental: Single $30, Double $45
Guided Nā Pali Coast Tour $145
Location: 2827A Poʻipū Road, next to Poʻipū Fire Station

Peddle and Power

Phone: (808) 826-9069
Rental: Single $20, Double $35
Location: Ching Young Village, Hanalei

Wailua Kayak and Canoe

Phone: (808) 821-1188
Rental: Single $25, Double $50
Location: Kūhiō Highway and Kuamoʻo Road, Wailua

Lū'au

It was the custom in early Hawai'i to celebrate special occasions with a feast. Hawaiians shared their bounty to mark such auspicious occasions as the birth of a child, victory in war, a successful harvest, or the completion of a new home or canoe. Originally called *'aha'aina* (gathering for a meal), the term lū'au came into use much later and refers to the edible taro leaves that traditionally were used to wrap the food prior to being placed in the *imu* (underground oven). Today, *lū'au* is a time to share traditional foods, enjoy songs and dances of early Hawai'i and other parts of Polynesia.

On the morning of the lū'au, a pit is dug and filled with kiawe branches and rocks. A fire is lit to heat the rocks and then a pig wrapped in banana and ti leaves is placed in the pit. The pit is covered with sand and the pig is left to steam all day. At sunset, the pig is unearthed and presented to the guests at the "imu ceremony." This main dish of the lū'au is called *kālua* pork and its slow-cooked meat is tender and succulent. The modern lū'au is set up as a buffet, which usually includes mahimahi, lomilomi salmon and poi, served along with many traditional American and Asian dishes. Poi is a starchy staple made from taro root and lomilomi is salted salmon with onions and tomatoes. If *laulau* is available, it is worth trying. It is chicken or pork mixed with butterfish and dark green taro leaf, steamed together in a wrapper of ti leaf. An open bar keeps the party spirit alive.

After the meal, guests continue drinking while entertainers sing and perform the hula. Reservations are needed for all of these lū'au. Seating usually begins between 5:00 and 5:30 p.m.

Drums of Paradise Lū'au
Phone: 742-1234
When: Sundays and Thursdays, 6:00 p.m.
Location: Hyatt Regency Kaua'i Resort, Po'ipū
Price: $62.50 adults, $31.25 children (6-12 years)

Kaua'i Coconut Beach Resort Lū'au
Phone: 822-6651
When: Daily
Location: Lū'au Halau Pavilion, Kaua'i Coconut Beach Resort
Price: $55 adults, $33 teen (12-17 years), $23 child (3-11), $50 seniors (55 and over). Mondays and Tuesdays are family nights, where one child is admitted free when accompanied by an adult.

Guests may watch the cooks prepare kalua pig in the *imu* at 10:45 a.m. At 6:00 p.m. the festivities begin with the torch-lighting ceremony, followed by a lei greeting and the culmination of the *imu* ceremony. Following dinner an all-Hawaiian Lū'au show, choreographed and arranged by hula master Kawaikapuokalani Hewett, is performed on stage.

Princeville Hotel Lū'au
Phone: 826-9644
When: Monday and Thursday, 6:00 p.m.
Location: Poolside and beachside, Princeville Hotel
Price: $59.50 adults, $47.50 seniors, $30 children (6-12)

Reflections of Paradise Lū'au and Polynesian Review
Phone: 245-9595
When: Monday, Tuesday, and Thursday, 6:30 p.m.
Location: Kilohana Carriage House, just west of Līhu'e
Price: $49 adults, $45 seniors (55 or over), $20 children (6-14)

The Kilohana Carriage House was built in the 1930s on a 35-acre plantation. Their menu is prepared in the kitchen of Gaylord's restaurant. The after-dinner show encompasses Hawaiian, Tahitian and Maori dances, as well as the popular Samoan fire knife dance.

Smith's Tropical Paradise Garden Lū'au and International Pageant

Phone: 821-6895, 821-6896
When: Daily
Location: Smith's Tropical Paradise,
 next to the marina on the south bank
 of Wailua River
Price: $54 adults, $27 juniors (7-13),
 $19 child (3-6); show only $14 adults,
 $7 child.

The gates open at 5:00 p.m., giving you time to stroll through the lovely gardens of Smith's Tropical Paradise before the *imu* ceremony at 6:00 p.m. Dinner begins at 6:30 while musicians provide entertainment and dinner music. At 8:00 p.m., the International Pageant begins in the Lagoon Amphitheatre. The traditional blowing of the conch shell and torch lighting starts the presentation. Then, with much drama, Pele, Goddess of Fire, emerges out of the darkness from atop a lava-spewing volcano. After that, a revue entitled the Golden People of Hawai'i presents dances from Tahiti, Hawai'i, China, Japan, Philippines, New Zealand, and Samoa. For a lesser admission price, visitors may skip the dinner and watch the show only.

Tahiti Nui Lū'au

Phone: 826-6277
When: Wednesdays, 6:00-9:00 p.m.
Location: Tahiti Nui Restaurant, Hanalei
Price: $52 adults, $30 teens (12-17), $20
 children (3-11)

In 1964, Louise Marston, owner of the Tahiti Nui restaurant, moved to Hanalei from her native Tahiti to found what was the only bar on the North Shore. In the 1970s she added a restaurant to the bar and began serving a family-style lū'au. Now the lū'au serves a huge buffet and a Polynesian revue features the Nani Hanalei Group, hula dancing, a Tahitian drum group, and a special contest for guests.

Walking Tours

Kapa'a History Tour

Guides of a newly launched walking tour of Kapa'a bring the intriguing history, people, and architecture of the east Kaua'i town to life. During the 90-minute tour, you learn about the devastating flood of 1921. Unfolded is what Kapa'a was like during World War II and the roles rice, pineapple, and sugar cane played in its development. Landmarks such as the Japanese stone lantern that was built in the early 1900s and stands in Kapa'a Park are pointed out.

The tour begins and ends at the Kapa'a History Shop located in the historic Kawamura Store in downtown Kapa'a. Tours are scheduled for Tuesday, Thursday and Saturday at 10:00 a.m. The cost is $10 for adults and $5 for children under 12 and includes refreshments.

DINING

Cuisine unique to Kaua'i has come to mean more than poi and pineapple. In the early nineties, some of Hawai'i's top chefs started to incorporate the Islands' extensive selection of fresh produce into their dishes, blending classic Asian and Western culinary techniques and starting the trend some call "Hawai'i Regional Cuisine." Using the bounty of fish from the sea, locally raised beef, and intensely flavored tropical fruits, these resourceful chefs have created dishes such as: 'ahi carpaccio, breadfruit soufflé and papaya cheesecake.

With visitors coming to Kaua'i from all over the world, restaurants cater to varied culinary tastes with cosmopolitan fare. For an economical taste of local-style cooking, try a plate lunch in the less-touristy areas of Kapa'a and Līhu'e. With plain white rice and cabbage, you'll get a choice of curry stew, teriyaki beef or kālua (roasted) pig, a beverage and change back from a $10 bill. Although it may not sound appetizing, a pupu is an appetizer.

Casual wear is acceptable at nearly all the restaurants on Kaua'i. Expensive restaurants may ask for "aloha wear," which means a shirt with a collar and long pants for men and a dress for women. Price categories are symbolized with $ signs and are the average cost for one diner without alcoholic drinks, tax or tips.

Reservations are not required unless so noted. Except for fast-food outlets, major credit cards are accepted at all restaurants.

$	Less than $15
$$	$15 to $25
$$$	$25 to $40
$$$$	Over $40

East Side Restaurants

Aloha Diner
Waipouli Complex, *mauka* side of Kūhiō Highway, Waipouli, 822-3851, Hawaiian, $

Aloha Diner is the place to go for economy-minded diners looking for local cuisine. The tiny restaurant has six tables, mural-painted walls and a kitchen barely hidden behind bead curtains. For lunch you can fill up on *kālua* pig or *laulau*, which is shredded pork roasted in ti leaves. Other choices include chicken lū'au, tripe stew, and lomilomi salmon, which is diced smoked salmon with tomatoes and onions (it looks like salsa). Rice or poi is included as a side dish. If you want to try poi for the first time, note that the portion size is generous and one bowl could probably be shared with your dining partner. For dinner service the portion sizes are increased. The restaurant is open 10:30 a.m. to 3:00 p.m. and 5:30 p.m. to 9:00 p.m., Tuesday through Saturday. They are closed Sundays and Mondays.

Beezer's Old Fashioned Ice Cream
1380 Kūhiō Highway, Kapa'a, 822-4411, American Nostalgia, $

If you are old enough, the decor will take you back to the 1950s. A long counter fashioned of glass blocks has red-topped stools that twirl. A jukebox helps to set the mood. There are the soda fountain favorites like root beer floats and extra thick chocolate malts. Food classics include burger and fries, meatloaf and chicken-fried steak.

Brennecke's

Across from Poʻipū Beach Park, 742-7588, $$

Brennecke's has been strategically located near the island's busiest beach since it was established in 1983. It is best known for fresh island fish char-broiled over kiawe charcoal. Pupus include sashimi, burgers, and prime rib sandwich served on sourdough bread. Seafood specials include mussels and pasta, Hawaiian spiny lobster, double jumbo shrimp skewers, and cioppino, a seafood stew. Prime rib steaks, oriental chicken stir-fry, baby back pork ribs and pasta primavera round out the menu. Each entree includes a trip to the salad bar or a cup of chowder with rolls and steamed rice, or herb pasta and fresh vegetable. Brennecke's is open daily from 11:00 a.m. to 10:00 p.m.

Bubba Burgers

Across from Kapaʻa Park, Kapaʻa, 823-0069, Burgers, $

The original burger stand in Hanalei was such a success that Bubba Burgers opened a larger burger restaurant on the east coast. The same lean burgers and fish sandwiches are available with an ocean view thrown in. The Kapaʻa location is open daily from 10:30 a.m. to 8:00 p.m.

Caffe Coco

4369 Kūhiō Highway, Wailua, 822-7990, $$

Diners are greeted at the restaurant's entry with foliage that has grown to form a tunnel. Greenery also creates a lush canopy in the back, shading the tables. Breakfast items include coco-custard French toast and lunch-time eaters might want to try the scrambled egg burrito. For dinner there's the Pacific Rim platter featuring potstickers, seared ʻahi (tuna), rice, Asian noodle salad and peanut dressing. A $10 corkage fee allows you to bring your own wine.

Coconuts

Mauka side of Kūhiō Highway, Waipouli, 823-8777, $$

Even though the Pacific Ocean is across the street, Coconuts has its own sandy beach in front of the restaurant. The interior is decorated island style with split bamboo ceiling, coconut furniture, coconut lighting and coconut-inlaid placemats. Drinks and pupus are served from 4:00 p.m. and dinner starts at 5:30 p.m. The kitchen stays open until 10:00 p.m. The pupu menu includes shrimp cakes and lobster ravioli. Dinner choices include grilled filet mignon and catch of the day. Wasabi mashed potatoes is an original recipe that is whipped up. Reservations are recommended for groups larger than eight. The restaurant is closed on Mondays.

Deli and Bread Connection

Kukui Grove Shopping Center, Līhuʻe, 245-7115, Deli, $

This deli counter is tucked into the back of a store that sells kitchen specialty items. Tables are provided for diners both in the deli and in the mall. Besides the ever-popular club sandwich, they assemble a sandwich called the Topss, piled high with turkey, pepperoni, Swiss cheese and sprouts.

Eggbert's

Kauaʻi Coconut Market Place, 822-3787, $

You can get more than eggs for breakfast at Eggberts—you can get eggs for lunch and dinner as well. Eggs Benedict come in five styles and two sizes. Omelettes can be ordered in two-egg and three-egg sizes with a choice of hash browns, rice, or toast. Salads, sandwiches, burgers and soups are available for lunch. For dinner, the menu includes New York steak, catch of the day, meat loaf, roast pork and stir-frys. Eggbert's is open daily from 7:00 a.m. to 9:00 p.m. The breakfast menu is available until 3:00 p.m. and seniors and kids menus are available.

Hanamāʻulu Restaurant and Teahouse

Kūhiō Highway, Hanamāʻulu, 245-2511, Chinese and Japanese, $$

This highly rated restaurant hides behind a demure facade in the former sugar plantation town north of Līhuʻe. The Hanamāʻulu Restaurant combines Japanese and Chinese cooking and serves it in a lovely garden setting complete with a fishpond. Your food is cooked in front of you in the Robatayaki Room. Reservations are needed to enjoy the Ozahiki Room, where diners sit on floor mats around low tables. They are open for lunch, Tuesday to Friday from 10:00 a.m. to 1:00 p.m., and for dinner, Tuesday to Sunday from 4:30 p.m. to 9:00 p.m.

Papaya's Natural Foods and Cafe
Kaua'i Village Shopping Center, Kapa'a, 823-0190, Vegetarian, $

Papaya's has 10 outdoor tables shaded by rainbow-colored umbrellas for those who like to eat outdoors. You can order fresh fish salad or spinach lasagna made with feta, mozzarella and parmesan cheeses and served with an organic green salad. A vegan special is baked tofu on brown rice and, for dessert: carrot cake, black mocha cake, or chocolate tofu pie.

Tip Top Cafe
3173 Akahi Street, Līhu'e, 245-2333, $

Locals recognize the Tip Top as a good-value restaurant for breakfast and lunch. The single large room is lined with booths and shows little in the way of adornment, except for a live orchid plant on each table. Breakfast includes very large pancakes with bananas or macadamia nuts and good coffee. Oxtail soup or beef stew are on the lunch menu. Daily specials are often breaded pork chops, breaded fish, and teriyaki dishes. The restaurant is open 6:30 a.m. to 2:00 p.m., Tuesday through Sunday, and is closed on Mondays.

Wailua Family Restaurant
4361 Kūhiō Highway, Wailua, 822-3325, $

This roadside restaurant, decorated with thousands of hanging lights, is open from 6:30 a.m. to 9:00 p.m. For breakfast, patrons order at a counter. Buffets are used for lunch and dinner and have something for everyone, including soba noodles, poi, lomilomi salmon, pigs feet and taco salads. A seafood bar is added at dinner.

Whalers Brewpub
3132 Ninini Point, Kauai Lagoons golf course, 245-2000, $-$$

Whalers Brewpub is located near Ninini Point with a great view of Nāwiliwili Bay. There is an outdoor deck that is the preferred place to drink and eat at sunset. Pupus are the favored menu fare to go with beer. They include fried flowering onion with ranch dip, chicken quesadillas, egg rolls, chicken skewers, and nachos. Slightly more filling would be the 20-ounce "Whale Burger." Fresh fish comes with a choice of soy-ginger, fruit salsa, and lemon-thyme beurre blanc sauces. Whalers is open from 11:00 a.m. to 9:30 p.m. daily and reservations are recommended.

North Shore Restaurants

Bamboo Bamboo
Hanalei Center, Hanalei, 826-1177, $$-$$$

In the former location of Cafe Luna, Bamboo Bamboo features open-air dining with wide views of Hanalei Valley taro patches, mountains and waterfalls, as well as a classy dining room. Lunch hours are 11:30 a.m. to 3:00 p.m. and dinner is served from 5:30 p.m. to 9:30 p.m., seven days a week. Popular dinner items include lamb, fresh 'ahi, potato-crusted mahimahi and an 'ahi pizza with wasabi cream topping. A variety of fresh pasta dishes are offered, as well as seafood stew and one of the restaurant's signature seafood dishes, Creole Hā'ena. Continental European, French, Asian and other cuisine are offered, along with a complete bar selection and cappuccino station. Dinner reservations are accepted.

Bubba Burgers
Hanalei Center, Hanalei, 826-7839, Burgers, $

Patrons can eat on a small porch at the yellow burger stand or on picnic tables and umbrellas thatched with coconut leaves next to Hanalei's main road. The menu features the Slopper, an open-faced burger with chili; the half-pound Big Bubba with three patties; and the Hubba Bubba, a plate lunch with rice, hotdog and chili. Chicken burgers, fish burgers, and fish and chips are available too.

Hanalei Dolphin
Makai of highway in Hanalei, 826-6113, Seafood, $$

The Hanalei Dolphin is in the first building you see as you enter Hanalei. It is situated on the Hanalei River and has outdoor riverside tables, although mosquitoes may want to make a meal out of you. The restaurant is open for dinner only, which centers around fresh fish or steak. Salad bar, steak fries or rice and bread comes with dinner entrées.

Hanalei Gourmet

In the Hanalei School Building, Hanalei, 826-2425, Deli, $-$$

Open for breakfast, lunch and dinner, the Hanalei Gourmet is a combination deli, restaurant and bar. The deli can make sandwiches to go for north shore hikers and beachgoers. Local musicians perform in cramped quarters most evenings at the Gourmet. If it gets too loud and smoky, you can eat on the porch outside the restaurant.

Hanalei Wake Up Cafe

North side of highway in Hanalei, 826-5551, Breakfast, $

This is basically a surfers' hangout with surfing photos and memorabilia hanging on the walls and ceiling. The cozy building and quaint decor doesn't guarantee good food. A restaurant specializing in breakfasts should certainly do better than microwave frozen pancakes.

Kīlauea Bakery and Pau Hana Pizza

Kong Lung Center, Kīlauea, 828-2020, Bakery, $

They bake and serve the best bread, danishes, muffins, and croissants on the island. Coffee is fresh brewed a cup at a time with filtered water. A few seats are available in the bakery, on the porch and on the patio. Expect it to be busy every morning. At 3:00 p.m. the bakery transforms itself into the Pau Hana Pizza. Their pizzas are made with organic olive oil, whole milk, mozzarella cheese, homemade sauce and with either whole wheat or traditional crusts. The Big Blue is their specialty pizza and comes topped with smoked mahimahi, tomatoes, capers, parsley, cheese and a squeeze of lemon.

Lighthouse Bistro

2484 Kaneke St., Kīlauea (next to Kong Lung store), 828-0480, $$

The Lighthouse Bistro recently opened in a renovated, plantation-style building with terra cotta floors, bamboo chairs and Hawaiian artwork. Live piano music is featured on Friday and Saturday nights. The kitchen serves up contemporary cuisine with an Italian flair.

Interesting menu items include seafood linguine, tortellini fresca, stuffed shrimp in phyllo and chicken satay with Thai peanut sauce.

La Cascata

Princeville Hotel, Princeville, 826-9644, Italian, $$$

Romantic views of Hanalei Bay appear through arched windows at La Cascata. Hand-painted murals and tiled floors give the ambience of an Italian villa. Menu items include potato-crusted crab cake with red pepper aioli or grilled 'ahi with risotto-fried capellini pasta topped off with one of the daily sorbet selections.

Postcards Cafe

Mauka side of the highway, Hanalei, 826-1191, Vegetarian/Seafood, $$

Gourmet vegetarian and seafood dishes draw diners to a converted plantation-style house in Hanalei. A breakfast specialty is the sunrise scramble, which features sautéed tofu with onions, garlic and herbs supplementing the eggs. For dinner you could try an organic salad or Thai summer rolls with spicy peanut sauce before the fresh fish or shrimp tacos. The taj triangles are crusty phyllo pastry filled with potatoes, peas, carrots and Indian spices served with tropical chutney.

Sushi Blues

Ching Young Village, Hanalei, 826-9701, Seafood and Steak, $$

Sushi chefs at this north shore restaurant and bar prepare traditional as well as cutting-edge style sushi such as crunchy, aloha, rainbow, Alaska, vegetable and rock & roll with baked spicy scallops. If you like your fish cooked, try the coconut shrimp with Thai chili plum sauce or fresh fish wok-charred with mango barbeque glaze or sautéed with garlic sake cream. Local musicians crank out the dance music most nights or live jazz is performed for more mellow moments.

Zelo's Beach House

Makai side of the highway, Hanalei, 826-9700, Burgers and Fish, $-$$

Located on the main road in Hanalei and not on a beach, Zelo's dresses up its hip and popular restaurant in South Pacific kitsch. The restaurant is centered by a bar area with a tin roof and ironwood poles. A canoe hangs suspended overhead. The best tables are next to the windows with flower boxes and mountain views. Lunchtime crowds will fill all of its 24 tables. Dinner reservations for groups of six or more are recommended. Lunch specials vary but there is always burgers and fries, Philly steak sandwich, Cajun chicken wrap, soft shell fresh fish tacos and stuffed baked potato. Happy hour lasts from 3:30 p.m. to 5:30 p.m. Dinner favorites are charbroiled or pan-blackened fresh fish or rib eye steak, Hawaiian chicken breasts marinated in teriyaki sauce and grilled with pineapple, and baby back ribs slathered in barbeque sauce.

South Side Restaurants

Beach House

5022 Lāwa'i Rd., Po'ipū (on the way to Spouting Horn), 742-1424, $$$

Be ready to experience such delicacies as wok-charred mahimahi in a ginger-sesame crust and lime ginger sauce or seared sea scallops with a polenta herb crust and papaya-avocado guacamole. A kiawe wood-burning grill adds a flavorful touch to kalbi-style lamb rack or pork tenderloin with jerk spices. Floor to ceiling windows showcase Po'ipū's best ocean view—especially at sunset.

Camp House Grill

At the signal light, on Kaumuali'i Highway in Kalāheo, 332-9755, $

Camp houses were built to house the contract laborers from China, Japan, Portugal, and the Philippines who toiled in the island's sugar cane fields. They were simple houses with tin roofs and brightly painted board and batten siding. The Camp House Grill operates in a remodeled camp house. The rustic restaurant has walls lined with black and white photographs and memorabilia portraying life in the old days of the Hawai'i sugar industry. One example is a framed pay slip and a note, dated 1918, where

a worker signed over his month's wages to the company store. Decorating the entrance is a reproduction of a food safe with pierced tin door panels. In the original camp houses, the food safe would have sat with its legs in sardine cans filled with kerosene to keep crawling insects at bay.

The fare at the Camp House Grill is delicious, simple and not geared to the diet conscious. The weight watcher breakfast special is two eggs any style, corned beef hash and a biscuit with gravy. Other options for breakfast are pancakes that can be topped with macadamia nuts, coconut, chocolate chips, bananas or blueberries. Their lunchtime menu is dominated by burgers. Camp House Grill serves the best burgers on the island. The patties are lean, ample and cooked medium-well unless otherwise ordered. A variety of topping choices are available. Delicious and appropriate for the locale is the Hanapēpē Burger with lettuce, tomato, pineapple, and teriyaki sauce. For lunch or dinner there is *huli* chicken—half a chicken barbequed with a blend of Hawaiian, Chinese, and Cajun spices. For dessert, they are famous for their pineapple cheesecake-macadamia nut pie.

Casa di Amici

2301 Nalo Road, Po'ipū (near Brennecke Beach), 742-1555, Mediterranean, $$

Patrons of Casa di Amici can dine on a lanai looking down to the ocean. Rattan furnishings and ceiling fans give the restaurant an island feel. The mainly Italian fare includes touches of Thai, Japanese, French, and Vietnamese influences. Many entrées can be ordered in light or regular portions. You can mix your favorite pasta with your choice of sauce, including pesto and salsa arrabiatta (a spicy tomato sauce with sautéed pancetta and crushed chili pepper).

Da'li Deli Cafe

5492 Kōloa Rd., Kōloa, 742-8824, Deli, $

Da'li Deli is an authentic European-style deli in the heart of old Kōloa town. Bagels and breads are baked fresh each day. Turkey, roast beef, corned beef and other sandwich fillers are prepared on the premises. They are open from 6:00 a.m. to 9:00 p.m., Tuesday through Friday, and 6:00 a.m. to 6:00 p.m. on Saturdays and Mondays.

Island Teriyaki

5330 Old Kōloa Rd., Kōloa, 742-9988, Asian, $

Step into the small restaurant under the big mango tree in Kōloa and you meet the heady aroma of papaya, coconut, pineapple, banana, guava, ginger, and curry. Specialties include wraps and bowls, plate lunches, fresh fish, chicken, pork and beef dishes served with delicious papaya teriyaki sauce. Wraps are served in a flour, sun-dried tomato or spinach tortilla. You can take your order without a tortilla and have it served in a bowl with rice or mashed potatoes. Breakfast burritos are available, as are smoothies and shaved ice. Island Teriyaki is open 7:30 a.m. to 9:00 p.m. daily.

Keoki's Paradise

Po'ipū Shopping Village, Po'ipū, 742-7534, $$

You'll be surprised to enter Keoki's and find a boathouse-style restaurant set on a peaceful lagoon with tropical foliage and a thatched-roof bar. Healthy-sized entrées include Caesar salad, fresh-baked bread, and herbed rice. Fresh fish, Kōloa pork ribs glazed with plum sauce, or Balinese chicken marinated in lemon grass and served with a lemon-shoyu sauce add a local flavor to the menu. Steaks and garlic mashed potatoes are served and for dessert, hula pie with an Oreo cookie crust.

Kupono Cafe

Hyatt Regency Kaua'i, 1571 Po'ipū Rd., Po'ipū, 742-1234, Vegetarian, $

"Kupono" means natural or balanced, and that describes the food and the setting of this courtyard restaurant at Anara Spa in the Hyatt Regency. You can have a fresh fruit smoothie, a vitamin-packed spirulina (blue green microalgae) smoothie or Anahola granola with fresh berries. Sandwich choices include grilled eggplant with olives, grilled onions and Alpine Lace cheese, or the Anara Veggie with fresh slices of ripe tomatoes, cucumber and avocado on whole wheat toast with Kīlauea leaf lettuce, spicy mayonnaise and roasted eggplant spread. They are open from 7:00 a.m. to 2:00 p.m. daily.

Piatti Italian Restaurant

Kiahuna Plantation, 2253 Po'ipū Rd., Po'ipū, 742-2216, Italian, $$-$$$

You can enjoy fine Italian food in a setting of gardens with torch-lit paths and rock walls, a rich wood interior, and verandah dining in a historic Polynesian home. The signature pasta dish, pappardelle fantasia, is a wide saffron pasta sautéed in white wine, herbs and spices and tossed with fresh garden vegetables and shrimp. A wood-burning oven will bake your pizza with portobello mushrooms, pancetta and fontana cheese.

West Side Restaurants

Green Garden

Highway 50, Hanapēpē, 335-5422, Local, $

It is hard to see this island-style restaurant behind all the tropical plants. Hanapēpē locals have been eating at the Green Garden since 1948. Its interior is cool and dark, with ceiling fans, display counters filled with a shell collection, and tables covered with orange cloths. There are dozens of Asian, local and American dishes on the menu, including a seafood special of breaded mahimahi, scallops, oysters and deep-fried shrimp.

Hanapēpē Cafe

3830 Hanapēpē Rd., Hanapēpē, 335-5011, Vegetarian, $$

You can sit at the black-and-white bar for an espresso drink or sit at a table while you dine on vegetarian food with a French-Italian flair. Menu items include garden burgers, Caesar salads, soup, croissants, and calzones. A vegetarian breakfast and lunch menu is available Tuesday through Saturday. Coffee and pastries are served until 3:00 p.m. Dinner, with live music by local guitarists, is served Friday when the art galleries on the street remain open late. Reservations for the Friday dinner are essential.

Waimea Brewing Company
9400 Kaumuali'i Highway, Waimea,
338-9733, Brewpub, $-$$

This micro-brewery is located in the Waimea Plantation Cottages. Pub fare is served on small plates for grazing. Choices include smoked chicken quesadillas, fried calamari, gado gado skewers and goat cheese dip with taro leaves. Regular-size servings of roasted chicken steak, short ribs, and *kālua* pork can be ordered. They are open daily from 11:00 a.m. to 11:00 p.m.

Wrangler's Steakhouse
9853 Kaumuali'i Highway, Waimea,
338-1218, Steakhouse, $-$$

The Western motif abounds; a wagon in the loft, log-framed booths with gas lanterns, and lauhala woven *paniolo* hats in the made-in-Hawai'i gift shop. Menu items include shrimp tempura with sashimi, beef teriyaki, *imu*-style roast pork with cabbage, and smoky and tender grilled mahimahi sandwiches.

ACCOMMODATIONS

The lower rate quoted is for the lowest-priced room for two people in low season without ocean view. The higher rate is for a deluxe room or suite in high season with an ocean view where applicable. State excise tax and transient accommodation tax will add 11.25 percent to the cost for both hotels and condominiums.

Resorts and Hotels— East Side

Aston Kaua'i Coast Resort
4-484 Kūhiō Hwy., Kapa'a
Phone: (808) 822-3441, (800) 922-7866
Website: www.aston-hotels.com
Units: 243
Rates: $140-$230
Beach: Waipouli Beach

Garden Island Inn
3445 Wilcox Rd., Līhu'e
Phone: (808) 245-7227, (800) 648-0154
Website: www.planet-hawaii.com/g-i-inn
Units: 21
Rates: $65-$200
Beach: Kalapakī

Holiday Inn Sunspree Resort
3-5920 Kūhiō Hwy., Kapa'a
Phone: (808) 823-6000
Website: http://holidayinn-kauai.com
Units: 216
Rates: $150-$275
Beach: Lydgate State Park

Hotel Coral Reef
1516 Kūhiō Hwy., Kapa'a
Phone: (808) 822-4481
Units: 24
Rates: $59-$79
Beach: Kapa'a Beach

Islander On The Beach
484 Kūhiō Hwy., Kapa'a
Phone: (808) 822-7417, (800) 922-7866
Website: www.astonhotels.com
Units: 196
Rates: $110-$195
Beach: Waipouli Beach

Kaua'i Coconut Beach Resort
Coconut Plantation, Kapa'a
Phone: (808) 822-3345
Units: 300
Rates: $150-$290
Beach: Waipouli Beach

Kaua'i Marriott
Kalapakī Bay, Līhu'e
Phone: (808) 245-5050
Website: www.marriotthotels.com/LIHHI
Units: 355
Rates: $259-$1800
Beach: Kalapakī Beach

Kaua'i Marriott's pool

Kaua'i Sands
420 Papaloa Rd., Kapa'a
Phone: (808) 822-4951, (800) 560-5553
Website: http://sand-seaside.com
Units: 200
Rates: $98-$135
Beach: Waipouli Beach

Radisson Kauai Beach Resort
4331 Kaua'i Beach Dr., Līhu'e
Phone: (808) 245-1955
Units: 341
Rates: $180-$410
Beach: Nukoli'i Beach

Resorts and Hotels— North Shore

Princeville Hotel
5520 Kahaku Rd., Princeville
Phone: (808) 826-9644, (800) 826-4400
Website: www.princeville.com

Units: 252
Rates: $360-$3500
Beach: Pu'u Poa Beach

Guests of Princeville Hotel enjoy magnificent views

Resorts and Hotels— South Side

Hyatt Regency Kaua'i Resort & Spa
1571 Po'ipū Rd., Kōloa
Phone: (808) 742-1234, (800) 742-1234
Website: www.kauai-hyatt.com
Units: 598
Rates: $310-$2950
Beach: Shipwreck Beach

Sheraton Kaua'i Resort
2440 Ho'onani Rd., Kōloa
Phone: (808) 742-1661, (800) 782-9488
Website: www.sheraton-kauai.com
Units: 413
Rates: $265-$740
Beach: Sheraton Beach

Resorts and Hotels— West Side

Waimea Plantation Cottages
9400 Kaumuali'i Hwy., Waimea
Phone: (808) 338-1625
Website: www.astonhotels.com
Units: 49
Rates: $160-$465
Beach: Lucy Wright Beach

Condominiums

Being more economical to rent than hotel rooms and offering more space, condos are the preferred choice for many traveling families. Although they don't provide the services of a hotel, vacation condos generally are located near beaches, golf courses and other recreation spots. Full-service condo resorts often have their own rental offices, restaurants and recreation facilities. Their rates can reach the levels of luxury hotel resorts. Condos rented directly from owners who list with vacation rental services on the Internet can be had for as little as $60 per night. Vacation rental condos come with fully equipped kitchens, which allow guests to save even more money by preparing their own meals. Another good source of condo rental listings is the classified ad section of *Hawai'i* magazine.

Internet Vacation Rental Listing Services

Vacation Spot
www.vacationspot.com

Vacation Paradise
www.vacationparadise.com

Vacation Rentals by Owner
www.vrbo.com/vrbo/kauai.htm

Great Rentals
www.greatrentals.com/HI/HI.html

A1 Vacations
www.a1vacations.com

Royal Vacations
www.royalvacations.com/kauai.htm

1st Choice Vacation Properties
www.choice1.com

10,000 Vacation Rentals
www.10kvacationrentals.com

Full Service Condos— East Side

Aston Kaua'i Beach Villas
4330 Kaua'i Beach Dr., Līhu'e
Phone: (808) 245-7711
Website: www.aston-hotels.com
Units: 113
Rates: $175-$330
Beach: Nukoli'i Beach

Banyan Harbor Resort
3411 Wilcox Rd., Līhu'e
Phone: (808) 245-7333, (800) 422-6926
Website: www.vacation-kauai.com
Units: 136
Rates: $110-$140
Beach: Kalapakī Beach

Kaha Lani
460 Nehe Rd., Līhu'e
Phone: (808) 822-9331
Website: www.aston-hotels.com
Units: 65
Rates: $180-$430
Beach: Nukoli'i Beach

Kapa'a Sands Resort
380 Papaloa Rd., Kapa'a
Phone: (808) 822-4901, (800) 222-4901
Website: www.kapaasands.com
Units: 20
Rates: $85-$124
Beach: Wailua Beach

Kapa'a Shore
4-0900 Kūhiō Hwy., Kapa'a
Phone: (808) 822-1457, (800) 801-0378
Website: www.kauaiproperties.com
Units: 81
Rates: $105-$135
Beach: Waipouli Beach

Lae Nani
410 Papaloa Rd., Kapa'a
Phone: (808) 822-4938
Website: www.outrigger.com
Units: 52
Rates: $195-$295
Beach: Wailua Beach

Lani Kai Resort
390 Papaloa Rd., Kapa'a
Phone: (808) 822-7700
Website: www.castleresorts.com/LKI
Units: 18
Rates: $201-$294
Beach: Wailua Beach

Plantation Hale
484 Kūhiō Hwy., Kapa'a
Phone: (808) 822-4941, (800) 775-4253
Website: www.plantation-hale.com
Units: 151
Rates: $125-$155
Beach: Waipouli Beach

Pono Kai Resort
1250 Kūhiō Hwy., Kapa'a
Phone: (808) 823-8427
Website: www.marcresorts.com
Units: 217
Rates: $169-$269
Beach: Kapa'a Beach

Wailua Bay View Condominiums
320 Papaloa Rd., Kapa'a
Phone: (800) 882-9007
Website: www.wailuabay.com
Units: 28
Rates: $99-$110
Beach: Wailua Beach

Full Service Condos— North Shore

Ali'i Kai
3830 Edward Rd., Princeville
Phone: (808) 826-7444, (800) 826-7782
Units: 30
Rates: $120-$150
Beach: Sealodge Beach and Pali Ke Kua (Hideaways) Beach

Cliffs at Princeville
3811 Edwards Rd., Princeville
Phone: (808) 826-9988
Units: 12
Rates: $125-$150
Phone: (808) 826-6219
Rates: $155-$225
Beach: Sealodge Beach and Pali Ke Kua (Hideaways) Beach

Hale Moi Cottages
5300 Ka Haku Rd., Princeville
Phone: (808) 826-6020
Website: www.marcresorts.com
Rates: $119-$179
Beach: Pali Ke Kua (Hideaways) Beach

Hanalei Bay Resort
5380 Hono'iki Rd., Princeville
Phone: (808) 826-6522
Website: www.aston-hotels.com
Units: 85
Rates: $170-$725
Beach: Pu'u Poa Beach

Hanalei Colony Resort
Highway 560, Hā'ena
Phone: (808) 826-6235 (800) 628-3004
Website: www.hcr.com
Units: 47
Rates: $145-$265
Beach: Kepuhi Beach

Pali Ke Kua
5300 Ka Haku Rd., Princeville
Phone: (808) 826-9066
Website: www.marcresorts.com
Units: 40
Rates: $179-$299
Beach: Pali Ke Kua (Hideaways) Beach

Pu'u Poa
5300 Ka Haku Rd., Princeville
Phone: (800) 344-6429
Website: www.marcresorts.com
Units: 56
Rates: $249-$299
Beach: Pali Ke Kua (Hideaways) Beach

Full Service Condos— South Side

Aston at Po'ipū Kai
1565 Pe'e Rd., Po'ipū
Phone: (808) 742-7424
Website: www.aston-hotels.com
Units: 285
Rates: $190-$390
Beach: Po'ipū Beach Park

Embassy Resort Po'ipū Point
1613 Pe'e Rd., Po'ipū
Phone: (808) 742-1888
Website: www.marcresorts.com
Units: 210
Rates: $299-$1000
Beach: Po'ipū Beach Park

Kiahuna Plantation
2253 Po'ipū Rd., Po'ipū
Phone: (808) 742-6411
Website: www.outrigger.com
Units: 193
Rates: $190-$470
Phone: (808) 742-2200
Website: www.castleresorts.com/KIA
Units: 333
Rates: $175-$610
Beach: Sheraton Beach

Lāwa'i Beach Resort
5017 Lāwa'i Rd., Po'ipū
Phone: (808) 742-9581, (800) 367-8020
Website: www.suite-paradise.com
Rates: $149-$215
Beach: Beach House Beach

Makahū'ena Resort
1661 Pe'e Rd., Po'ipū
Phone: (808) 742-7555
Website: www.castleresorts.com/MKH
Units: 79
Rates: $139-$309
Beach: Po'ipū Beach Park

Nihi Kai Villas
1870 Ho'one Rd., Po'ipū
Phone: (800) 367-8020
Website: www.suite-paradise.com
Units: 45
Rates: $146-$218
Beach: Po'ipū Beach Park

Po'ipū Crater Resort
2827 Po'ipū Rd., Po'ipū
Phone: (808) 742-6464
Website: www.suite-paradise.com
Units: 30
Rates: $115-$141
Phone: (808) 742-7400

Website: www.grantham-resorts.com
Units: 30
Rates: $111-$124
Beach: Po'ipū Beach Park

Po'ipū Kai Resort
1941 Po'ipū Rd., Po'ipū
Phone: (808) 742-6464
Website: www.suite-paradise.com
Units: 150
Rates: $115-$340
Beach: Po'ipū Beach Park

Po'ipū Kapili
2221 Kapili Rd., Po'ipū
Phone: (808) 742-6449
Website: www.poipukapili.com
Units: 60
Rates: $170-$400
Beach: Po'ipū Beach Park

Po'ipū Shores
1775 Pe'e Rd., Po'ipū
Phone: (808) 742-7700
Units: 39
Rates: $192-$307
Beach: Po'ipū Beach Park

Sunset Kahili
1763 Pe'e Rd. Po'ipū
Phone: (808) 742-7434, (800) 827-6478
Website: www.sunsetkahili.com
Units: 27
Rates: $115-$155
Beach: Po'ipū Beach Park

Waikomo Stream Villas
2721 Po'ipū Rd., Po'ipū
Phone: (808) 742-7220
Website: www.grantham-resorts.com
Units: 60
Rates: $89-$129
Beach: Po'ipū Beach Park

Whalers Cove
2460 Pu'uholo Rd., Po'ipū
Phone: (808) 742-7571, (800) 367-7052
Website: www.whalers-cove.com
Units: 39
Rates: $310-$550
Beach: Beach House Beach

KAUA'I ON THE WORLD WIDE WEB

News

Garden Island Daily Newspaper

www.kauaiworld.com

This is the electronic edition of Kaua'i's daily newspaper.

Kaua'i News

http://www.hawaiian.net/~kuai/kauainews.html

Radio station KUAI archives its news stories and posts them on their website.

Weather

Real-Time Weather Conditions

You can check on the current weather conditions at different locations on the island.

Kīlauea

www.aws.com/aws_2001/asp/obsForecast.asp?zipcode=kilauea%2C+HI

Kekaha

www.aws.com/aws_2001/asp/obsForecast.asp?zipcode=kekaha%2C+HI

Kapa'a

www.aws.com/aws_2001/asp/obsForecast.asp?zipcode=kapaa%2C+HI

Līhu'e

www.aws.com/aws_2001/asp/obsForecast.asp?zipcode=lihue%2C+HI

Visitor Information

Hawai'i State Vacation Planner

www.bestplaceshawaii.com/vacplanner/kvp

This state-sponsored travel planner includes listings of most hotels and activity businesses, plus Kaua'i weddings and marriage information. There is also information on Kaua'i vacation rentals, bed and breakfasts, and activity services, including golf, scuba, fishing, hiking, camping, and boating.

County of Kaua'i Official Visitors Site

www.kauai-hawaii.com

Information is provided on Kaua'i's sights and attractions, parks and beaches, local culture and island events.

Kaua'i Visitors Bureau

www.kauaivisitorsbureau.org

They answer frequently asked questions and have a calendar of events.

Live Cameras

Po'ipū

www.staykauai.com/Live_Camera/

Princeville

www.800hawaii.com/webcam

INDEX

The author welcomes any comments, contributions, or updates to information contained in this book. He may be contacted at: exploreparadise@msn.com

Mana Waipuna (Jurassic Park) Falls, 1915